The Thinking Crisis

The Thinking Crisis

The Disconnection of Teaching and Learning in Today's Schools

T. Ellen Hill and Joel Shatzky

Authors Choice Press

San Jose New York Lincoln Shanghai

The Thinking Crisis
The Disconnection of Teaching and Learning in Today's Schools

Authors Choice Press
an imprint of iUniverse.com, Inc.

For information address:
iUniverse.com, Inc.
5220 S 16th, Ste. 200
Lincoln, NE 68512
www.iuniverse.com

ISBN: 0-595-19679-9

Printed in the United States of America

Contents

Introduction to The Thinking Crisis: The Disconnection of Teaching and Learning in Today's Schools

For the past five decades, the schools of this country have been under scrutiny by parents, educational experts, social critics and political figures for inadequacies in the way children and young adults learn. In the past few years, a number of remedies have been offered to improve student learning, the most recent being vouchers, the increased use of the Internet, and a "back to basics" philosophy. We believe that in order for educators to address properly the problems that we as a nation face in educating our students, we must examine more carefully not only what students learn and how they learn it, but what they perceive the learning process to be. Unfortunately this continuing gap prevents students from achieving the level of writing and critical thinking that is vital to academic success in college.

Of course, a significant percentage of students can learn no matter what the mode of instruction. They are not only highly motivated, but many have been given certain cultural and intellectual advantages that enable them to thrive in almost any educational environment, provided, of course, that the minimal requisites of instruction are available. This, as we know, is not always the case in schools that not only lack the basic tools of learning such as books, equipment, and well-trained teachers, but also a safe environment. We feel that such matters must be addressed in order to improve the chances of learning for a greater percentage of students. We also recognize that there are schools with far fewer resources than others in which students perform quite well, and educators can cite statistics in which per capita expenditure in some districts might be far higher than in others with less positive results.

Certainly, money must be made more available to districts that are lacking the essentials for a healthy educational environment, and the new technologies that are being publicized such as the Internet, can be very useful teaching tools. But, unless the class room teacher, and the college educator who is responsible for teaching those who are to teach fully understands the dynamics of what is going on in the classroom in the learning process, abundant resources themselves will not solve the problem of poor learning. And, as we have been told by social critics, the consequences of poor learning can be a major contributory factor in turning a potentially productive, law-abiding citizen into a young felon and, eventually, a professional criminal. A disproportionate number of people in jail exhibit serious problems in reading, writing, and other skills essential to success in school.

The reason we are writing this book is to call attention to the simple fact that good teaching has to be looked at from the point of view of what the student sees when coming into the classroom as well as what the teacher assumes he or she sees. The present trend to greater reliance on technology as a means of instruction as well as what we believe to be unfocused, "feel-good" methodology as a substitute for hard, demanding, and carefully coached teaching will result in a greater percentage of students who could be educated to fall by the wayside and be tempted to deal with their failure in school with success on the streets and outside the law.

Our purpose is not to offer a simple panacea for the problems of learning, nor is our aim to suggest the elimination of such programs as multicultural studies and collaborative learning, but to point out some of the problems of these programs as presently taught. We want to point in a direction that we feel has not been adequately examined and addressed: how the students view learning as reflected in what and how they think. We believe that only through a systematic and thorough examination of the cognitive processes that students adopt in the classroom can we begin to address the problems that can be described as a disconnection between the mode of teaching presentation and the way in which students learn.

An anecdote illustrates this point. Several years ago, one of the authors was teaching the novel "Native Son" by Richard Wright. When he asked the students if they had "learned" anything about Black history, or culture, or literature, very few of them responded at all. When he then asked how many of them were "taught" these subjects, almost all raised their hands. The fact that students think that what they are taught and what they learn are not really connected should be a warning that unless we begin to address this issue, all of the technology and educational dynamics that have been experimented with over the past five decades may be effective for those students who have the ability and/or the background to absorb them, but might prove useless to a much more significant number. The growing gap between teaching and learning not only endangers our future economic and cultural well-being, but also the continuation of our democratic society.

Chapter One

The Basis of the Basics

If we look carefully at the nature of what is going on in the classroom and why a lot of basic learning seems not to be happening, there are about a half a dozen factors that we must take into account that are often highlighted individually in various studies on student learning, but have not been considered in their totality. They are: the make-up of the teaching pool, the proportion of students attending, the social and cultural backgrounds of students, the needs and goals of students, the pressures of the socializing process, and the economic consequences of success and failure in school. All of these have a direct impact on what is going on in the classroom and how and why students learn or don't learn. They also have an impact on what kind of models of learning teachers use and how students respond to them.

1. **Who are the teachers today?** Whatever else that can be said about today's teachers, whether or not they are adequately prepared for their jobs, one thing is definite: the pool of teachers has changed drastically over the past fifty years. Prior to World War ll, the majority of classroom teachers in the grades K-12 were women. At one point, in fact, teachers had to be single women, rarely giving up their careers to marry. And they were the self-selected group of women who valued the teaching profession highly enough to make this sacrifice.

In other words, they were very bright, very dedicated and, in most cases, very effective in teaching because they were among the very best and brightest women in this country. The young women of today who have many alternatives to the teaching profession can be found in business, government, and professions other than teaching, especially law and medicine. Those among this group who do choose to teach generally go into college teaching and research at universities. The intelligence, the intellectual curiosity, the dedication and the ingenuity of past generations of women who chose to go into a profession are now dispersed over many areas besides teaching. This is not to say that women students who choose K-12 teaching today are necessarily less intellectually gifted, but having taught for thirty years at what is predominantly a teachers college I would say that of the thousands of students who have passed through my courses few K-12 teacher candidates were among my best, and many among the worst. By worst I don't necessarily mean students who are just dumb, but those who seem to have the smallest intellectual curiosity or background to give to their own students in need of a rich, developed perspective on learning.

I can recall in my own experience going through grade school in the late 40's and early 50's several terrifying teachers and a number who were very kind and gentle. With one exception, I cannot recall any who were not bright and one in particular, Miss Capo Di Ferro, my sixth grade teacher, was incredibly gifted and gave her intellectual gifts to any students who would avail him or herself of them. The knowledge these teachers had of history, art, music, literature and even science gave us a background that, regardless of our home environment, introduced us in many ways to the life of the mind.

The generation of students who are now going out to student teach have themselves been educated by teachers who were raised on television. The thinning of the rich cultural milieu that was produced by grade school teachers who had been print-oriented instead of image-oriented has by now been reduced to the point where, except for rock and roll references, there is hardly any common knowledge students today share with each other. But of course there are still students who have gifted teachers, enriched learning experiences, and are very well prepared to go on to higher education. There is little reason to believe, however, that they are more than a small proportion.

2. **What proportion of high school graduates today are attending college?** Although statistics may be disputed, there is little doubt that a tiny proportion of high school graduates attended college prior to World War ll. The number may be as small as 10%, but certainly it was far less than the 50% of all students who graduate high school today and attend college. The purposes of a college education fifty years ago, of course, were far different than they are today, in most cases.

When my parents attended college in the 20's and 30's, they were both primarily interested in a job, but they were also both intellectually gifted. None of their siblings and few of their cousins attended, and although they were first-generation Americans, they had mastered English and excelled in grade school. They both attended what is now branches of the City University of New York, my father going to CCNY and my mother Hunter, and there were many working-class students among them. But in most parts of the country, even the large mid-West universities, the predominant reason for attending college was for "social values," not vocational ones. Most people could get a decent-paying job with a high school degree, many even without one, in factories and small businesses. And a much larger proportion of young people lived on farms and needed no more than an eighth-grade education to be successful farmers. And an eighth-grade education meant that the student could read on an eighth-grade level, something we can no longer take for granted from students who have graduated from high school.

Now a minimum degree for any decent job is at least an associate's degree from a two-year school, and even that is not sufficient in many cases if someone wants to move up the career ladder. Thus, the proportion of young people who might have been able to get a decent-paying job two generations ago with a basic education is diminishing rapidly and the number who must attend college in order to achieve any economic well-being continues to grow. The gap now between the average salary of a college graduate and someone with a high school diploma, until recently, had been rapidly increasing. For any young person, regardless of interest, background, economic status, or emotional maturity, there is no real alternative to college in order to have a decent life. And this leads to an increasing proportion of students who are unsuited and certainly unprepared for college-level work.

George Will stated that one of the reasons for this lack of preparation is that: "most institutions of higher learning have, essentially, open admissions, [therefore] many high school students feel little incentive to exert themselves" (84). Will goes on to decry the amount of remedial work going on in colleges, and the recent attack by Mayor Giulliani on the remedial courses in the City University of New York is indicative of one line of criticism of higher education. But the elite schools in this country have no problem in getting their numbers for selective classes. And to say that the colleges must be more selective when, in many cases, their survival depends on enrollment, is, to say the least a little disingenuous. Moreover, to assume that the reason students do not do well in high school is due to their perception that they can go into college no matter what their performance is to ignore the fact that high schools have the task of getting students to perform better regardless of their motivation. Half of the students who graduate from high school do not go on to college and their education must be attended to as well as the college-bound. Remediation is often a necessity because the resources or standards at many high schools have not adequately prepared students, regardless of motivation.

At the college where we teach, in the SUNY system, enrollment is THE number one factor in determining the revenues we receive for the running of the institution. If we were as selective as Mr. Will suggests, we would have a much smaller school but certainly not a better one.

This is confirmed by the fact that we have been getting smaller by over 25% in the last fifteen years and the consequences have been the loss of many of our best and brightest faculty and an increase in the number of part-time instructors from less than 10% to almost 50%. Good as many of these instructors are, they are unable to devote the time necessary to be a pervasive presence on campus, the kind of presence that, as we shall indicate, is necessary for the learning and teaching needed to make a measurable impact on students.

3. **What are the social and cultural backgrounds of college-bound students today?** Although many students attending college today come from college-educated families, an increasing proportion are first-generation American, coming from predominantly Asian and Latin American backgrounds with a significant number of Eastern European immigrants as well. But there are many American-born college students that are the first in their families to attend college. At the school in which we teach, this is quite frequently the case. For them, college is not only a unique experience in their families, but serious and concentrated reading may be as well. In many families, books are not something that young children see their parents reading as they are growing up; all the books in the house may not be more than a Bible and a phone directory. And regardless of the advent of the computer, print-oriented education is still the predominant form of instruction. In fact, computers demand a certain level of sophistication in the type of instruction one must master. A poor reader will have problems with computers beyond a basic level.

Another factor, then, in the background of almost all students is the predominant influence of television. Many books have been written on the negative influence television has on learning, and since most students have been exposed to literally tens of thousands of hours of television before they enter a grade school classroom let alone college, they are far more sophisticated visually than linguistically. The most enthusiastic and attentive response I have had from average freshman to a writing course is when I taught the course using videotapes as the basic teaching tool. Although there was required reading, it was supplementary rather than primary in instructing the students in developing their writing skills. And these students, many of whom had limited reading skills, demonstrated exceptional ability in remembering details from video tapes, especially images which they could retain far better than I could. It was in finding the words to describe these images, however, that the students began to have difficulty. And when they were shown tapes of events that required their following arguments and ideas, such as the Kennedy-Nixon debates or the McCarthy-Ed Murrow controversy, they found it more difficult to express their impressions and defend their ideas.

In contrast, however, the most stimulating classes in freshman composition I have ever taught were ones in which not just texts were used as the basis for writing themes, but classic texts. The students in this class were expected to read and understand Goethe's *Werther*, Stendahl's *The Red and the Black*, Dostoyevski's *The Gambler*, stories from Kafka's *The Metamorphosis*, and Camus' *The Plague*. As a treat, the class read and then watched the movie version of Fowles' *The French Lieutenant's Woman*. Few of these students expressed any problems or reluctance in reading these texts. But they had been selected as part of the Honors Program. What differentiated them from many other incoming freshmen was not only that they had somewhat higher grades and SAT scores but, in most cases, believed that they deserved to be Honors students. But there is no doubt that their general knowledge of history, the arts and literature was more extensive than the average student's in my other classes. Yet once they were in a "regular" class with non-Honors students, I noticed that their responses became fewer, their enthusiasm, which they had exhibited in the Honors class, became subdued, and they were "dumbed down" to the level of the other students. It wasn't that the Honors students didn't know the answers any longer; rather they felt they would "stick out" if they displayed greater knowledge than the rest of the class.

This is due to the cultural backgrounds of many students in this country which teach them to be anti-intellectual. It is part of our heritage as a pioneering society in which "intellectuals" were associated with aristocrats and success was equated with economic enrichment. The expression: "If you're so smart why ain't you rich?" is a typically American sentiment. And the portrayal of bright students as "nerds," "geeks" or the earlier term, "egg heads" embodies the negative stereotypes portrayed in media and especially television programs. Therefore, it is difficult for students who have truly intellectual interests and a thirst for knowledge as an end in itself to thrive in such an environment. Despite the many awards assemblies, prizes and scholarships talented students are given by their high schools, the cultural norms often contradict these outward shows of veneration for learning. Physical appearance, success in sports and "being cool" are considered far more desirable attributes by most students than intellectual achievement. This is not to say that most students who are college-bound disdain good grades; just so long as it doesn't seem that they are "learning" anything.

And thus another aspect of the social and cultural background of today's college student is a consumer-mentality toward learning. It's as if they see knowledge as a commodity that they must acquire in some way and once it serves the purpose of getting a grade, it can be dispensed with as if it had no more value than an out-of-date video game or an empty soda can. This is one of the reasons, we believe, that knowledge retention among students in so many areas is so poor: they don't see knowledge as a cumulative development of elements of information that can lead to a professional level of mastery of a subject. They too often see it as discrete and unconnected tasks that they must perform in order to get on with their high school and college careers.

This fragmented mentality can be attributed in part to the increasing emphasis on consumption as an end in itself. But one of the most devastating things that television and the media in general achieve is to give the impression that everything can be trivialized as entertainment; that the death of a movie star is equivalent to the assassination of a head of state. There is little of a holistic view of the world that can be discovered in the "white noise" that constantly bombards the child growing up in this so-called "information age." What we are finding more and more is that the barrage of facts that we are presented in the media often obscures any knowledge that can be gleaned from them.

Many students, then, take refuge in the one subject which most all share: the world of MTV, Soaps, and Rock. In these areas, their retention of information about who Rick is sleeping with or when Betsy and Jack will marry is far more effective than any knowledge of American history or Shakespearean drama. Ask almost any group of high school or college students to name the Top Ten hits on the charts or TV videos and you will get a much greater response than from their knowledge of most academic subjects. Yet, the Life of the Mind is still the ideal many faculty would like to advance for students who have little experience with thinking at all.

Even in matters of listening and concentrating on what is being said in the classroom, students have a difficult time. There is mounting evidence that a significant number of students, by the time they enter college, have experienced some hearing loss because of the high decibel level at which they have been listening to music through their early years, not only at rock concerts, but by turning up their head sets so their friends across town can hear what they are hearing at the same time. We have often experienced the response of students in the classroom who need to have a question repeated, not necessarily because they weren't concentrating, but because they could literally not hear what was being said by the instructor, clear and loud as her voice might be.

But another aspect of this problem in understanding is what is being increasingly diagnosed as "attention deficit disorder" or ADD. Students have confessed to me that they cannot concentrate for more than a few minutes at a time on a text before their minds begin to wander. This is true in the classroom as well. Although I now give a five-minute "break" after the first fifty minutes of a seventy-five minute class, I still feel that many students have a maximum concentration time of less than even those fifty minutes. This happens despite the variety of teaching techniques I have used in class besides lecture, understandably the most off-putting form of instruction and still the most commonly used in the college classroom.

In addition, many students who enter college come not only unprepared in their writing and critical skills but with a very poor vocabulary. Words that people of my generation might have taken for granted as basic in grade school are now unfamiliar or unknown to college students. This problem might be remedied if students were more willing to look up an unfamiliar word in a dictionary. But since many believe that spelling is more important than a sophisticated vocabulary, or that a thesaurus is a way of dealing with an inadequate one, they do not show much more than an eighth-grade level vocabulary both in reading and writing in their in-class papers. Even worse, they often misunderstand the words I am using in classroom discussion or lecture and are reluctant to reveal this by asking me what a word meant. In their writing, this ignorance is consistently reflected.

A recent incident illustrates this serious deficiency. I was proctoring an exam for a colleague; it was a poetry course and the instructions included permission to request from the proctor the definition of words unfamiliar to the students. Several asked me for the definition, not of some obscure fancy of poetic diction, but "prevail," "starkest" as an intensive of "stark," and "divinest" in the sense of to understand something intuitively. Granted that the third of these words has an archaic meaning, what possible excuse could a college student have for not knowing the word "prevail?" And yet average college students do have problems with many words in a basic 2000-word vocabulary when they should have mastery of six or seven times that many in order to understand not only their texts but the lectures and discussions in class that are conducted concerning those texts.

Finally, and what is most important an objective in this book is for us to point out that students are not adequately prepared to think, not just think critically, but, it seems, think at all when they enter college. To us, "thinking" means taking knowledge and information and learning how to apply it to different situations demanding different responses from those demonstrated in class. An example of a "critical thinking" exercise is to take a character from one play and show how he or she would respond to a situation in another play, given basic character traits. Or what had once seemed to be the most basic assignment: a comparison and contrast of two works from different periods, taking into account the changes in society reflected in the way characters respond to comparable situations. This exercise, once self-evident to my classes of twenty-five years ago, is now almost undoable for my students. The only task they seem comfortable doing in a literature course is plot summaries. Their ability to compare and contrast aspects of different literary works is so limited, I find, that it is almost necessary for me to point out the examples and ideas myself, one by one, and then hope that the students will be able to knit together an intelligible paper through my coaching.

In the English department where we both teach, moreover, even among the best and most advanced students, the ability to distinguish critical works and evaluate which ones are better than others and why is sadly lacking. In conclusion, most college students come unprepared to do college-level work for a variety of reasons; thus, it is vital that we as teachers respond in effective ways, without necessarily "dumbing down" any further the level of expectation and the nature of the materials we expect our students to read and master.

4. **What are the needs and goals of students?** This, of course, leads us to realize that the needs and goals of students, certainly as they perceive them, are often not the same as the needs and goals of their teachers, particularly college teachers (Profs are from Saturn, students from Mercury). Statistically only one in four students today majors in what

we would consider the liberal arts with another quarter in business and the rest in predominantly vocational programs.

The key problem in this mix is that the purposes of higher education, and the high school preparation now being focused on students getting into college, is quite different from the objectives most students have in attending college. The origins of the university system going back to monastic times, were founded on the concept of the *trivium* and *quadrivium*, the classical disciplines of mathematics, the sciences, philosophy and the arts. Most students during this time attended to obtain a degree in law, medicine, or theology so they themselves could become university professors. Harvard was founded for the purpose of training Protestant clergy.

In the more recent past, higher education was almost exclusively reserved for the wealthy and privileged to send their sons and, finally, daughters to a more advanced level of "finishing school" where they could cultivate an appreciation for the arts, literature, philosophy and impress their peers with a smattering of foreign languages. In Europe, the old guild system and apprenticeship programs provided clever and ambitious young people with the opportunity to master a craft. The United States, with its vast agricultural resources, began to establish "Ag and Tech" institutions where students could learn these vocational skills with a direct practical purpose. Vestiges of these two cultures can be seen at one of the Ivies, Cornell, which has both an outstanding liberal arts university and a first-rate husbandry program as well.

Since the late 40's and the establishment of the GI Bill in which hundreds of thousands of bright, able and enthusiastic servicemen and women were given the means of going to college, however, the liberal arts college and the Ag and Tech programs have begun to merge in what is now the "comprehensive" liberal arts school. Few of the traditional Ag and Techs still consider themselves to be so and have attempted to present themselves as all things to all students. The more specialized, vocationally oriented institutions are now housed in the two-year community colleges, many of which have excellent programs in such areas as nursing and other health-care professions. Yet, still, many students who receive an associates degree believe that they will be unable to have a truly rewarding career unless they continue in a four-year school and receive a bachelors.

The original purpose of the liberal arts as it evolved from the medieval models was to "cultivate" the tastes and sensibilities of students so they would have the social graces necessary to fit into privileged society. However, since a great proportion of students today have no such background or the slightest interest in literature, classical music and art, philosophy, the sciences, or foreign languages, there is a clear disconnection between the stated objectives of most liberal arts programs and the needs and goals of students as they enter the college classroom.

This disconnection, this cognitive dissonance, can best be seen in the way in which General Education or distribution courses are treated in the university system. The one vestige of the traditional concept of a liberal arts education is found in the vast variety of "gen. ed" requirements that still remain at most liberal arts colleges. These provide the excuse we academics try to give ourselves that we are presenting all our students with the opportunity to become "well-rounded" and "liberally educated" despite the vocational focus most of them enter the classroom with. And yet, since most general education courses are taught at universities by graduate assistants or inexperienced instructors, in large lecture rooms, with few opportunities for students to interact with each other or the instructor, students are unlikely to find such courses interesting, engaging or "relevant" to their needs and goals.

It is one of the paradoxes of the contemporary institution of higher learning that those first few years in which students need the most hands-on instruction, the most attention from faculty in small classes, the most intellectual guidance, they are "dumped" into large, impersonal lecture halls for their "required" courses in General Education. Is it any surprise, then, that as little value as most students see in these courses, the institutional practices reinforce these perceptions?

In his article, George Will observes that one in four college students does not return for a second year. Given the fact that they are put into a strange and often alienating environment as eighteen year olds, one in which they have really had little preparation for intellectually and emotionally, and then find themselves in classes in which they are no more than a number, is it any surprise that a large proportion of freshmen either flunk out or leave voluntarily? If the objective of a college education is to get students to learn how to think, read widely, and be able to make connections between various disciplines so as to come up with new ideas and insights, the general education programs at most institutions are not conducive to such learning. The lack of articulation between disciplines, the negative attitude toward teaching general education that many faculty show, and the conditions under which these courses are conducted merely reinforce students' perceptions that the only study of value is the "real stuff" in the major.

Certainly, there are attempts at articulation between courses at some institutions. There are reformers everywhere that realize the inadequacy of these distribution programs for the purposes for which they were intended. But as long as the university and, to a lesser extent, college system "back loads" its resources for the juniors and seniors and scants on the freshmen and sophomores, the attrition rate, which is actually over fifty per cent between freshman and senior year at many institutions, is unlikely to be reduced.

As long as a majority of young people in our society find it necessary to attend college as a way to economic survival, their goals and needs will be at odds with many of the objectives of a liberal arts education. And paramount among these, we believe, is to teach them to think. Only in freshman writing courses are first-year students placed in reasonably small sized classrooms, but their experience there is too often contradicted by their experiences in other introductory courses. And the amount of writing required and level of instruction in writing in other courses often is at variance with what is expected of them in freshman composition.

If there is no consistency in demands and requirements when it comes to thinking and writing about what they think, students will perceive that much of what they are supposed to be learning in college is a "game" which they can play by mastering a few basic rules and then figuring which apply to which teacher. Any holistic, comprehensive view of learning, writing, reading and thinking is lost in those first two years and quite easily since most students do not come to college with the goals and objectives they were supposed to bring with them.

Their culture does not value critical thinking: just feelings and impressions; their home environment often has not enhanced their sense of the life of the mind: just getting good grades; their values have been geared toward consumption as a way of life: not retention of what they consume; and they have been socialized into believing that a love of learning for its own sake is "not cool" and nobody wants to be considered a nerd.

Yet, there are certainly earnest, eager, focused and well-prepared youngsters who enter the academic life with grace and good humor and come out of those four years truly well-educated. But, of course, they could do so regardless of the quality of instruction and personal attention they get (Though generally these students are the ones who do get personal attention because of their qualities). This book is not addressing that segment of the student population. They don't need much help. It is the other group, the under-prepared, unfocused, often resistant and resentful majority of college students on which this work is focused.

Sadly, as evidenced by drinking practices and violent behavior on campuses, the goals and objectives of many students are to have a good time for a semester or a year and then leave. And their self-destructive behavior too often has a negative effect on that portion of the students who could be "saved" to do well in their studies and complete their degree. An example of these goals and objectives—"get high, get sloshed, get laid"—was boldly expressed in a banner that had been put on graduation day several years ago across the front of one of the fraternity houses next to the campus where we teach: "Flunk finals, don't graduate, so you can party for another year."

One of the most depressing periods for students who do not have "connections" when they graduate is the fear and uncertainty that they might not get a job, or not a job for which they are qualified. Part of this, of course, is that many current jobs are not those for which these students received their degrees or to which they aspire. But another reason, we believe, that students do not necessarily look forward to getting a job with the eagerness that one would expect is that they know that they have not had an adequate education. Despite the validation of the degree, the passing of all requirements, the assurance from the institution that they have achieved the necessary objectives set for them, they know that much of what they have passed through is to them a sham. THEY KNOW.

Once I attempted to reintroduce the practice among my colleagues to return to the comprehensive examination as one of the requirements for graduation at our institution. The suggestion got nowhere. And one of my friends in the chemistry department confided in me that the last time his colleagues administered such an exam, the results were so discouraging that they never did it again. And yet our institution, that graduates among the largest proportion of elementary school teachers in the country, many of whom are marginal students at best, scored the highest nationally on the National Teachers test. If our students are doing so well, what is the nature of the test? And what of the teachers who do not pass? What level of knowledge, of thinking ability is needed for someone to go into an elementary school and "instruct" the next generation of students?

This is not to say that there aren't many able teachers in the public schools of this country, but the common practice of allowing people to teach "out of license" with minimal or no training is, to say the least, disconcerting (Several of my undergraduates have been able to get substitute teaching jobs in the local schools without a degree. I doubt they are the exception.).

And so yet another dissonance between the goals and objectives of students and the institutions they attend is evident in the way teaching is too often regarded in this country: anyone can do it so let's give anyone who wants to a chance. To put this in perspective, how many pre-med students or pre-law students would be licensed to practice law or medicine in any court or hospital in this country? But these are "professions": teaching really isn't, is it? With such a perception, when teachers are being questioned about their curriculum by parents and agenda groups both liberal and conservative, and when politicians, media experts, and columnists weigh in with their wisdom, it should not be surprising that students who are college bound might not see the life of the mind as a meaningful objective or goal for their education. In some respects, it's a wonder that as many students attend who do regard the love of learning as something more than a slogan.

5. **What are the pressures of the socializing process?** The experience of college, both single-sex and co-ed, is an abnormal experience, unique, in fact, among late adolescence. Although they are gathered together five days a week for six hours a day from the age of five to eighteen, at no time before or after do students have constant contact with each other, day and night, incessantly, seven days a week as they do during their college years. Of course, there are more and more non-traditional students attending college in which their only contact is when they attend classes. But still, for the overwhelming majority, this is a period in which a concentration of adolescent and post-adolescent behavior, role models and socializing occurs with little, if any, impact from adults.

This is not to say that faculty and other staff are not at times present during extra-curricular activities. Some even schedule events along with students and there are courses, such as botany and field studies in various areas, that require the presence of an instructor. But for the most part, on a day-to-day basis, most student contact is with other students.

We touched on drinking and the drinking culture that seems to pervade so many colleges including some of the very best. There are many reasons for this, not the least of which is peer pressure. We would not want to idealize our own college careers during the 60's. We can imagine that students then did their share of drinking. But we both attended college during the years in which social activism, concerning Civil Rights and the Vietnam War, was a major element in the cultural and social milieu of college students. Even if the majority never actively participated in demonstrations or protests or any political activities on campus, there was a sufficient critical mass that set the tone and social agenda for the campus as a whole and the rest of the student body responded to it in some way. The point is, there was a clear objective to key elements of campus life, regardless of whether or not a significant number of students agreed with it. And in those days, it was relatively easy enough for most college graduates to get a decent-paying job after graduation. This is no longer the case: the future of a decent-paying job is not that certain; and the social and cultural objectives of college are no longer clearly defined.

The results, we believe, manifest themselves in the attraction so many college students have today toward drugs, chiefly alcohol, but illegal ones as well. It is a symptom of alienation, a word too often used in the past to mean almost anything unpleasant but, we believe, now can be aptly used to express the confusion, anger and frustration many students feel in being where they don't want to be, doing what they don't want to do, and getting into debt to be there and do that. Binge drinking, anti-social behavior, the lack of civility that some students are beginning to exhibit more frequently at campuses throughout the country is the result of all the factors that we have already indicated: they simply have not been trained, socialized, intellectually and emotionally prepared and given the goals that would enable them to be comfortable, accepting and eager to be part of the college community.

The leap can be an enormous shock to many students, from parental involvement in a high school in which assignments are often spoon fed and individual initiative is limited, into a world in which the social and cultural norms are, in large part, determined by their peers and little or any adult guidance is available. The freedom to do what you want when you want it, as often as possible, after the constraints of home life can be fearful and emotionally devastating. This is why a significant number of students who leave school do so in the first two weeks. And although we, as well as a number of other institutions are attempting to address this problem of adjustment by conducting summer orientation and first semester College 101 courses, there are simply too many experiences that flood the students in their first semester for these measures to adequately compensate for the alienating and unfamiliar modes of life that they are often exposed to for the first time.

We are convinced that if in-depth studies were conducted to explore student attitudes toward college, a considerable number would confess that they don't want to be there, not because of the social and sexual opportunities that many of them will be having, but despite them. Since a large proportion of them has never really been exposed to serious learning, they are frightened or contemptuous of it. And since if we are to feel we are successful in educating students by getting them to "love" learning when many of them can barely tolerate it, we are often working at cross purposes with them. This may sound harsh, but in my thirty-five years of teaching, and in similar experiences described by my colleagues, this is the state of higher education today: students increasingly need to be "converted" before accepting the responsibility of learning, especially when they have little or no reason to know what it is or how to value it.

Finally, the costs of a college education have increased considerably proportionate to the students' and their families' ability to pay them. Figures vary, but one of them indicates that in the past five years average student debt has gone from $8000 to $18000 upon graduation. And this is only the money owed to college. Student consumer debt through credit card use has also recently escalated. Since many students do not get high-paying entry-level jobs, they are often faced with a situation in which they are tempted to file for personal bankruptcy which, of course, ruins their credit rating. And although an increasing number of students works part-time to help pay their bills, the pressures of such additional work can often distract them further from their studies.

Given this added economic pressure, those students who take their studies seriously are more burdened by the possibility that if they are going to be conscientious about paying off their debts, they must get a good-paying job. And those students who have come to college as a social experience, studies being an incidental annoyance, are also pressured by the economic consequence of being in debt for one or two years of "the college scene" with little to show for it.

While students, then, often come to college with a very skewed perspective of what is expected of them and what they can do about it, the majority of faculty teaching in college approach learning, teaching and thinking from a very different perspective. While only a small proportion of students elect to go into college teaching, and considering the predominance of part-time over full-time positions, that choice of profession becomes more and more dubious, almost all faculty come from that intellectual elite who have chosen teaching, or, at least, "professing" in an institution of higher learning.

The overwhelming majority of the students they teach in most institutions outside of the elite ones are not nearly as enthusiastic or interested in their studies, nor are they, unlike those teaching them, as intellectually or culturally equipped. Given the sad fact that most college and university teachers have had little if any training in pedagogy, some of which is actually useful, and many never learn very much or have much interest in teaching as opposed to lecturing or "boasting," there is a significant cognitive and affective dissonance between the perspective the average college teacher brings into the classroom and the point of view of the average student. They are very often simply not on the same wavelength. This is not only true in terms of the level of commitment and expectations brought into the classroom by college teachers who have as their role model their own professors in generally elite colleges or elite programs within college; this is also reflected in their expectations developed from their peers who were generally as intellectually curious, gifted and culturally developed as they were.

Perhaps sixty or seventy years ago this was not the case. Students who attended college were much closer in background and interests to their professors than they are today. Even the children of the privileged who settled for their "gentlemen C" had similar cultural backgrounds and could understand, if not entirely appreciate, the purposes and methods of learning that they would find valuable in their own social circles. And while it is no longer common to have the gentleman or lady professor who would contribute the pittance they received as a salary to the alumni fund, and most of the people teaching in college really need the money they earn, the habits of mind brought to the classroom by the instructor have not really changed very much in all those years since the university system hasn't changed very much. But the students have: radically. And the problem of reaching them in effective and meaningful ways is not really being addressed, as much lip service as institutions make toward doing so.

The recent attacks on remedial education among politicians, the recent rejection of bi-lingual education—with all its flaws admittedly—in California, and the continued push for "distance learning" and increased reliance on computers and "nets" as a substitute for—not supplement to—instruction, indicate that the trend is going to be toward a further distancing of the instructor from the student, resulting in a further alienation of those considerable proportion of students from the learning process. I would pose the simple question, in regard to this rush toward technological "fixes" to teaching: if it's so good, how is it that the elite institutions in this country are not rushing to distance learning?

To put all of these factors into a specific application, consider the average student at Normal U. Susie B. is eighteen years old and has never been away from home for any length of time. She has been required to do about three-four hours a week of homework in high school, if that, and has been able to maintain a "B" average. She has never read through a "classic" novel or, if she has, she has understood little about it except for the plot summary she was requested to do as an assignment. She has never really written a research paper, hardly ever been required to revise her work, and has some difficulty concentrating on a task for more than ten minutes before she needs a "break."

Since she has done little reading, having watched tens of thousands of hours of television as a substitute, she has command of a seventh grade writing vocabulary and an eighth grade reading vocabulary. In school, she was socialized into believing that any student that took school work seriously was a "nerd" and anyone who volunteered to answer a question in class was a "brown-noser." Most of all, in terms of her sense of social identity, she was taught to "fit in," which often indicated that she had better show a healthy contempt for the life of the mind, and a vast and up-to-date knowledge of the latest rock hits, stars, their lives, and the lives of their families and pets. She will probably have some serious problems in note-taking given her limited vocabulary and some noticeable hearing loss due to many hours of attending rock concerts which were performed at mega-decibel level and the thousands of hours of listening to rock music on headphones at only slightly lower decibel levels.

Of history she knows nothing, or, more to the point, remembers nothing since, like any other information she receives in high school, it is "disposable." It is more than likely that some of her attitude comes from a family background in which a book is rarely seen and if so, rarely opened by parents and other family members. Since she does want the material benefits of the "good life" which she either sees in her parents' lives, those of relatives, or, certainly, those projected on the television screen, she knows she ought to go to college, so she does make a half-hearted attempt to "get through" high school; and since she has some native intelligence, she manages to do so without having gotten very much benefit of any instruction she was given there.

She has little if any study habits since she didn't need to cultivate them in order to do satisfactorily in high school and her concept of college is often predicated on those social high school experiences that could be considered "extra-curricular." That is, she is told that two of the chief activities one does at college is to get drunk and, with some concern about the possibilities of getting pregnant, get laid. She may also be told by her parents that since they cannot afford the total costs of her college education, she will have to get a job for fifteen to twenty hours a week and learn how to balance her time, which she has never done before, between work and study, which she has never experienced before, in a social environment which is almost openly hostile to the purposes for which she purportedly came to college: to learn to think in order to get a good job and do well in it. One thing is fairly certain: there is nothing in her preparation in high school, or practically nothing, that would lead her to think.

Coming into the classroom on the first day, she is greeted by an instructor, sometimes a graduate assistant, a part-time teacher and, rarely, if ever, in a large university, a tenure-track or tenured faculty member. This teacher has little if any training or preparation in the kind of teaching that our student would need, especially in a class of fifty to five hundred other students. Susie B. is presented, when in an "-ology" course, with a text that is huge, often poorly or boringly written, with many words that she has never seen in print let alone heard spoken in some intelligible context. And she will hear, if she can hear well enough to understand it, a lecture which is often nothing more than a reading of a text with a few illustrations that she will probably find hard to follow since the class meets at 8:00 A.M. and she has been partying until 2:00 A.M.

The instructor's background is often very different from hers. Prof. A. was the "nerd" in high school who hung out with her "weird" friends and might even have listened to classical music although she had time to master the rock and roll culture as well. If her parents themselves weren't college-educated, they had some value for learning or, if not they, some dedicated teacher who took her in hand. If a teacher in the humanities, she had a love for reading from the time she was six, if in the sciences, a fascination for science at about the same age. She had a twelfth-grade vocabulary by the time she was eleven and would devour about a book a week. She was at the top of her class in almost all subjects. Although she had a decent social life—varsity tennis, high school orchestra, debating team—she devoted twenty hours a week to learning and thinking, not solely to her high school assignments which like Susie B. she could also do in three to four hours a week, but those "outside" activities and projects for the science fair or the literary magazine or year book where she learned to apply some of the things she had read and thought about. She also hung out with like-minded friends who read and thought about the same things, and they would actually discuss them at times. In this way, she also developed her thinking skills.

In college, Prof. A. was well-prepared for her studies since she had not only been "taught" history and literature and biology and a language and all of the "enriched" and optional subjects that she willingly took in high school, but she actually "learned" and remembered what she was taught. Fairly early in her college career, she was already singled out as an exceptional student and given the kind of attention and nurturing which was helpful, but far less essential for her to succeed in her studies than it would be for Susie B.

When Prof. A. graduated from college at the top of her class, she was offered a graduate scholarship to one of the elite universities in the country where the teaching model she would learn from was the brilliant, sometimes elusive and recondite, but always straight lectures delivered by her brilliant, elusive and recondite professors. Sometimes, in her university studies, she would come across someone who knew something about teaching, but since that was rare and often, in higher academia, suspect, it made little impression on her. Finally, as preparation for her teaching career, she spent two years doing research on a subject obscure, elusive and recondite, written, often in a language no one she would ever teach could understand, including many of her future colleagues who had learned by then that the proper use of language is to communicate. She would undoubtedly get some "practice" in college teaching at the university where she would be given little if any instruction in how to teach, the assumption being that like her, the students she taught would "absorb" the material just by having it presented to them. And although she might experience difficulties with some of these students, chances are that since they, too, attended the elite university where she was getting her degree, they would be better equipped and more responsive to Prof. A.'s form of instruction than would Susie B.

At the end of four or five years of graduate school, in which most of her experiences would be focused on the life of the mind, with fellow students as exceptionally gifted and committed as she is, Prof. A. would then get her first job teaching at Normal U. And as she enters the class for the first day, there is Susie B. with her perspective on learning, looking at this creature from another planet, Prof. A. And what do we have: Profs are from Saturn, students are from Mercury.

As exaggerated as these profiles might seem, they encompass most aspects of the differences between the backgrounds and attitudes of the average student and average college teacher in this country. There are certainly many exceptions to each profile, but there is also mounting evidence that the gap between the two is widening. Not just a rise in anti-intellectual behavior among college students but a notable increase in cynicism and despair among college teachers about the lack of preparation that students have coming to college is manifest on today's campuses. The rise in binge drinking is complimented by the increasing number of faculty who choose early retirement, faculty many of which could have spent another ten or fifteen productive years in the classroom had they felt it was worth their effort.

Our concern, then, is that the dynamics of the learning process in the classroom, or, more precisely, the thinking process, are not being properly understood or addressed as is manifested by the "solutions" being offered in the educational community. How Susie B. got into college without learning how to think or even knowing that she had to, what kind of "preparation" she had in her high school, will be the subject of our next chapter.

Work Cited
Will, George. "Disorder in the Schools." *Newsweek*. 13 April 1998: 84

Chapter Two

The Secondary Learning Trap: From Learning for Knowledge to Learning for "Success"

When considered in their totality, the social and cultural factors contributing to the erosion of student learning might seem insurmountable. However, what many fail to understand is that the burgeoning secondary culture in which Susie B. was educated for four years systematically instilled many of the anti-learning habits with which she and her peers now begin their higher education. Susie B's intellectual and attitudinal roadblocks to learning, to a large degree, were firmly implanted within the walls of American Public High. The concerned public needs to take a more rigorous and analytic look at the in-school practices that stymie the secondary student's academic achievement. Most prominent is an entangled web of affective outcomes which has gradually fragmented and diluted secondary education's primary mission of helping students build the prerequisite knowledge and skills for college. The three with which we will deal in this chapter—self-esteem, cooperative learning, and multicultural education—contribute significantly to the disconnection of teaching and learning that teachers and students have been programmed to accept. When viewed from the learner's perspective, these affective goals form a powerful force suppressing students' academic success.

For the last two decades, as standardized test scores and overall literacy skills have declined nationwide, educational theorists, school reformers, and educational capitalists disguised as consultants have dedicated their talents to designing programs that meet the secondary student's ever-changing needs. Unfortunately, these change agents have been more concerned with injecting specific value-driven agendas into the curriculum than with strengthening the reciprocal process of teaching and learning. As a result of these progressive reforms, secondary affective programs are now awarded the same curricular status as the development of subject knowledge and related skills. During this time, proponents of value-oriented curricula pressured schools to adopt prepackaged programs aimed at curing the psychosocial ailments of contemporary adolescents. The high school where I taught in the 80's and early 90's added to its academic curriculum a trinity of affective goals—self-esteem, concern for others, and self-direction. From the standpoint of policy makers, this treatment plan dovetailed perfectly with their academic mission. Although each secondary school's affective goals are unique and responsive to cultural change, the resulting split curriculum, the crammed affective-cognitive model, factors strongly in the shockingly weak thinking, reading, and writing skills with which many students now begin college. These programs make up a large but little scrutinized piece of the curricular pie.

While the affective/cognitive model of learning is by no means a new educational concept, the affective component mushroomed into full-fledged educational learning outcomes by the late 70's. This shift occurred as schools capitulated to the public's demand for school-based programs that address the behavioral and social problems invading and disrupting the classroom. During the 80's, the high school where I taught joined the nationwide trend to pack the academic curriculum with carefully aligned value outcomes. By the new millenium, secondary students have had a hefty spate of nonacademic objectives added to the rigorous academic standards New York and many other states now mandate. Self-esteem, cooperative learning, diversity tolerance, behavior modification, AIDS education, character education, and teenage parenting rank high in the expanding slate of affective goals that, according to Stanley Pogrow, have transformed secondary education into a testing ground for mere corollaries of the learning process: "We keep creating reforms that focus on everything but learning. For example, in the 1980's we became absorbed in developing student self-concept and computer literacy. So far in the 1990's we are absorbed with de-tracking, empowering, eliminating labels, sex equity, changing tests, and increasing democratic participation. While all of these are important and are related to learning, they are not learning" (659). Consequently, the time, ways, and means for teachers to effectively impart and students to adequately learn content knowledge and language skills have been slashed to make room for a socio-politically correct and, therefore, inherently transient affective curricula. By the start of the 21st century, affective education has ironically become a prime tool for marketing and selling reigning cultural values with no proven effect on the learning needs of secondary students.

E.J. Hirsch's analysis of American public schools' century-old debate over their fundamental mission also provides the historical and theoretical context from which to reexamine affective education. He traces the debate back to two early documents, the 1893 *Report of the Committee of Ten on Secondary School Studies*, and the 1918 *Cardinal Principles of Secondary Education*. While the earlier report made the traditional humanities disciplines, a core academic curriculum, its overarching value, the latter proposed an eclectic mix of six affective goals for secondary students, including health, citizenship, and ethical character, and one potentially academic outcome, the [c]ommand of fundamental processes," (Hirsch 171). From Hirsch's overview, it can be inferred that the first document valued the building of integrated subject knowledge, the second the nurturing of the well balanced, integrated individual.

When viewed broadly, these documents together reflect the fractured theoretical model to which the contemporary learning and literacy crisis can be traced. Secondary schools' current effort to engineer and impose fluctuating self-concept formulas while raising academic standards threatens to erode student learning more than ever. This dichotomized model confirms the continuing "shift from subject matter to social adjustment" (Hirsch 171) to which secondary students are still subjected.

Her high school's self-esteem curriculum most likely enabled Susie B to cope with those difficult days when she was an unhappy denizen of her secondary world for any number of extracurricular reasons. There was the day she sat in class fuming, resenting her mother's refusal to buy her the outfit she planned to wear to the school dance that weekend. Or the time in class when she started crying over the rude comment her boyfriend made to her the night before. Or the fact that she did not read the assigned novel chapter because she was so upset. But after these letdowns, just by showing up for her English class she could have her self-esteem lifted high by the personally comforting practices of her teacher or the communal praise of her entire class, whether or not she did her homework. She knew that in class she would always be awarded just for being herself. Unfortunately, the educational self-esteem Susie B and her peers nationwide have been generously awarded directly contradicts the experience-based form of self-esteem we have all genuinely earned at one time or another, particularly where real intellectual achievement is concerned.

Educational self-esteem, as Lerner reminds us, came into being when educators all of a sudden assumed that "children with high self-esteem forge ahead academically, easily and naturally; children with low self-esteem fall behind. They cannot achieve excellence, or even competence, in many cases, until their self-esteem is raised" (9). By now this misconception about the nature of learning has raised students' identity component to the status of a required learning outcome at many secondary and middle schools in New York State. Viewed erroneously as a prerequisite rather than a reward for learning, educational self-esteem is equally distributed by teachers to all students in the class, regardless of whether or not they actually need regular doses of self-enhancement. However, the critical question the public fails to ask is, how is educational self-esteem integrated into the academic curriculum? The schools have come up with a solution that is simple in theory only. The general practice is that teachers "simply" incorporate practices and activities into any unit in any subject so as to give students equal opportunity to have their ideas both recognized and valorized. When administrators designate self-esteem as a uniform, district-wide learning outcome for all students, secondary teachers must consistently and coherently inject this element of the student's self-concept into either the subject matter being taught or the methods and formats by which students apply their new knowledge.

Susie B's 11th grade English teacher could have given her the opportunity to read to the class her journal entry on how she felt about the controversial ending to Kate Chopin's *The Awakening*. If her entry was poorly written, superficially developed, or illogically reasoned, the teacher would still find a way to administer the requisite dose of self-esteem and self-gratification just for sharing her response. The reasoning here would be that doing so would encourage Susie to feel positively about herself and hopefully encourage her to transfer this feeling to the academic work at hand. On the other hand, this raises serious questions about the amount of time it takes for every student in the class to read a journal entry in order to receive esteem-building feedback; and about the impact such "feel good" learning activities have on students' equally important academic task of understanding and applying a novel's difficult learning objectives of literary conventions, figurative language devices, and literary analysis.

Suppose the teacher assigned Susie B to work cooperatively with her group, writing and orally presenting or even acting out an alternative ending for the novel. Even if her group's presentation fell far short of the published criteria for effort, content, and delivery, Susie and her group still would have their egos boosted by the applause and verbal support of their classmates and teacher. Within this affective model of learning, one that is not concerned with students' development of subject knowledge per se, teachers are coached in ways to make students feel successful about themselves even when they know that educational self-esteem is disassociated from the self-reflection, self-discipline, and critical thinking that produces new knowledge and earned self-esteem. Educational self-esteem is a way for students to quickly and often undeservedly feel good about themselves instead of their academic effort and accomplishments. Unfortunately, it is also another factor underlying the apathy students today have toward the arduous self-discipline and hours of study per day upon which successful college learning depends; and even toward the secondary and college teachers brave enough to keep demanding intellectual rigor from them.

On the other hand, suppose another student, John A, did put considerable thought and effort into planning and developing his personal journal response to the novel's ending. Suppose he wrote what he considered to be not just his own original ending, but one that reflected the author's development of literary conventions and implied point of view. According to the self-esteem ethos, he still would receive his fair and equal share of praise and self-esteem for his intellectual effort from teacher and students. Yet what would probably go unnoticed would be the self-esteem John A awarded himself for his effort to compose a personal response reflecting his newly acquired literary knowledge. John A would have felt this self-awarded self-esteem, regardless of the reactions of teacher and classmates. However, in schools where self-esteem is the precondition for learning rather than the end-product of difficult individual study and knowledge-building, why would students choose challenging, discipline-based work like literary study when they can have their egos flattered for spouting personal views? Almost a decade ago, Charles Krauthammer warned educators that the "fixation on feeling is leading to the Balkanization of American education" (78). What he might consider saying these days is that this fixation has led to the Balkanization of the secondary student's, and in turn the entering college student's, entire learning process. The educational myth of self-esteem is a factor to keep in mind when we consider that the majority of secondary students have lost the ability to adjust their effort and thought processes to the more complex subject matter, reading material, and writing tasks required at the college level.

We have found most recently that first-year students overall lack the basic writing conventions and critical thinking skills to apply thought processes like classifying, defining, summarizing, or analyzing to initial academic writing tasks. Many, in fact, require extensive remedial instruction and conferencing in the principles of academic thinking and writing, basic concepts they should have learned in high school. For many, recovery of knowledge and reasoning lost in the suspended animation of secondaryland is unlikely in a single, fast-paced, concentrated college course. Still a growing number of these students expect to be made to feel good about themselves and their work, regardless of how superficial or substandard. As the products of sustained nourishment by self-esteem—the unearned, school-awarded, and identity-promotion version—their adaptation to the forms and standards of academic learning is rendered all the more difficult, if not impossible.

The affective learning paradigm extends far beyond the enhancement of the student's self-concept via self-esteem building activities and lessons. Today it encompasses a broad range of learning programs designed to educate not so much the mind as a variety of social and psychological needs that students bring to bear on their learning processes. Besides endowing the secondary student with a more positive and successful self-concept, the secondary classroom now must provide the proper dynamics for helping students become successful in almost every category of social and psychological well being. Having extended itself well beyond self—esteem ideology, secondary school's affective curricula routinely includes two other programs directly related to the learning-thinking disconnect, cooperative learning and multicultural education. The common values upon which these programs rest can not be disputed. In addition to educators, all democratic citizens recognize the urgent need for social institutions to nurture respect for other people and for other cultures in an increasingly uncivil and violent generation. Similarly part of our shared legacy, the values of self-discipline and legislated policies of equal opportunity buttress behavior modification and inclusion programs while vying for prominence in the newly amalgamated affective curriculum. However, besides self-esteem, we believe that cooperative learning and multicultural education are the value-based programs most closely associated with the divorce between student's thinking and learning at the heart of our book. Given their highly publicized and visible role within the secondary curriculum, these affective programs have had the strongest impact on how students perceive learning and what they are actually taught in preparation for college. We can here only begin the task of clarifying the inflationary effects these combined affective programs have on not so much adolescent identity, as students' potential as academic and life-long learners.

Concurrent with the swift advance of affective programs in the secondary curriculum over the last two and a half decades have been educators' growing concerns over the impact of broad social changes—particularly in family structure, demographics, and media influences—on students' ability to learn. The effects of these radical cultural shifts on students' perceptions of and attitudes toward learning have been the subject of extensive theorization in all relevant disciplines. All told, the response of the educational community to the increasing alienation of adolescents from their traditional support systems, as well as from their developing intellects, is best summed up by Mikalachki: "Cognitive learning cannot take place in a state of affective disorder, and we can no longer assume that the family or some other agency will take responsibility for the student's affective development. It is imperative that school systems devote both their wits and their financial resources to the production of programs of affective learning" (19) Proclamations of this sort were allowed to raise secondary affective education to the level of importance and implementation it now shares with academic or discipline-based educational objectives. Many secondary teachers, consequently, have reconceived their main role as the "facilitator" of their district's combined affective and academic goals. From this perspective, they have been relegated to professional enforcers of their district's preestablished learning model. The balancing act these teachers must play is particularly difficult; they often must fight the clock to even minimally prepare students to meet subject area standards. While each of these corollary programs began as an outgrowth of experts' efforts to offset the erosion of common values caused by decaying social institutions, secondary school's affective curricula must now be held accountable for contributing to students' declining motivation and preparation for academic learning. We are, moreover, especially concerned with interpreting the far-reaching effects of schools' behavioral and sociopolitical agendas on students' preparation for thinking and learning critically about academic disciplines, and also on the teacher's ability to help students achieve these goals.

During the '90's, cooperative learning has become the leader in the new affective category of interactive or group learning strategies. Conceived and formulated during the '80's, this interactive strategy has blossomed into a learning objective in its own right. Its aim, as one text geared for middle and secondary school clarifies, is to "encourage students to work together and help each other toward common goals, and because of this, they have been found to be successful in fostering positive inter-group attitudes in multicultural classrooms" (Jacobsen 232). Another source, written for elementary grades, echoes this correlation of social values and learning format: "Of all grouping options, cooperative grouping may represent the best opportunity for every student to contribute to the group...[a]ll group members have responsibilities for group and individual learning" (Radencich and McKay 33-4). Cooperative grouping, capable of simultaneously enhancing socialization skills and multicultural awareness, is the favored K-12 methodology. This learning approach can create in-class opportunities where students can practice getting along with not only other students, but with students of diverse cultural backgrounds. Most tellingly, up-to-date texts on instructional approaches for elementary, middle school, or secondary levels, with their extensive analyses of the nature, purposes, and forms of this popular affective vehicle, reflect the degree to which cooperative learning has become synonymous with effective teaching/learning nationwide. For the sake of concreteness, however, let us consider Susie B's personal viewpoint on the educational advantages of cooperative learning.

To recall, Susie B has entered college with what she considers a commendable secondary achievement—a "B" average sustained throughout her entire four years of high school. Looking back, she is convinced that her teachers provided her with an excellent academic background, while giving her many opportunities to "interact" with her friends. As one assessment of students' understanding of the unit on Edgar Allan Poe's short stories, her 11th grade English teacher designed a cooperative learning project. Each group, abiding by the rules of cooperative learning, had to work together writing a short story imitating the ironic point of view and symbolism Poe used to satirize numerous aspects of his hypocritical society. Upon completion, each group would present its verbal creation to the class, replete with costumes and props. Susie penned the following account of what her group accomplished during their last of three group sessions:

When I arrived at English class, Mrs. O had us get into our groups and said we could work together the entire period finishing our Poe projects. Peggy, Sara, Tom, and I were all so relieved! We thought we were going to be tested on the last three stories in the Poe collection. Thank God I had the schedule mixed up! I didn't even read "Premature Burial" last night

because of cheerleading practice taking so long. That wasn't my only surprise. Mrs. O let us get to our project immediately—not even a five minute
lecture on what we were supposed to do or how we should do it. Just a
quick reminder of some guideline sheet she gave us last week for the project,
but my group had forgotten to bring their copies. Oh, well, we pretty much
have a great idea and know we are writing a story if not as good as Poe's, at
least a lot more interesting and relevant to readers like us today. Like our
teacher keeps telling us, we just need to let out the "author" in all of us. We
are rewriting "The Tell Tale Heart" from the point of view of the victim—
finally a chance to let this poor old man set the facts straight about his
"grotesque" looking eye that started the whole cycle of horror in the first
place. We all thought we could make this detail gorier and more elaborate
than Poe! Before class, I checked with some other kids in the class. They all
were at different stages of their Poe story. Joe's group still had no clue as to
what kind of project they were going to do but they are good at looking
busy in class while trying to keep their motorcycle magazines concealed as
Mrs. O goes around checking on everyone's progress and giving us tips. We
got right to work planning out the ending of our story so we'd be on track—
ours goes into why and how the narrator threw acid on the old man's eye to
make it so repulsive in the first place. We argued a lot the week before but
finally agreed the story would be a lot more entertaining if readers had all
the cool details about the argument that led to this attack. Today we
debated until we all accepted Peggy's idea that the old man's ending of
their long-term homosexual affair would really add spice. Since Peggy and
Sara wrote most of the part finished last week, today I got to describe the
mutilation of the eye as Tom offered great details. Then we took turns
rereading this part until we got it chucked full of fear, suffering, and gore.
We got so involved we had to skimp to bring our story up to where Poe's
begins. The end of class came so quickly. We ran out at the bell, happy to
finish and anticipating the class's reaction to our warped slant on the story.

    In microcosm, Susie B's entry reflects the same disconnection of
thinking from learning that is becoming a common occurrence in

introductory college courses. The most interesting, organized, thorough, clear, and varied instructional formats become powerless when students are unable to synchronize these mutual paths to knowledge, the way they are conditioned to think with the ways they are compelled to learn. Whatever has caused this intellectual chasm, it has something to do with the highly social and cooperative learning formats that have become the centerpiece of secondary learning.

From Susie's perspective, her group seems to have all the characteristics of model learners. They bring enthusiasm and personal relevance to their project; they are actively involved in discovering and controlling their own learning projects. Based on her account, the group also cooperates in making decisions and contributing to the completion of their writing task. Not only do they work together, they enjoy writing about a personally relevant concept, violence, while interacting and cooperating with each other and the teacher as she checks each group's progress and addresses specific concerns. Both Susie and her teacher would concur: the activity could not be more student-centered, "hands-on," and cooperative!

The teacher also plays an important role in this hypothetical classroom scenario. She has designed this cooperative project as a way to assess both what her students have learned throughout the unit, and how creative and cooperative they can be in doing so. Instead of using precious class time further demonstrating the literary elements her students should by now have learned, she relinquishes her teaching capacity to provide a maximal opportunity for them to apply their new understandings about Poe's original contributions to the short story genre. In fact, she feels certain she has made a wise pedagogical decision, grounded in the theory that students become more involved in their learning when permitted to select and engineer the ways in which it is to be applied. Above all, she is most likely using this student-directed and cooperative learning project to best enable her students to demonstrate the balance of affective and academic objectives they are required to achieve.

We certainly recognize the affective benefits Susie B and her group can reap from their cooperative endeavor. However, a group's cooperative spirit in either a figurative or literal classroom is no guarantee that the group will involve thoughtful students—seriously thoughtful students who can all equally make the mental connections needed to not only exhibit or display their learning objective, but understand it as well. In this case, her group's combined effort is expended on the tangible, visual, hands-on cooperative activity; learning remains divorced from specific efforts to review and emulate Poe's short story conventions of point of view, symbolism, and theme in an original story. Chances are the class had carefully taught lessons on these literary conventions involving a variety of teaching and learning formats, including the teacher's thorough explanations and presentations of these short story techniques and opportunities for the students to identify and analyze them in their assigned stories. At least one would hope so. Yet Susie makes no references to these complex literary conventions, let alone to the novel twists given them by Poe that her group was required to incorporate into their own short story. Any ideas on how the group planned to give a Poe-like treatment to each element while integrating all three into their story line are equally missing.

The tedious mental processes required by easy to assign and easy to apply cooperative projects have not been awarded the same attention and scrutiny as the students' affective agenda. Any cooperative project in which students are engaged takes up an entire class period from an ever-diminishing number of days in school. Even the three periods allotted to this project seem insufficient for accomplishing the strenuous mental operations required by this task: the conceptualization and analysis of three different literary elements; the comparison/contrast of Poe's and other short story writers' treatments of these conventional elements; and the difficult synthesis of all three literary components in an original story line. Such expectations would constitute nothing short of cognitive overload for students inadequately prepared for multiple levels of abstract reasoning.

Clearly, the cooperative, interactive, and student-centered merits of this activity remain divorced from the project's more important cognitive dimensions and requirements: the review and analysis of Poe's unique point of view, symbolism, and vision, and the effort to synthesize these into the group's own short version of gothic horror. In the classroom, students' thought processes end up shortchanged by overemphasis on outward behavior and activity. In this hypothetical case, they are unable to consider the larger literary and social contexts in which Poe's tales are framed or to understand the required connections between his tale and theirs, or between the violence and victimization of his culture and theirs. Focused, or "fixated" as Krauthammer asserts, on the display or performance of learning, the journal entry mirrors the growing insignificance students have learned to award subject matter and critical thinking as a result of secondary school's overarching affective goals.

One easily overlooked subtext of this cooperative learning project is the availability of chances secondary students have to avoid applying the academic knowledge most teachers take great effort to impart. Another is that the critical space between learning and thinking—the space where strategic teaching and learning of the critical thought processes of conceptualization, analysis, comparison and contrast, synthesis, evaluation, and others should occur—is increasingly usurped in the secondary classroom by activities dedicated to anti-thinking, behavior-based outcomes. That this teacher was asking these students to think so much attests to her commendable agenda for shaping more thoughtful learners. That she is also powerless to control the amount of time and the instructional resources students require to interweave new knowledge and critical thinking into cooperative writing tasks attests to her school's prioritization of affective over discipline-based learning.

Susie B's hypothetical journal entry is our way of relying on the power of metaphor to illuminate intangible conditions like the alarming gap between secondary students' thinking and learning. In this case, the fictive foursome drift almost effortlessly through their project, planets away from the more formal kind of learning—teacher-directed, discipline-centered, objective-driven, criteria-based, content-overloaded, and literally mind-boggling—to which they must soon adjust in college. This is not to deny that the same learning formats to which secondary students are accustomed will also be offered by their college teachers. But whether or not they are, it is certain that their academic achievements in college will be much more dependent on their individual effort and motivation, and because of this, all the more difficult.

Unfortunately, the suppression of Susie B's developing thought processes has not been the only long-range consequence of her high school's cooperative activity blitz. This learning format figures strongly in her lack of preparation for the teaching and learning formats that dominate the college classroom. Long exposed to congenial, non-threatening, unchallenging, experience-based, hands-on, and socially interactive cooperative learning activities, Susie B and her peers are all the more resistant to the lengthy verbal instruction, full-class in-depth lecture presentations, copious note-taking sessions, one-on-one critical questioning, painstaking written summaries and analyses of reading sources, and preference for individual as opposed to social learning for-mats that comprise the bulk of college learning. Co-dependency on affective-high and thought processing-low lessons of the cooperative brand, for all the wonders they might do for ailing interpersonal skills, has blinded a generation to a more connected and intellectually liberat-ing concept of classroom learning.

There is no doubt that cooperative learning can be an effective vehicle for imparting the discipline-based knowledge that is still the cornerstone of higher education. However, when cooperative learning is conjoined with a shallow content objective or, by contrast, a complex, inadequately presented, or missing content objective, then social interaction unhinged from relevant learning and thinking goals and a display of mere business are the only outcomes for unchallenged, justifiably bored, and turned-off high school students. As a student teacher supervisor, I have noted the increase in activity-driven as opposed to knowledge-driven lessons in English classes, 7-12. Values teaching more and more substitutes for the complex, demanding instructional process that aligns content teaching with students' developing language and thinking skills. In fact, the more lessons are in cooperative and socialization factors, the less the emphasis on, and the shallower the students' understanding of a short-range content objective. The following lessons illustrate this basic principle of deintellectualized teaching/learning formats:

* A 7th grade student teacher organizes a double period lesson on the concepts of poetic tone and descriptive language around five different cooperative group activities. These include: writing and reading journal responses to a model poem; listening to and describing the tone with which the teacher reads the poem; group readings of the poem's descriptive language; group readings of the poem in monotone and then in an appropriate tone; finally, writing and reading another journal entry on the difference between the two readings. There were no verbal or other kinds of instruction for giving students even a minimal analytic breakdown of the poetic concepts of tone or descriptive language; no guided practice allowing students to inductively or deductively learn these concepts; and no way to assess whether or not students were actually learning either poetic concept in this engaging, very cooperative, interactive, and multiple activity-driven lesson.

* To teach the 9th grade class how to paraphrase Shakespearean dialogue, in *Taming of the Shrew*, the student teacher neither introduced this complex reading and writing skill nor provided adequate ways for students to conceptualize and analyze it. After the teacher briefly defined this skill, students worked cooperatively in pairs, switching back and forth between two sets of activities

from the same handout: 1) "translating" sets of dialogue from this and other Shakespearean plays into their own words and reading their versions to the class; 2) identifying the main character traits suggested by their "translations." Lacking adequate initial instruction on paraphrasing and ways to check their initial understanding, these students went almost directly to a cooperative activity. Thus they had no chance to first integrate this important reading and research skill with either their prior knowledge or critical thinking skills. There was a great deal of cooperation between students as they worked in pairs, but they ended up with slim to no knowledge of either paraphrase or Shakespearean comic characterization in this content-overloaded, instructionally weak, and thought-deprived lesson. Obviously, the more important goals from this novice's perspective were met: the students worked cooperatively, focused on their activities, and brought Shakespearean language down to their level of diction.

* To facilitate students' progress on their research paper, both the 11th grade cooperating teacher and the student teacher brought them to the school library for a period-long session in which they were required to work cooperatively on whatever stage of their paper that they happened to be at. Throughout the period, students sat at tables in groups of three or four, as they worked on different stages of their draft while socializing with their group. The session lacked the most basic criteria of a lesson, whether activity-driven or content-driven: a specific research writing objective relevant to a phase of their writing process; an understanding of the critical thinking skill subsumed by that writing objective; an organized series of steps for motivating students, and for teaching and learning the objective; and a valid method for measuring all students' learning of the new knowledge.

Considering the pervasive use of cooperative learning at the secondary level, many questions need immediate answers. These include: To what degree can this secondary classroom orthodoxy improve not only social interaction but also the understanding and application of critical thought processes necessary for thoughtful and connected learning of difficult language arts objectives such as upper level literary concepts, writing processes, or grammatical skills? Can this affective strategy increase subject matter depth and knowledge, while also preparing secondary students to think more critically about their expanding content knowledge? Will a lesson's academic goal be accomplished because of or in spite of using a learning format in which all students are made accountable for their contribution to the group, or in which they can practice interacting cooperatively with other students? Can the academic goal, the main reason why students are being taught in the first place, become overshadowed or subsumed by an activity's overt behavioral objective? Finally, is cooperative learning more apt to produce independent- thinking learners or well-socialized, activity-dependent learners?

We are raising these questions as a way to stimulate critical reflection, scrutiny, and evaluation of the affective program whose overuse or misapplication distorts and fragments the secondary student's perception of and attitudes toward learning in general. Those about to enter college have gone through high school as the decade-long activity blitz overtaking public education reached its apex. The student teachers I have recently supervised at two different colleges have been indoctrinated threefold into the gospel of cooperative learning: via their K-12 education; their undergraduate education courses that trumpet cooperative learning and other affective goals; and their student teacher experience in which they often spend considerable time observing cooperative activities and designing their own for specific lessons. In our college courses, both first-year and upper-class students are quick to convey their familiarity with and preference for this learning format. They do so by repeatedly requesting to work in groups; lavishing the consenting teacher with gratitude; and even basing their course evaluations on the degree to which the teacher used cooperative group activities.

Yet neither in oral nor written responses have we found students making explicit connections between their cooperative projects and their learning. They do not connect them with their development of either specific content knowledge such as the principles of child development or economic factors that shaped the public school system. Nor do they associate this affective vehicle with the specific thinking skills needed to sustain, expand, and apply their knowledge in meaningful ways to discipline-based learning tasks or workplace tasks. Does this secondary learning format really prepare students for the highly concentrated, laborious, and recursive task of acquiring and extending discipline-based knowledge? We contend that this over-exposure to and over-reliance on cooperative learning formats, especially when disconnected from the content material and thought processes vital to understanding, have done more to widen than to bridge the gap between prospective college students' learning and thinking. Reconsider the surfeit of external stimulation that the lengthy cooperative "literary" project affords Susie B. While her affective needs are sated by the constant social, auditory, and visual stimulation of her group, her application of specific thinking, reading, and writing skills to important literary objectives is suspended in a state of inertia for several days. Can a program that conditions students to connect their learning with a system of external gratification and rewards minimally prepare students for the solitary, self-sacrificing, highly concentrated, and intellectually rigorous forms of learning and thinking that will lead them to discipline mastery and college success?

Thirdly, secondary education's emphasis on multicultural education throughout the decade has brought another kind of success to untold numbers of students—the character growth they are conditioned to feel when guided to view an unfamiliar culture from a new perspective of tolerance and respect. As such, multicultural education has played a commendable role engendering in American students a better understanding of and in turn respect for the many cultures that have immigrated to the United States. But to what degree does this affective outcome help second-ary students build coherent subject matter, critical thinking, and language skills, especially the rigorous reading and writing skills, that a college preparatory program has the responsibility to impart?

For all its contribution to students' cultural awareness and esteem, multicultural education is essentially just that—not a knowledge base to which to apply thinking and language skills, but a new disposition of thinking; not a specific and coherent body of concepts and information, but an immeasurable subjective element of feeling and attitude. Specifically, it implies a new appreciation and open-mindedness for an ever-shifting kaleidoscope of populations once considered different, strange, or simply unknown; a new habit of mind that assumedly can be cultivated by educators, administrators, and a rising corps of diversity experts and trainers licensed to be mind-shapers. Yet the "what" of multi-cultural education—the "what" as in, what are the students learning today?—remains subtly obscured by proponents' narrow focus on its ostensible goal of raising student consciousness to an unmitigated cele-bration of the equality of all cultures and their ways of life. These homages to cultural diversity reverberate like mantras, over and over again, throughout newly formatted secondary textbook lessons and class-room activities dedicated to inculcating a multicultural disposition of thought. Whether or not this multicultural perspective is a critical and knowledge-building disposition of thought seems to be of little concern.

This brings us back to a major premise of our book. In assuming the role of mind-shaper, secondary schools compromise their fundamental responsibility to the teaching and learning of knowledge. By taking on the added role as manager and director of students' cultural consciousness, schools are not just shaping predetermined ways of perceiving and think-ing about impartially presented cultures, but going beyond imparting widely shared values of self-esteem and cooperation. In the case of multi-cultural education, educators transgress the line separating intellectual freedom from indoctrination. They do so when they decide how students must think about different cultural groups without first giving them the thorough knowledge from which to infer reasonable conclusions of their own. They also do so any time they make the classroom a site for transmitting arbitrary positions, uninformed assumptions, and biased notions of other cultures to promulgate the diversity and the equality of every existing culture. In doing so, they forfeit their responsibility to teach students the knowledge needed to formulate their own carefully reasoned views; and to model the processes of reason and logic upon which the development of advanced knowledge in any field ultimately depend.

An in-depth and coherent knowledge gained incrementally and painstakingly on a year- to-year basis throughout high school has been the curricular model capable of guiding secondary students to learn thoroughly and analytically, concretely and abstractly, reasonably and open-mindedly about traditional disciplines of English, history, mathematics, and science. Certainly they deserve to have this same curricular model of a core knowledge, and its underlying assumptions about learning, to insure a critical understanding of their own and other cultures. On the contrary, Susie B's secondary multicultural program, now regularized in schools nationwide, clashes sharply with the discipline-based model, sending her contradictory messages about the complex process of developing knowledge. This affective program has moved secondary students further from the thoughtful habits of knowing and learning upon which academic excellence has been and continues to be based.

Hopefully, a closer examination of the "contents" and nature of popular multicultural lessons will encourage others to also suspect the long-range detrimental effects they can have on secondary students' preparation for higher learning. As a secondary program whose purpose is fundamentally affective, in this case the generation of tolerance and respect for diverse cultures, multicultural education lacks a shared body of knowledge like that upon which core subjects of English, history, and science, as well as sub-disciplines of literature, U.S. government, and chemistry, are based. The contents of multicultural education, as currently taught in high school, are erratic and unpredictable. Any culture from Egyptian to Chinese, Native American to Latin American can be transported into the classroom for the sake of showcasing the uniqueness of a people and their achievements. A quick search of the latest journal articles touting this influential program is all that is needed to recognize the shifting forms and perspectives this approach to learning can take. The only staple of this pedagogy is that it is frequently appended to a traditional discipline, literary studies being a favored site for attachment. There are no consistent state or district guidelines for determining which cultures students must be taught, in bits and pieces, to celebrate and revere; no logic to which cultures will next be appended to long established disciplines for the purposes of teaching cultural tolerance.

This program's lack of a shared body of knowledge also has a harmful impact on the teacher's role. From the teacher's perspective, multicultural units in literature and social studies, with their shallow and mercurial content, make it impossible to plan and teach an integral, sequential knowledge upon which students can consistently build new knowledge from one year to the next. The transmission of this sweeping panorama of cultural information and trivia prevents teachers from mapping out and implementing a program of sequential instruction. Two principles of instruction—-the organization of a discipline into interrelated segments or units that students can build on year by year, and the ability to help students acquire enough related knowledge to think, read, and write critically about it—are negated by multicultural education. Even if a teacher is able to quickly gain a sufficient knowledge of another culture such as ancient Egypt, she is denied the conditions needed to provide students the depth and breadth of knowledge necessary for thinking critically about a newly learned culture. In Global Studies, currently taught in 9th and 10th grade, students presumably learn about a smorgasbord of cultures, including ancient Egypt, Greece, and Rome, while spending as little as two weeks to three weeks on each vast chunk of history. For the secondary teacher, multi-cultural education can easily devolve into a sophisticated act of cutting and pasting together pieces of a culture to fabricate another glowing and superficial image of cultural diversity.

Since teachers most directly impact secondary students' intellectual development, their views on multicultural education are paramount. Articles by history and English educators voice wide-ranging complaints regarding the program's fundamental lack of a substantive content for teaching, despite the elevated status being awarded multicultural education K-12. These professionals repeatedly stress the defective nature of a multicultural lesson's or unit's content. Common assessments of *distorted, truncated, fragmented, amalgamated, piece-meal, painless,* and *shallow* reflect teachers' widespread evaluations of this secondary learning program as fundamentally incoherent and inadequate. Theodore Sizer effectively conveys the difference between knowledge- and thought-generating programs, on the one hand, and trendy affective programs like multicultural education, on the other, that permit teachers to give only a fleeting taste of learning: "The typical American high school offers an abundance of opportunities and curricula, and most kids sample this and that, becoming informed about many things but unable to make much use of anything. The essential offerings are those which are most useful and most generative—that is, the most effective in leading to more knowledge. They must connect with one another and be as coherent as possible" (105). Clearly, this sad commentary equally applies to the latest engines of grocery store education that continue to offer students no space, mental or physical, to construct genuine critical knowledge and understanding.

Classroom teachers contribute vivid snapshots of the glaring divorce between activity and knowledge, learning and serious thinking that educational multiculturalism has incurred. Diversity awareness activities recently observed by former history teacher and director of the National Council for History Education, Elaine Wrisely Reed, reflect this appalling disconnection we have also discovered in many cooperative learning activities. She describes one lesson on "the treatment of Native Americans [which] notes that the Cherokee Nation had their own newspaper, the Cherokee Phoenix. It then goes on to suggest creating a newspaper about your class. The second activity in the lesson indicates that Sequoyah developed a written alphabet of the Cherokee language; create an alphabet of your own." Another multicultural lesson on "exploring world cultures, in a recent issue of a social studies magazine, provides instructions for making multi-colored beads from strips of magazine paper, cut into triangle pieces. This is intended to address the theme of 'time, continuity, and change,' and is meant to be a discovery project for 'beads around the world'" (Reed 26). These lessons, reflecting a trademark of tolerance instilling lessons, replace thoughtful, criteria-based processes of teaching and learning with student-centered social, hands-on, and kinesthetic activities. That teachers at any grade level would teach such truncated projects can only be explained by two factors. Either they lack adequate knowledge of the diverse cultures they are required to teach to be able to implement coherent lessons from which their students can learn or, worse, they have succumbed to a form of educational "tolerance" that is their way of coping with illegitimate and top-down anti-learning programs. When a principal educational goal is to teach students to respect and equalize all cultures, the reciprocal teacher/student drive for excellence in teaching and learning is precluded.

This takes us to the most drastic effect of multicultural education—the impact it has on the teacher's and student's mutual perception of the learning process. What was once secondary history has slowly metamorphosed into the politically correct social and global studies programs. Due to the multi-culturalization of American history, huge chunks of information and concepts that shaped an American culture have been gradually eliminated, deemed incompatible with the dominant values and ideals of multiculturalism. This blanket chopping of the traditional history curriculum is advocated at all levels of education, but most by those factions within and without education with high stakes in lucrative multicultural grants and textbooks. As Linda Chavez reminds us, "Multiculturalism is not a grassroots movement. It was created, nurtured, and expanded through government policy. Without the expenditure of vast sums of public money, it would wither away and die" (494). Recent essays such as Alexander Stille's "The Betrayal of History" bring starkly to light multicultural education's other hidden agenda, the booming multicultural/social studies textbook industry, and its long-range impact on what and how students are taught to learn in the once rigorous knowledge and thought-generating discipline of history.

But whether the driving force of multiculturalism is corporate greed, political agenda, or educational outcome, our key concern is the impact this program has on what students can learn and to what degree it disconnects their learning from their ability to think and construct knowledge and meaning. Sean Wilentz, professor of history, clarifies this impact as he decries the gradual reduction and elimination of the once integral content and context of American history: "Areas of history that cannot be easily connected to current priorities inevitably get neglected. Diverse ideas and cultures are reduced to one-dimensional subjects or 'factors'" (15E). By this, we can infer that as secondary programs' long-established history curriculum regressed to its current social studies/global studies/multicultural format, the traditional model of knowledge-based teaching and learning was replaced by another. What was the integrated and coherent American history curriculum, within which students progressively strengthened critical thinking and language skills, has been supplanted by a flattened, decontextualized, and values-based process of recognizing, memorizing, and momentarily esteeming fragments of American culture and other cultures—fragments that have been severed from their comprehensive and truth-affirming historical contexts.

In 1991, history professor Kenneth Jackson also sounded the alarm on public education's betrayal of both teaching and learning as it yielded to

multiculturalism's corrosive processes of amalgamating and diversifying, fragmenting and diluting the intellectual framework within which
students learn the discipline of history: "[u]nder a curriculum presumed
to be Eurocentric, students in New York spend no more time on Britain
and Western Europe than they do on Africa, Asia, Latin America, or the
Soviet Union. Equally important, they have little time to consider the
history of any of the regions, whatever their location on the globe. Most
students get around to Europe only in the last quarter of their sophomore year, and then the focus is on contemporary problems, not history.
Only 1 percent of students takes a year-long course in European history,
and those are the kids in advanced placement classes. Everyone else must
make do with an ahistorical concoction known as global studies" (483).
Jackson's point is clear. Teachers are being stripped of their most challenging skill of generating students' critical knowledge of American history. Students, concurrently, are being denied a fuller understanding of
their own history, let alone the histories of all those who have immigrated to the United States in the last half-century.

Ironically, New York State's Education Department, the agency
empowered to revamp both social studies and English, has subsumed
the combined tenets of multicultural education, self-esteem, and cooperative learning into its revised learning standards documents which
govern these curricula. The most recent language arts K-12 document
directs students to successfully listen and read, speak and write for four
main linguistic purposes: information and understanding; literary
response and expression; critical analysis and evaluation; and social
interaction. Each of these language-based standards, furthermore, is
aligned with performance indicators, elaborately outlined forms and
ways by which students need to develop their speaking, listening, reading, and writing skills throughout grades K-12. This language-based
model is the state's answer to the literacy crisis resulting from the rapid
linguistic and cultural diversification of its public schools. However, the
net impact of this additional paradigm shift on the gap between how

student are taught and how they think is the marginalization and erosion of secondary programs dual commitment to helping students build rigorous discipline-based knowledge and critical thinking skills.

To date, there has been no commensurate replacement model for preparing secondary students for the specialized, discipline-based knowledge they must soon learn to think, read, write, speak, and critically think about to meet college standards of learning. However, further diminishing the twin academic goals of knowledge building and critical thinking are the new social studies standards. These standards, also revised to accommodate multicultural education, reduce United States history to a single learning outcome on par with global studies. Not surprisingly, the multicultural approach figures strongly throughout the performance indicators or learning displays recommended in the social studies learning standards document.

We now return to Susie B. and the esteem-raising, cooperation-enhancing, diversity-affirming, literacy-building, content-reducing, surface-skimming, past-eliminating, and thought-flattening programs for learning to which her secondary education delivered her mind. All while she was supposed to be preparing for college. Her learning habits are not just a matter of free will, neglect, or carelessness. Since she herself has been denied the ability to construct a dense and connected knowledge of what should have been her core disciplines, why would anyone—who gives the matter much thought, that is—expect her to bring intellectual and critical depth to her college courses? It is not so much that many of her generation "have neither the aptitudes nor the attitudes that should be prerequisites for going to college," as George Will and other writers themselves superficially reason (84). It is easy for those looking into this learning crisis from the outside to make snap judgments and to blame students or teachers, the most likely scapegoats, for habits of teaching and learning themselves produced by a divisive learning model that severs students from their learning process.

Works Cited

Chavez, Linda. "Demystifying Multiculturalism." *Current Issues and Enduring Questions.* 4th ed. Sylvan Barnet and Hugo. Boston: St. Martin's, 1996. 490–94.

Jackson, Kenneth T. "Too Many Have Let Enthusiasm Outrun Reason." *Current Issues and Enduring Questions.* 4th ed. Sylvan Barnet and Hugo Bedau. Boston: St. Martin's, 1996. 481-85.

Jacobsen, David. *Methods for Teaching: A Skills Approach.* 4th ed. Upper Saddle River, NJ: Prentice Hall, 1993.

Krauthammer, Charles. "Education: Doing Bad and Feeling Good." *Time.* 5 Feb. 1990: 78.

Lerner, Barbara. "Self-Esteem and Excellence: The Choice and the Paradox." *American Educator.* 20.2 Summer 1996: 9+.

Mikalachki, A. "Youth Alienation and the School System." *Orbit* 4.5 1973: 19.

Pogrow, Stanley. "Reforming the Wannabe Reformers." *Phi Delta Kappan.* June 1996: 657–63.

Radencich, Marguerite C., and Lyn J. McKay. *Flexible Grouping for Literacy in the Elementary Grades.* Boston: Allyn and Bacon, 1995.

Reed, Elaine Wrisley. "Projects and Activities: A Means, Not an End." *American Educator.* Winter 1997-98: 26+.

Sizer, Theodore R. *Horace's School: Redesigning the American High School.* Boston: Houghton Mifflin, 1992.

Stille, Alexander. "The Betrayal of History." The New York Review. 11 June 1998: 15–20.

Wilentz, Sean. "The Past Is Not a 'Process.'" *New York Times.* 20 April 1997: 5E.

Will, George. "Disorder in the Schools." *Newsweek.* 13 April 1998: 84.

Chapter Three

Successful Students: Failed Reading and Multiple Draft Writing

At the college level, one needn't search far to discover the cumulative effect of the watering-down of the secondary curricula by a success-touting ideology on students' learning habits. The most immediate, tangible proof of their thinking/learning disconnect is their writing. To us, what students' failed writings bluntly mirror is their failed readings of academic texts. Where Susie B is concerned, college writing becomes not so much an index of writing proficiency as a readily available blue-print of her current habits of thinking and knowing—most of all her reading skills. This first required essay, more than any other dimension of writing, reflects the processes for building knowledge and critically thinking about that knowledge to which the student writer has become conditioned. At the college level, academic writing is not only a sub-dis-cipline comprising a set of related information, concepts, and skills like history, biology, chemistry, literature, mathematics, or art. It is also a complex skill that enables students to write from different frames of ref-erence and create different kinds of meaning; to synthesize and contin-uously expand content knowledge; and to apply and strengthen their developing thought processes. In fact, it is perhaps their most impor-tant tool for developing knowledge across the disciplines. Yet while first-year students are expected to immediately integrate their thinking, reading, and writing skills with developing content knowledge, they have not been taught to do so at the secondary level.

The erosion of content knowledge and the ability to reason critically about that knowledge is nowhere more manifest than in students' initial college writings. The same clutch of educational and cultural factors disconnecting secondary thinking from learning has also disconnected fledgling college students' thinking from their writing. In reducing the depth and breadth of content knowledge about which students must read and learn, high school's "feel-good" learning programs and textbooks rob them of the cognitive bedrock upon which critical thought processes can be developed. For instance, when college students lack understanding of the rudiments of literary interpretation, the literal, artistic, and metaphorical dimensions of conventions like characterization, they cannot be expected to coherently analyze a character in a play or a novel. Nor can they be expected to make meaningful connections between a literary character and the real world when they have had no practice reading closely so as to grasp the character's full literal development and meaning. Inadvertently or not, many secondary programs have been instrumental in mass-producing the increasingly shallow and disconnected thinking, reading, and writing of first-year students.

Writing about literature, as diverse college essays confirm, often reproduces the superficial and muddled treatments that secondary students are taught to give reading sources extending beyond their personal frame of reference. Unfortunately, we suspect that students with a deficient secondary reading background will make little headway improving their reading and writing skills by their second or third year of college. A strong premise supports our reasoning here.

Literature texts, like those used in all college courses, are densely contextualized. Each literary work embraces a complex set of conventions that reflects the larger genre to which it belongs, although many elements may appear in other genres as well. Students are taught how to recognize and use these literary conventions—for example, point of view and foreshadowing in short story; internal characterization and conflict in drama; figurative language, rhythm, and rhyme in poetry—as springboards for understanding and appreciating the art of literature, as well as for achieving new perspectives on the shared concepts underlying the human condition. In a novel, play, or story, the literal level of meaning alone involves a complex hypothetical reality in which readers can make original connections among fictional characters, places, and events, and, in turn, similar aspects of their real lives. Yet inherited passive reading/writing habits stymie the college students from taking advantage of literature's ever-available and limitless context for intellectual and creative thinking and writing. Their writing about literature often reflects their inability to read for a work's literal meaning. And even more frequently, their overly personalized literary analyses suggest both a misunderstanding of the purpose and content of literature and inexperience digging into, grappling with, and thoughtfully interpreting literary conventions. Where literature is concerned, college students lack the concepts, skills and intellectual tools for reading and writing about a mode that simultaneously offers three fertile grounds for thought—the literal, the literary, and the metaphorical. Along with this, they lack the prerequisite skills for reading non-fictional texts across the academic disciplines.

For the same cognitive overload and print-resistance occur when introductory writing courses require students to write about brief, culturally relevant discursive essays in a common text, usually an up-to-date thematic reader or essay collection. For years, I have taught a broad range of undergraduate writing courses at my college—from developmental, to introductory and intermediate, and also Writing for Teachers, an advanced writing course. At all levels, I have been consistently shocked by the difficulty many students have reading and writing about relatively short—no more than 10 pages on average—and varied academic essays. Each semester, I select a common text that includes essays on a wide range of cultural and disciplinary interests. Despite the variety of topics from which to choose, numerous students wait until the last minute to select one. Some claim they are unable to make a personal connection; others confess they are intimidated by the task of writing about a topic from another writer's perspective. All told, no more than a quarter of the students in each class bring anything resembling enthusiasm or passion to the objective, informational topics of their integrated thinking, reading, and writing tasks.

However, it has not taken me years of seeing increasing student anxiety and apathy toward writing about other writers' ideas to understand the main cause of students' initial resistance to college reading and writing tasks. Given their lack of consistent secondary training in reading and writing from dense and impersonal informational contexts and their parallel overexposure to both visual media and passive forms of learning, students' minds invariably resist the rigors of navigating and synthesizing an alien world of academic print. Whether writing about a chapter analyzing the effects of steroids on the cardiovascular system, or a study documenting the recent causes of homelessness, "average" students like Susie B submit initial drafts that make only the thinnest, generic connection with an academic source's dense context of information and concepts. These spare source-based drafts reflect reciprocal reading deficits: an inability to read for selective information and meaning in daunting, data-packed academic sources; also, an inability to apply the essential critical thinking patterns of summary, analysis, and comparison/contrast to these sources. From this, we draw three conclusions. First, the majority lacks methodical instruction and practice in the art of sifting through and making sense out of the purposes and contents of diverse texts, including sources that do not appeal to their personal interests. Second, prior to college most were not taught how to apply critical thinking skills to integrated reading and writing tasks. Finally, given first-year students' frustration with and apathy toward source-based writing, they seem to have little emotional or intellectual stake in what they can learn from the words of others.

The Trouble with College Analysis

Varying degrees of content-resistance emerge in academic writing as soon as students are asked to write a substantive analysis of a reading source. This reading block occurs, despite varied, time-consuming activities for discovering, applying, and learning the structural elements of informative and persuasive texts. The paragraphs below have been excerpted from four initial drafts of full-length analyses of popular argumentative texts. These passages, additionally, were randomly selected from several intermediate or second-semester writing classes that already had extensive practice applying analytical and evaluative thinking to controversial essays. The essays they chose to analyze were respectively: A) Barbara Huttman's "A Crime of Compassion" which advocates the right of the terminally ill to deny life-sustaining technology; B) Thomas Stoddard's "Gay Marriages: Make Them Legal" which argues the unconstitutionality of banning gay marriages; C) Ronald Takaki's "The Harmful Myth of Asian Superiority" which refutes the misconception underlying the general public's view of Asian-Americans; and D) Patricia Williams' "Hate Radio" which claims hate radio violates First Amendment rights.

A.   *Barbara Huttman writes this essay from her own perspective. There wasn't any other outside sources such as statistics or another author. She gets the reader to a point where they feel sorry for Mac and his family. There is one point in the essay where Huttman writes about Mac, "His doctor was one of the several who believe we must extend life as long as we have the means and knowledge to do it" (90). Here Huttman tries to make the pro-life argument look wrong.*

Excerpt A conveys the difficulties college students often have when asked to incorporate relevant textual material into their writing for a specific purpose, in this case the integrated act of reading to understand a specific component of an argument and writing a paragraph that adequately presents and explains that element. The writer begins with a point that could have been followed up with an identification of the persuasive element toward which it seemed to be leading: Huttman's detailed narrative account of Mac's horrific suffering, the case at the heart of this nurse's implied stand on active euthanasia. In fact, due to her extended narrative structure, Huttman does not need to provide "other outside sources such as statistics or another author." However, the reader of this student's analysis learns nothing about the graphic and moving personal narrative at the heart of this essay, only the unsupported point that Huttman makes the reader "feel sorry for Mac and his family." This student's untrained, non-analytic mind never identifies or examines the horrific phases that make up Mac slow, agonizing death, or explains how these parts relate to the author's argumentative purpose. The ability to reason analytically about alternative perspectives remains untapped when students are long trained to associate meaningful reading with personal relevance.

From reading to writing, this incompetent reader transmutes Huttman's story into an exercise in constructing nonsense. The first four sentences establish four disjointed points, reflecting a serious inability to consistently develop units of thought. The only unified purpose this brief "paragraph" seems to serve is to resist any reflection on, let alone controlled analysis of, Huttman's brief but packed narrative. On one hand, the writer could have misconstrued the task. However, several sentences in other sections of the essay display at least a scattershot approach to analysis, suggesting the student had an inkling of her own rhetorical purpose. Yet despite a few erratic stabs at hinting at the graphic suffering of Mac, the disciplined and detached task of analytic reading and writing gives way to more familiar habits. Conditioned to not read for the author's purpose and meaning, the student moves without direction from printed page to written draft, confirming her dead-end learning cycle. Why else would a concise, detailed, and tightly knit essay metamorphose into a mishmash of bland and incoherent ideas? The excerpt and the text subsuming it betray an imperviousness to the carefully organized and vividly detailed images of Mac's suffering; to the controlled focus on his physical, emotional, and psychological suffering that Huttman provides in her appeal to the reader's logic and emotion. Huttman's extended case study should have been easy for a first-year student to analyze due to her clear, coherent organization of the key phases of Mac's suffering. However, these five sentences themselves remain as disconnected from each other as the student's analytic thinking from her reading context, another writer's frame of reference.

B.   *Stoddard uses two women as an example in the essay because it is easier to understand and sympathize with then if it was two men he was discussing. Stoddard realized that dealing with two women was more emotionally appealing because even in this day and age, most people do not like to think about two men getting married, it is easier to think about women.*

Here the student writer similarly forsakes the integrated task of closely reading the extended case study Stoddard presents in support of his stand, and fairly representing this important supporting evidence in a coherent paragraph. This sub-topic, in fact, like all others in the student's essay, eschews the steady part-by-part examination of analytic reasoning, replacing it with the writer's easier, spontaneous habits of personalized thought: snap judgment, unsupported generalization, and gender stereotype. Reading for information and meaning gives way to the uncontrollable urge to deliver personal opinion. The first sentence rushes directly to judgment and an incoherent one at that, washing mindlessly over the concrete information shaping Stoddard's extended example. Instead of analyzing the detailed parts of Stoddard's tragic tale of Sharon Kowalski and Karen Thompson, this writer chooses to flaunt her built-in assumptions: that "we" are more apt to sympathize with lesbian couples than homosexual couples simply because the former are women; that for "most people" it is "easier to think about women" getting married than men; and that Stoddard must have "realized that dealing with two women was more emotionally appealing" to his audience. Nowhere in his essay does Stoddard give any evidence to support these assumptions. Conversely, Stoddard culminates his argument by emphasizing, "gay American adults,"…"their families and friends, together with fair-minded people every where, should demand an end to this monstrous injustice" (59). The student's pretzel logic could have been avoided had she, in the first place, read the essay to objectively analyze another writer's main lines of reasoning and related evidence, and to find out what new insights she might learn from this new vantage point.

From the perspective of standard writing conventions, this brief two-sentence paragraph exhibits serious incoherence at the level of sentence structure. Misunderstanding of concepts of subordination and coordination dovetails with the student's lack of reasoning. As unfocused, incoherent, and unfounded as this sub-topic is, however, our more pressing concern lies less with what is there, than what is not there. As with many literary analysis samples we have examined, students' academic source-based essays convey a disarming indifference to and disengagement from the rhetorical purpose and underlying structure of academic sources. Excerpt B suggests that the reader, instead of reading the three packed paragraphs devoted to this case, skimmed right over Stoddard's efficiently wrought tapestry of interrelated facts, details, and images making up his powerful case study of humans mistreating humans. More careful analysis of the case's presentation would even have led the student to infer that the same cruel series of injustices inflicted on the two women could have just as easily been inflicted on a male couple. As it stands, the student's curt references to the "two women" suggests the missing link of caring about the views and experiences of others which prevents many beginning college students from becoming critical readers and writers.

Just as serious, the passage trumpets the student's immunity from the intricate and strange world of the "other" that is tightly woven into

Stoddard's content. The personal, legal, and social discrimination these "two women" suffered did not merit a painstaking analytic reading and writing. That these "two women" have no more significance than the two impersonal words used to refer to them is worthy of scrutiny. The unwillingness to explore the ideas of others and the others whose lives they in turn can illuminate, the apathy toward other perspectives and experiences, is just as instrumental as the lack of training in critical reading and writing in the deterioration of student learning. Because of the overarching self-centeredness of passage B, objective analysis of the contents and structure of texts, a requisite skill in college reading and writing at every level, is automatically negated. It is replaced by chatty, even substandard expressions of personal feeling and opinion. This writer lacks both motivation and skills to carefully sort through, select, and discuss relevant contents of this brief but riveting case. Absent analytical reasoning, the passage offers nothing of substance or meaning to pass on to an audience, thus perpetuating the cycle of reading and sense-making. Having failed to grasp the relationship between Stoddard's own purpose and his information, the student's thinking also remains impervious to objective standards of evaluation.

C.   *Mr. Takaki used some facts in deceiving ways as well. He tended to give a lot of examples that compare Asian-Americans to other Asian-Americans or he uses comparisons to Caucasions as well. That is okay as he is trying to get the point across that they do not compare favorably to Caucasions yet since his thesis deals with the idea that there is tension between themselves and African-Americans I would have like to have seen some comparisons between those to groups. An example of this idea that he didn't compare the groups he should have compared is evident in the beginning of the essay. He states that the only reason why Asian-Americans compare favorably to Caucasions is that they have to go to school longer and work harder for this equality. Yet, the fact that they are equal almost defeats the thesis he is giving. They do compare will with Caucasions therefore, the belief that they are superior is supported.*

When we examine this excerpt from the standpoint of what the writer communicates from Takaki's frame of reference to the reader, the lack of training in critical reading and the desire to want to think critically about another's view are confirmed. This third excerpt intersperses superficial and bumbled analysis of Takaki's supporting evidence with individual preference, irrelevant opinions, and incoherent evaluations. The writer shifts erratically from informing to feeling, generalizing to opinionizing, trying unsuccessfully to go through the motions of analyzing Takaki's use of evidence. The source's groundwork of hard-core facts and statistics is swept aside, the writer preferring to transmit his own banalities about the author's purpose ("He tended to give a lot of examples that…"; "he uses comparisons to Caucasians as well"; and "he is trying to get the point across that…"). He also displays his preference for personal opinions ("That is okay…" or "…I would have like to have seen") and contradicts his opening evaluative position when he states, "Mr. Takaki used some facts in deceiving ways as well."

The intellectual implications of students' passive reading habits cannot be underestimated. Proof of this student's failure to actively use writing to learn is his flagrant omission of Takaki's statistical evidence, including, "Twenty-five percent of the people in New York City's Chinatown lived below the poverty level in 1980 compared with 17 percent of the city's population," and "A 1987 California study showed that three out of ten Southeast Asian refugee families had been on welfare for four to ten years." In fact, he refuses to recognize or selectively analyze any of Takaki's supporting data—over 12 combined statistics and concrete examples in one compact argument. Whether unwilling or unable to analyze the source of the author's evidence, the writer ends up producing a stream of incoherent ideas instead of expanding his and his reader's understanding of an important cultural issue. What this excerpt points to is not so much a case of illiteracy as long-promoted thinking and reading habits greatly at odds with the critical reading and writing tasks expected of first-year college students. Much more than remedial lessons in basic writing skills is needed to fix this case of failed learning. Until secondary students learn how to analytically read sources for specific meaning such as supporting evidence, and value reading about alternate views on broad, even impersonal, social issues, they will remain unprepared for essential college learning tasks. Concerning another aspect of this excerpt, the number of errors in syntax, grammar, and mechanics in this single paragraph are also excessive enough to suggest illiteracy. However, these are but a linguistic by-product of much more serious reading and writing deficiencies being promoted and ever rewarded at the secondary, college-preparatory level of education. When secondary standards in content knowledge and critical thinking erode, so do standards for the crucial language arts of reading and writing. Faulty grammar, mechanics, diction, and syntax are to be expected from students not in the habit of reading and thinking critically about the dense information, specialized knowledge, and unconventional views presented by others in the first place.

As the paragraphs from these randomly chosen essays confirm, the erosion of critical reasoning and reading skills runs parallel with public education's disparagement of rigorous knowledge and learning standards in all core subjects. As Hirsch has already incisively warned, "Critical thinking is always predicated on relevant knowledge: One cannot think critically unless one has a lot of relevant knowledge about the issue at hand. Critical thinking is not merely giving one's opinion. To counterpose 'critical thinking' and 'mere facts' is a profound empirical mistake" (qtd. in "Core Knowledge" 7). Until educators at all levels decide to ground secondary reform in the complete and integrated ways by which students need to learn new content knowledge, the sad state of thinking and writing exhibited in these three excerpts will continue to be passed on.

In contrast to the first three passages, the following two paragraphs from another student essay showcase the benefits that critical and inspired reading has for analytic reading and writing tasks:

D. *Williams uses melodramatic examples to collect agreement through pity. First she paints a picture of herself as a victim: poor, naive Patricia is trying to wash her wineglasses when she is forced to hear "filth" on the radio (582). The reader can envision the annihilation of Patricia's mental picture of the harmonious world where everyone loves each other. Although she acknowledges that bigotry is not something new, she thought that the civil rights revolution had conquered it (586). She must have lived in a cave on a deserted island for the last thirty years with earplugs and eyes closed to be surprised at the radio conversation that she cites. In actuality, Williams is a law graduate of Harvard University and a professor at Columbia University. Nevertheless, she is manipulating her readers into believing that she is naive because she knows childlike naivete is a quality that evokes pity. She is using the corruption of her innocence, the revelation of the horrible truth that hatred exists, to gather empathy from her readers. If she were to present herself as a Harvard law graduate and professor at Columbia University and give logical evidence instead of manipulative, emotional evidence, she would lose her pathetic quality, but gain more respect and have a stronger argument. Eliciting pity is not a proper argument, but manipulative pity is both dishonest and improper.*

Williams also uses illogical reasoning in her interpretation of the radio conversation that she uses as an example. The radio conversation refers to Americans of African descent as "Blafricans," stating "they can't make up their minds [about what] they want to be called" (582). Williams argues that "Blafrican" is a "stand-in for nigger" (583). The radio conversation uses the term "Blafrican" to mock the inability of the black population to decide on a generally accepted term that no one takes offense to (582). Although Williams is rightfully offended by the conversation as a whole, she is over-exaggerating when she compares Blafrican, a blend of the words "black" and "African," to "nigger" (584). She also accuses the radio conversation of deeming black people to be "without intelligence" (583). The radio conversation only said that Clarence Thomas was without intelligence (582). Thus Williams is using faulty logic. Assume that Clarence Thomas was without intelligence. Clarence Thomas is black. She wrongly deduces that the radio conversation was judging all blacks to be without intelligence. The radio conversation is guilty of the common practice of insulting the intelligence of a politician, but Williams wrongly infers that since this politician is black, the intelligence of the entire black population is also being insulted.

This fourth excerpt is an exhilarating change from the other three. It analyzes adequately, documents solidly, evaluates reasonably, and also reaches beyond the text to make some original and refreshing connections with Williams' prior knowledge and experiences. It reflects the writer's awareness of her own purpose as a source analyzer, her source's purpose as an arguer, and her audience's needs for certain writing standards—three different frames of reference the other writers failed to acknowledge or to impart. Moreover, she seems to anticipate an audience of intelligent, information-hungry people who expect to have those traits validated by the sources they read. What most drives this student's heightened proficiency in written communication, besides her range and precision of diction, is her capacity and desire to rigorously apply analytic reasoning to the components of another writer's argument. Both paragraphs reflect a reciprocal process of analytically reading for and writing about two selective and relevant components of the source's argument, "melodramatic examples" and "illogical reasoning." The documented quotes and paraphrases of Williams' persuasive strategies woven throughout both paragraphs, as well as the use of coherent transitions between ideas, confirm this student's disciplined effort to read and write analytically about another writer's thought process. Also this excerpt conveys what is increasingly rare in beginning college writers—a keen interest in and scrutiny of how another writer uses language devices and thought processes to persuade the audience. Unlike the first three, writer D brings to her work the desire and capacity to reflect on, question, and give deeper meaning to her own and others' ideas that is the true mark of a critical thinker.

Unlike the others, these two paragraphs pulsate with the writer's uncommon excitement for making sense out of another's ideas. Fully activating her analytic reasoning, the student searches for and examines the subtle, easily overlooked ways Williams uses "melodramatic examples" and "illogical reasoning." Her method of composition is testimony here to her willingness to explore and better communicate the deeper ways the "other" both thinks and writes. Besides recognizing Williams' own thought processes, the student's analytic thinking generates a vibrant rhetoric for capturing the nuances of this arguer's interrelated tasks. "[P]aints," "acknowledges," "is manipulating," "argues," "is rightfully," "accuses," "deduces," and "infers"—each term clarifies a different thought process of the source author. More importantly, her close scrutiny of the author's mental acts reflects the degree to which she has acknowledged and shifted her focus to another writer's frame of reference. She is absorbed in the process of scrutinizing, identifying, naming, illustrating and explaining how someone else uses language to affect others' thinking.

This excerpt, thus, reflects a heightened form of analytic reading and writing. Yet while we gain new insights into the arguer's science of manipulative thinking and writing, we learn nothing about the student's personal feelings, attitudes, or convictions regarding either the controversy of hate radio or the writer condemning it. Unencumbered by irrelevant opinions and subjective views, the audience, like the student writer, can move logically from analysis to evaluations grounded in evidence. The trap of dead-end has been transcended. The smooth connections between this writer's thinking, reading, and writing reflect the generative cycle of knowledge from writer, to reader, to written text.

Without a preliminary analytic reading, this student could not have established the author's argumentative components or the related examples to which to apply standards of reason and logic. Her acknowledgement and documentation of Williams's lines of reasoning and evidence confirm her rare habit of reading analytically for the rhetorical purpose and content of others' written texts. Clearly, she has naturalized the processes of analyzing others' thinking and information and has used her writing to communicate this meaning. Most likely, she will be able to competently and enthusiastically analyze and evaluate a full-length novel or a chapter on a key sociology concept when required to do so. This is not to say her writing is flawless. In several sentences, unconnected ideas and needless repetition of "uses" destroy coherence. Greater audience sensitivity also could have directed the student to extend several quoted passages for fairer representation of the author's meaning. However, when students fail to acknowledge and represent a source author's purpose and content, as do writers A and B, surface errors will abound. Simply put, these students have failed to read enough to internalize the thought processes and writing conventions of those they read. When the right audiences are inspired by self-transcending, thought-expanding, and other-affirming student insights like, "the reader can envision the annihilation of Patricia's mental picture of the harmonious world where everyone loves each other," or "she uses the corruption of her innocence, the revelation of the horrible truth that hatred exists, to gather empathy from her readers," then they will take the right steps to guarantee all secondary students can think, read, and write critically by the time they enter college.

Part II—The Trouble with College Synthesis

Fear of reading and writing about academic texts fills the classroom when first-year students are asked to compose a synthesis of three or more authors' views on an academic issue of their choice. Synthesis, the critical thinking skill needed at the intermediate level of academic writing and as students advance in their discipline, involves the ability to combine three or more authors' views on specific aspects of a shared concept like freedom of speech or a controversial topic such as affirmative action programs. This ability to analyze and integrate varied source views around a common idea is the key building block of advanced expository, argumentative, and research papers. It is also the academic writing standard teachers take most for granted. Recently, several students in my intermediate academic writing class with a strong interest in the issue of homelessness, chose to write informative research essays synthesizing up to six different writers' views on the causes of the new homeless population. From the start, the students found the thinking and reading skills needed to accomplish this multifaceted task exceptionally hard to integrate, and unlike any learning task done in high school. Their initial response to academic source synthesis, particularly its level of difficulty and unfamiliarity, was right on the mark. Yet by carefully examining how other writers use and benefit from this knowledge-building skill, they took the first step toward making this empowering thinking skill an integral part of their learning process.

In contrast with synthesis, analysis involves both categorizing and elaborating on specific elements of a source's content or structure, one at a time and in-depth. The students found that analyzing the causes of the new homeless in a single source first involves reading for and accurately summarizing underlying causes like reduced subsidies for low-income housing and large scale downsizing/layoffs in the manufacturing sector. We have already illustrated the incoherence, shallowness, and resistance that can result when students first attempt to analyze specific attributes of unfamiliar topics like gender discrimination, terminal patients' rights, or minority stereotypes. However, when required to extend their critical thinking to include synthesis, the written result often resembles illiteracy due to a cognitive overload. As this group of students discovered, multiple source synthesis includes summary and analysis of the causes of homelessness posited by different authors. In order to achieve synthesis, they needed to make valid inferences about the subtle ways these sources compare and contrast in their causal reasoning; to discover and communicate the deeper relationships among multiple contexts. Because source synthesis simultaneously requires close analysis of shared categories across texts, and broad generalization about how diverse experts relate in their views on important public issues, acritical thinkers unused to writing about others' ideas in the first place often erect a variety of defense mechanisms. For academic writing teachers, source synthesis becomes a telling indicator of two interrelated problems of first-year students: lack of training in critical thinking skills and lack of interest in exploring the views of others on public issues and abstract concepts. Considering the many ways students convolute the objective and methodical process of source analysis, one might wonder exactly how they fare with their first full-length, multiple source synthesis.

Struggling to synthesize three different views on two different aspects of our freedom of speech, one student with poor basic writing skills to begin displays a not-so- infrequent coping strategy in these back-to-back sub-topics:

A.   *Should or shouldn't freedom of speech be regulated. Susan Jacoby feels that any regulation would be against free speech. Jacoby states that the government is powerless in trying any type of regulation because the Constitution is a document that cannot be argued against (Jacoby 16). On the other hand, Derek Bok feels that if speech were to be regulated it would be the responsibility of the community. By making it the responsibility of the community instead of any one organization or institution less tension is created. Some instances there is way to much inappropriate speech used. So Bok feels that the community as a whole can better help speech regulation than any one given institution, because community can better shape the attitudes of people (Bok 255-26). Lawrence feels that there is a constitutional basis for regulation. He feels this way because displaying some speech in certain situations is against the law. Laws are all derived from breakdowns of the constitution. So indeed there would be a conditional basis for regulation of speech in some situations (Lawrence 682-685).*

The authors also touch on the topic of censorship in their writings. Jacoby feels that censorship could help reducing inappropriate conduct, but my not be the best way. Although at the same time Jacoby feels that censorship would not be a good way in dealing with speech (Jacoby 16-18). Lawrence feels that censorship can be avoided. Avoiding it all relies on being able to conduct intellectual arguments. Intellectual arguments make for conversations that are less heated and look more at the issues (Lawrence 682-686). Bok views censorship as dangerous. It is difficult to define when to use it and when not to. If censorship were in place it would come into play at the wrong time on some occasions and create a problem bigger than originally what was at hand (Bok 25).

A cursory reading of the first paragraph suggests an analytic mind at work. The writer gives a focused and balanced summary of three writers' stands regarding free speech regulations. It also conveys the student's effort to synthesize views by explaining how they differ in their stands. The tally is clear: Jacoby opposes all regulation on constitutional grounds; Bok favors public regulation according to democratic principles; and Lawrence favors regulation of speech only in certain situations on constitutional and legal grounds. Nevertheless, this student adheres to the "slim pickings" school of source analysis and synthesis. He gives a minimalist's account of all three views on speech regulations, omitting authors' specific lines of reasoning and underlying premises. In other words, he conveys no interest in reading for and fairly representing each source's distinct claim, or meeting the audience's need for clear, adequately represented and documented source views. This skimpy attempt at multiple source synthesis raises a battery of questions. How close to Jacoby's original meaning is the student's paraphrase that the Constitution "cannot be argued against"? To whom or what is Bok referring with vague terms like "community" and "any one given institution"? Why doesn't the student bother to provide the reader with adequate textual information to clarify these views? Could Lawrence have been so vague as to leave his reader with no specific examples of the kinds of speech "situations" that should be subject to existing laws?

As this excerpt suggests, college students' lack the ability to scrutinize and fully analyze the structural or conceptual parts making up a single informative or argumentative text. Not only do they lack training in analytic reasoning, the groundwork of synthesis, but also in actually synthesizing or inferring relationships among multiple source views. Such thinking/writing is totally new to them. They have learned to write in student-centered learning formats like personal journal responses, and collaborative learning groups or peer evaluation sessions involving socially mediated activities. At college, they must abruptly shift to rigorous thinking and writing, independently and critically, about other writers' ideas and views on public-interest topics. This task poses an intimidating intellectual challenge for which typical first-year college students have little, if any, preparation. Academic writing is not a process which students can teach themselves. Their success as source synthesizers depends largely on individual, focused readings of sources, the teacher's instructional formats, and disciplined effort to understand and intentionally apply their innate skills of analysis and synthesis to academic reading and writing. Students today cannot discover, on their own, the complex, multi-strand learning tasks that involve, almost simultaneously, critical thinking, reading, and writing. Nor are the majority of secondary teachers trained to teach integrated learning tasks like source synthesis, for that matter.

On one level, this student's failure to thoroughly analyze multiple authors' main claims, particularly their different premises or underlying beliefs, reflects weak composing skills, specifically sub-topic development. Yet when we factor in the missing dimensions of the student's learning process, what this excerpt really reflects is the lack of training secondary students receive in critical learning tasks. The omission of authors' more precise lines of reasoning, verbatim ideas or carefully paraphrased evidence for supporting these thoughts, reflects the student's failure to understand the process of analyzing academic sources, as well as inexperience in reading in an investigative way about the structural parts of an argument. This surface-skimming approach to analyzing and synthesizing three authors' main stands or claims on free speech regulation, the get-me-to-the-finish-line approach to writing, does nothing to offset the widening chasm between self-based and other-based writing. But this is also one of the most common coping strategies of students unfamiliar with the critical thinker's exploratory mode of reading, one free of bias and always open to new perspectives, that is at the heart of multiple source synthesis. Unfortunately, the prominence awarded students' personal views in secondary writing pedagogy could not clash more with the dominant value awarded the ideas and thought processes of others at the college level.

But what about the question, is this real synthesis? The answer, of course, depends on which concept of writing the student has internalized. According to the writing paradigm operative here, source views merely need to be quickly summarized, one after another, like so many items on a grocery list. The problem is, academic synthesis deals not with fixed, quantifiable properties like groceries, but rather with the diverse reasoning processes of thinking writers. Two authors may agree on one common point like speech regulations or psychological effects of homelessness, but not on another. Two may be linked by subtle shades of agreement in support of mandatory drug testing that need to be clarified for a knowledge-hungry audience. Just as well, two may argue the same stand against capital punishment, but develop vastly different types of supporting evidence. Since comparison and contrast of three or more thinkers' views is the hallmark of academic source synthesis, the ways these views can relate to one another are limitless. Thus the more pressing question is, how can students avoid severe technical and cognitive difficulties when suddenly expected to acknowledge, scrutinize, analyze and synthesize numerous source views when most have had no experience examining the minutiae of one. Academic/critical learning poses an overwhelming burden for a generation of passive learners that has grown accustomed to discussing, reading, and writing in an intellectually "lite," but socially meaningful way.

The student's effort to synthesize these three views boils down to the transition, "on the other hand," signaling stark opposition between Jacoby's and Bok's main positions. From the student's perspective, this is the first step into a vastly more strenuous and independent realm of thinking and learning. To expect the student to elaborate further on this contrast, by explaining more subtle distinctions between these two views, is tantamount to expecting a child to progress directly from crawling to running. As in genuine synthesis, the ability to draw inferences about how varied writers' thinking compares and how these views alter the reader's view as well involves an open, reflective orientation of thought, one that seeks to penetrate the deeper levels of meaning beyond a textual surface. All told, the learning process expected in college far exceeds the average first year student's superficial reading and writing skills, while challenging self-centered views and habits of learning. Most have had inadequate opportunity reading in structured and critical ways beyond textual surfaces, and tend to be stingy at communicating even this level in writing. As I have found in my own academic writing classes, entering students for the most part lack basic competency in critical thought processes of analysis, synthesis, evaluation, and argumentation, particularly as they apply to their reading of dense and critically written academic sources. Interestingly, some students can apply a variety of critical thinking skills in classroom oral discussions and reports. Yet their attempts to apply these thinking skills to college reading and writing are often exacerbated by the difficult syntax and technical vocabularies of discipline-based experts.

In the second paragraph, the student introduces the second common point of the free speech issue addressed by all three sources, that of censorship. To synthesize multiple views on an additional shared aspect requires a second reading of all sources involved. Obviously, the student did this. However, beyond this step in the source synthesis process, the student fails to go. For the remainder of the paragraph, he abandons all effort to fairly and accurately represent multiple perspectives on an extremely relevant and stimulating aspect of this issue. His attempt to synthesize others' views gives way to spouting personal opinions about what these authors feel, as he now views their ideas about censorship through the blurry, self-referential lens of his narrow personal point of view. This defense mechanism, the sudden shift from public to personal writing, is increasingly prevalent in first-year students. The only standard applied consistently to this excerpt, in fact, turns out to be an anti-standard: the repetition of the verb, "feel," eight times in these two paragraphs and generously throughout the entire draft. Why is it that students, prior to college, have not learned at least a dozen verbs of mental action for what writers do when they write, and thinkers when they think? In their first source-based, academic essay, many college students display a mental block for using any but the personally relevant, "feel," and its stand-in verb, "believe" and "think," to denote the vast and precise functions of a writer's mind. Overtaxed by thinking about others' thinking and the demands of a public audience, students often abruptly revert to the comforting habits of writing from their personal frame of reference.

On one level, this distracting writing habit is a powerful index of college students' language impoverishment and deficient reading experience. Going further, it also mirrors the failure of secondary programs to develop active and reflective readers who care about what the authors of their high school texts think, mean, and communicate. Secondary programs that condone passive states of feeling and learning ultimately suppress students' innate ability and desire to think, read, and write in the empowering, transactional mode of academic writing. Ironically, these are the very students who urgently need the cognitive and social benefits of transactional writing to transcend their narrow, self-referencing modes of thinking and learning. Also, we need to view the incoherence and inaccuracy of the entire second paragraph as not so much the student's fault and carelessness, as just one more flagrant reminder of how poorly prepared, intellectually and affectively, students are for the complex college learning tasks demanded across the disciplines. They will remain unprepared as long as behavioral goals, whether self-esteem, cooperative learning, multiculturalism, or the latest slant on character education, continue to fragment and erode secondary students' integrated thinking, reading, and writing skills.

A longer excerpt from another essay on the same synthesis topic vividly illustrates the degree to which "touchy-feely" writing habits negate the knowledge-building and self-expanding benefits of academic writing:

B.   *All the authors feel that there is some way to make people feel better about the thoughts on censorship. Susan Jacoby feels that writers should be able to print what they feel is appropriate and be able to do this without interference from anyone, but the they fact is, not everyone will think everything printed is acceptable, and not think it is offensive in some way. Derek Bok also feels that the first amendment should be protected without exception, because if the government imposes restrictions on people, they are restricting the Constitutional rights of United States citizens. Charles R. Lawrence III regards the first amendment by saying there should be restrictions put on hate speech because this will inflict psychic injury on certain people, and this is as bad as inflicting physical injury on someone.*

The three authors feel there should be some sort of censorship. Susan Jacoby feels that there should be a sort of self-censorship. If one regards a certain type of material offensive then do not subject oneself to that material. Derek Bok also feels that if one does not feel comfortable with a certain type material then stay away from it as much as possible, this is no difficult to do. Bok also feels that people should use self-censorship in being sensitive to minorities, and counseling those who do not sensor themselves. Certain types of magazines such as Playboy and Hustler are usually regarded as offensive, and if someone finds it offensive, then the individual should not go out and purchase the magazines. This seems to be the easiest way to avoid being offended by such material. Charles R. Lawrence III believes there should be a regulatory standard of some material, mostly against hate

speech. Lawrence believes that the use of free speech as hate speech is caus-
ing the bigotry to continue in this country. Regulation of hate speech seems
to be the only way to eliminate racism, according to Lawrence.

This student bluntly states her first point of synthesis, how other writers "feel" about the ways to "make people feel better about thoughts on censorship," and indirectly presents the second, their feelings about forms of censorship, mainly self-censorship, through example. This passage at least consistently demonstrates a capacity to critically read for and understand the larger context of factors involved in a controversial issue that can eventually lead to valid and thoroughly grounded inferences. However, the sensitivity and skills needed for recognizing the broader conceptual framework of an issue—definitions, legal and ideological grounds, causal factors, historical context and precedents, and the many processes, participants, effects or other attributes that could be involved—are acquired only through time-consuming and structured reading activities and follow-up discussions on these attributes. Such arduous reading lessons are resisted by most high school students. Systematically reading deprived, college students today are gravely under-prepared for reading and thinking beyond the flat surface of a controversial issue or academic topic for its complex conceptual elements. They cannot read the forest through the trees.

Often undermining the ability to think critically about the thinking of other writers is students' current obsession with subjective states of feeling and expressing opinions. Here the student incessantly filters the ideas of Jacoby, Bok, and Lawrence and the concrete facts upon which they are grounded through a hazy screen of personal feeling and opinion. This unrelenting subjective filter controls her thinking and shapes how she perceives others' thinking as well. So locked is she in this narrow, self-centered view—a view essentially of how she and everyone else feels and expresses whatever comes to mind—that no objective and meaningful synthesis of external views can occur. Any more expansive and critical vantage point from which to examine the outer world of ideas and facts is precluded. Perhaps the most frightening aspect of this perspective is the corresponding linguistic habit that could have been offset had prior schooling been different. Sadly, the suffocating rhetoric of feeling dominating many students' writing history, the narcissistic language promoted by student-centered approaches and activities, makes it difficult and unnecessary to learn a precise and varied vocabulary. Secondary students lack adequate knowledge of verbs for denoting myriad ways of knowing and constructing meaning since such mental processes have been awarded no educational significance.

This first-year writer bluntly states the three authors' first point of synthesis, how other writers "feel" about the ways to "make people feel better about thoughts on censorship," and their second, their feelings that "there should be some sort of censorship." Throughout, her fixation on her own and, in turn, others' subjective feelings and opinions on this issue suppresses her desire to think critically about others' views and their shared points of analysis. Almost incessantly, she filters the main ideas of Jacoby, Bok, and Lawrence and the concrete facts upon which these are based through an obscure haze of personal feeling and generalization. This unrelenting subjectivity controls her thinking and limits what she can learn from different sources. She cannot, for example, get beyond this mindset to notice and attempt to represent each author's separate line of reasoning on what should be fairly easy to identify commonalities. Locked in a self-centered frame of reference, she remains impervious to using reading and writing to identify, analyze, and interrelate the common points of others' views that is the exploratory goal of source synthesis. Sadly, college students can avoid such regression to self-centered, feeling-based writing, and its compliment, the all-purpose rhetoric of feeling, but only if they are intentionally and rigorously guided to learn in active and critical ways about the world of ideas beyond themselves.

The student's overly personal point of view, together with a very limited vocabulary, prevents her from recognizing, representing, and communicating the specific ideas and concrete data communicated by only three experts. The original words Jacoby, Bok, and Lawrence use to convey their exact thoughts on both sub-topics are also not noticed, let alone accurately summarized, paraphrased, quoted, or documented for an audience seeking valid representation of others' meaning. The student merely reminds us, in sledge-hammer fashion, that these authors also think, feel, and believe something. The informative and thought-provoking views of reputable, knowledgeable sources are, in fact, relegated to a litany of monotonous and vague opinions: Jacoby "feels that there shoud be a sort of self-censorship..."; Bok "also feels that if one does not feel comfortable with a certain type material then stay away..."; Lawrence "believes there should be a regulatory standard of some material...." So vague is the writer's language, and so self-preoccupied the thinking, that while some sentences reflect the complex process of subordination, they fail to communicate anything of substance. The student is unable to recognize, convey, or elaborate on any of these authors' scrupulously gathered supporting examples, facts, cases, statistics, or other hard data for the transactional purpose of expanding her own and her reader's understanding of this controversy.

Academic writing, when restricted to the writer's personal frame of reference, betrays its twin commitments to objectively representing and interconnecting diverse perspectives, and effectively communicating these to an implied public audience. As this student's perspective implies, the exciting intricacies of how, what, why, to what degree, and by what standards writers inform or argue about any matter of human interest and concern have been devalued and pushed aside by the vague, standardless, painless student-centered school of thinking and learning. For this acritical college thinker to become a critical reader and writer will require a degree of self-discipline and effort of which she may be capable. We have witnessed amazing transformations in students' learning process. Yet even when passive learners are motivated toward critical learning, there is no shortage of personal and extracurricular factors at college that continue to undermine their achievement of this goal.

Because they lack critical thinking skills, students are also unable to read for—to comprehend and strategically examine—the broader conceptual framework in which a writer presents a concept. They have not been trained to read for the more precise attributes that make up abstract concepts such as freedom of speech, for example; for the exhaustive definitions, legal and ideological grounds, causal factors, historical contexts and precedents, processes, participants, effects and other attributes that knowledgeable writers routinely analyze or argue about, and that critical readers automatically anticipate when they read a new view on this concept. Such critical learning habits can be acquired by secondary students as they prepare for higher education, but only through time-consuming, structured in-class reading and writing lessons that slowly and repeatedly walk them through the processes of critical and conceptual thinking until they become automatic. Until secondary students are trained to be critical learners, they will arrive at college unable to read and think beyond the literal surface for the structural parts of a writer's argument, or the complex elements of a textbook chapter's underlying concept. This is one learning crisis that others can prevent.

There are instances when students, even those infected by the epidemic use of "feel" for predicating anything a writer does, do succeed in objectively synthesizing the intellectual content of academic sources. Invariably, what most distinguishes these proficient college synthesizers is a long-practiced habit of actively and critically reading a variety of genres, especially for the unique twist or turn a new source gives to an old topic. Because the following model reflects this more critical and anticipatory disposition of thinking and reading, the writer's distracting repetition of "feel" turns into an easily revisable writing convention, rather than the mark of a self-centered writer:

C.*Just as there are distinct variations of opinion on which expression should be protected, there are also substantial differences among the three authors' opinions on community regulation of expression. Derek Bok feels that "communities do have the right to regulate speech in order to uphold aesthetic standards…" (Bok 26). By "aesthetic standards," Bok means any form of expression that could possibly disturb or harm the public and its environment. He feels that even with such regulation by the community that there should exist a consistent enforcement of such regulation (Bok 26). Similarly, Lawrence agrees with the general consensus of court rulings on the manner of community involvement in the regulation of expression. Lawrence writes, "the regulation of otherwise protected speech has been permitted when the speech invades the privacy of the unwilling listener's home or when the unwilling listener cannot avoid the speech" (Lawrence 684). Lawrence specifically discusses the dormitory with this point. He feels that the dormitory is an example of a "safe haven" where a student should not be subjected to racist media. He considers it an invasion of a student's home to allow racist material to permeate his or her living area (684). In contrast to the opinions of Lawrence and Bok, Susan Jacoby feels that the community has no place in the regulation of speech and expression. She contends that it is more the duty of the individual, or if that individual is a child, the duty of an adult, to regulate what material is seen and what isn't (Jacoby 18). Generally, she feels that it is the individual's right to censor what he or she is subjected to. Overall, discussion of community involvement in free speech regulation creates a more defined picture of the authors' positions on the issue.*

This synthesis sub-topic exhibits a more fluent and controlled alignment of writing and critical thinking skills. Perhaps this is because it emanates from the student's deep enthusiasm for the act of reading what Freire calls the "word worlds" of others. Within Freire's brilliantly conceived model of learning, as thinking beings we are existentially driven to critically read and to understand the deeper significance of the two interrelated contexts from which we can learn—the expanding context of our lived world, and the expanding context of our reading world. For Freire and Shor, our negotiation between these two contexts for learning and knowing, our lived world and the "word worlds" of others, determines our level of literacy and critical consciousness by enabling us to "become more and more critically communicative beings" (Freire and Shor 13). So tightly interwoven are these two evolving contexts for reading and understanding that:

> Reading is not exhausted merely by decoding the written word or written language, but rather anticipated by and extending into knowledge of the world. Reading the world precedes reading the word, and the subsequent reading of the word cannot dispense with continually reading the world. Language and reality are dynamically intertwined. The understanding attained by critical reading of a text implies perceiving the relationship between text and context (Freire 5).

Within this conceptual model for literacy and learning, academic writing, with its goals of teaching the next generation to critically read the word worlds of others while continually synthesizing these new views with their expanding knowledge and experiences, plays an indispensable role in shaping more literate and critical learners.

Diction alone conveys the student's initial digging into the word worlds of these articles to discover the finer shades of others' reasoning, the "distinct variations" and "substantial differences" among source views for which he carefully read. Rather than skimming for only diluted and distorted views, this first phase of objective synthesis involves critically reading each source, perhaps several times, until discovering a specific sub-topic shared by all. Once this common point is determined, the student then must read even more closely for the unique ways it is developed by each writer. This second step, moreover, is enhanced by the reader's awareness of the many possible components of any issue over which experts may differ, as well as an ingrained respect for the highly individual, ever-shifting frames of reference in which each writer's view is shaped. This passage, with its consistent trajectory away from self and toward writers' variable perspectives on a given attribute, the community's regulation of expression, captures these critical traits at work. The student struggles to accurately represent and document the individual context, notably the underlying belief or value, that shapes each view, while also clarifying distinct forms of regulation espoused by two.

The culminating phase of this synthesis model is deeply tied to the writer's overarching interest in the word worlds of others, the infinite shapes they give to abstract concepts. Having established and substantiated each writer's view on "community regulation of expression," the student then moves through the final, looping-back phase of mature, multiple source synthesis. He achieves this by using his writing to contribute his meaning to these views by inferring their precise interrelationships. First, by using the conjunctive adverbs, "similarly" and "in contrast to," he infers and communicates the connection or interrelationship between these sources. Then to complete the cogent loop of synthesis, however rudimentarily, his original synthesis or rearrangement of separate views triggers additional insight into the differences within this similarity. For instance, the similarity he makes between Lawrence's and Bok's stand on community regulation generates his keener realization that Lawrence "specifically discusses" a dormitory "safe haven" which would require regulation against hate speech. By reflecting on and clarifying the specific ideas and techniques that others use to develop common lines of reasoning, students internalize their use or writing as a powerful tool of critical assessment. This student's implicit recognition of how source writers both converge and diverge will continue to generate his interest in using writing for synthesizing not only the multiplicity of views presented in traditional print, but also those flowing incessantly from electronic sources.

Nevertheless, only after first formulating denser analyses and representation of others' views can students take this first step in expanding thought beyond the literal surfaces of sources toward the mature, recursive, knowledge-generating, and self-liberating process of critical thinking called academic synthesis. This student's struggle to create his own transactional text testifies to how "language and reality are dynamically intertwined" in the academic learning process. Yet who is preparing students for building these critical connections between their word worlds and their lived worlds that form the core of a critical higher education? Certainly, several of this students' points are vague or awkward; however, overall he succeeds in representing three separate views in an original rearrangement, an interrelationship, that is new food for thought, both for himself and his readers. Unfortunately, this level of focused objective synthesis, which meets the standards for in-depth analytic reading and writing by first year students, is becoming a rarity.

Sadly even this adequate level of synthesis can be achieved by only a small number of entering college students today who have developed critical habits of reading and writing. Thus we cannot overstress the importance of understanding and ameliorating what is a more tangible, educational root of the crisis in learning today. The reason why the majority of students now entering college have also become part of this crisis in learning is the least publicized and debated. They have been denied the learning conditions necessary for acquiring the critical reading and writing skills, at the secondary level, for communicating and learning within an academic community. Also, from a more philosophical stand-point, as Freire would say, they lack the one impetus that determines human potential, the human desire to "become more and more critically communicative beings." It is this desire that most strongly differentiates college synthesis sample C from the two preceding college excerpts, and from the problematic secondary samples presented in the next section.

The Trouble with Secondary Literary Analysis

By contrast, those secondary students who cannot read and write critically about their interrelated real and print worlds lack the fundamental desire to do so. But why wouldn't they when countless social, cultural, and educational factors have converged to stifle their need to develop more critical—more questioning and penetrating—ways of reading and writing about the limitless world of concepts, facts, and views that make up academic knowledge? The student-centered approach having now inundated secondary schools, another educational paradox has come full circle. What began as a secondary effort to align teaching and learning formats with changing needs of students has gradually replaced the fundamental learning tools of critical thinking, reading, and writing, with student-centered activities that only superficially instill targeted behaviors like self-esteem, concern for others, and ethnic tolerance. The secondary literary and history word worlds, the traditional wellsprings of pre-college critical thinking, have also been progressively watered-down in level of ideation and language. From the new social studies texts, much of the past has been excised, replaced by politically correct illustrations and shallow, disconnected sub-topics that provide no substantive analysis and, in turn, invite no critical dialogue between reader and text. Soft-cover novels, written by authors of unproven literary merit to entertain adolescent readers, appear out of nowhere even in high school, supplanting mentally and linguistically challenging classical texts because the latter were written by dead white males and/or fail to meet the school's current diversity standards. Reader response was originally a literary approach for linking students' personal experiences with legitimate study of literary texts. However, this approach now leads to exhibitions of learning that have everything to do with validating students' individual lives and self-centered thinking, and little to do with the actual analysis and interpretation of the literary conventions. In these and countless other ways, public education's preoccupation with affective goals and identity politics denies students the learning standards and preconditions that produce critical and college-ready minds. Understandably, when students like Susie B begin their college education, the chasm between old and new ways of learning and thinking appears unbridgeable.

Among the many skills and aptitudes that secondary English education students must display during their student teaching experience is the ability to create and apply analytic scoring guides to students' assigned literary essays. These rubrics are designed to help students view writing as a complex set of concepts, processes, and skills they must learn to control, evaluate, and continuously revise. They also identify and weight the specific writing standards such as clear thesis, coherent sub-topics, audience awareness, sentence structure, and mechanics upon which their score will be based. As one of their requirements, my student teachers provide me with secondary literary analyses, reflecting different levels of competency, they have commented on, evaluated and scored according to these rubrics. In all but a handful, the common denominator has been secondary students' inability to analyze literature. These essays reflect both students' deteriorating knowledge of literary conventions, and their inability to analyze these conventions at their literal, artistic, and metaphorical levels of meaning. At the secondary level, the use of writing to explore and communicate these multiple levels is rapidly eroding. Like writing about academic sources, writing about literature is more and more the end-product of impoverished thinking, reading, knowing, just one more sign of students' fragmented learning agenda.

The three following 10th grade literary analyses were selected by a student teacher to display her ability to respond to and assess what she believed were three different levels of competency. Her students' primary task was to compare and contrast the development of the main characters' ethical or moral conflicts in at least two short stories read during a brief three-week unit. Prior to this literary task, students discussed each story in collaborative and large group formats, focusing on analyzing the development of the main character's internal conflict. As a way to conclude, the student teacher asked the students to explain whether the ending was happy or not, and, if not, to propose changes that might render a "happier" ending.

A.   *Interior and exterior conflicts in the stories of Barn Burning and Teenage Wasteland, are shown through two important characters that are in the story. Mr. Snopes the father of a boy who has many conflicts with-in himself, known as interior conflicts. Low self-confidence in himself, does not like anybody around him who shows to be better or have more than his family. Another interior conflict is maybe he is unhappy to the way his parents had brought him up which could caused him to react the way he does. Most of the conflicts are shown exterior towards other people. Example he goes around burning down barns to people who have not done anything to him expect work hard for what they have. Not knowing that it would be destroyed by some selfish person who can and is capable of working too. Because of Mr. Snope conflicts with himself it caused his own son to have conflicts with in himself and others around him. Sartoris loves his father no doubt about that but the main conflict dealing with interior had to do with his father. For the fact that he was very abuses to the family as will as himself. Sartoris also didn't like or believe in what his father was doing to other people or the way he makes a living. The conflict between the father and other people was dealt with by dieing because his son had told on him and he was shot in the act. The conflict with Sartoris was dealt with him by running away and never looking back to the past. The story could have had a happy ending if the father was willing to change his ways and start a new way of life for the family and himself that would have also solved the conflict with his son and been a good start for a happy ending.*

Teenage Wasteland has many interior conflicts and exterior conflicts dealing with it's two main characters the mother and the son. Because of the son conflicts it caused his mother to have conflicts herself. Most of the mother conflicts are interior conflicts. She has portray herself as a mother. She feels that she had failed as a mother because her son is having some problems. The most problem she have is facing the fact that she tried as a mother therefore it caused all the problem above and more but it also caused exterior conflicts. She hates people who think or question her able to be a good mother. She does not like it when people put down her son not when he is look bad upon because that does not make people think highly of her neither. An example of this is when the teacher had called to let her know that her son was still failing the class, she got very mad because it seem like the teacher was still putting down her son not realize how far he really has come. The son problems had to do with the fact that he thought very low of himself did not like where he was from or what he become. He thought he was not good at anything and didn't have a reason to live. All those emotion that he show are all interior conflicts within himself. Exterior conflicts have do with his mother and his dad. They really didn't give him room to grow or space that he need which caused him to revolt and cause so many problems around him. That was the most exterior conflict he had. He really didn't have any problems with anyone else it just got reflected on to them. The conflict with the mother was never really solved because her son ran away so she has more conflicts. The son old conflict was resolved by running away but he faces new and hard ones to come. The story could have had a more happy ending if there was more communication with in the family.

Interior conflicts and exterior can be shown through many types of attitudes. The situation can have a good outcome or a bad one that all depends on how the characters solve the problem. Barn Burning and Teenage Wasteland outcome with the conflicts were solved the best way for the situation.

B.   Two stories that display internal and external conflicts are "Barn Burning" by William Faulkner and "The Catbird Seat" by James Thurber.

In "Barn Burning" there are both internal and external conflicts. Sarty, the son in the story, has an internal conflict with himself. He has, in fact, more than one internal conflict. The first conflict he faces is whether or not to lie in court to protect his father, who burns barns and other buildings. He knows that it is morally wrong to lie in court, but he is afraid of what his father will do to him. Sarty's father threatens to beat him if he doesn't lie in court. Sarty would have told the truth in court if he was asked to testify, but it ended up that he was not made to speak. This is how that conflict is resolved. It is not a good or gad ending, because Sarty did not have *to speak and defy his father. Evidence of this conflict was that you can tell what Sarty is thinking when the print is in italics. This is how you know that he has an internal conflict, because you can tell what he is thinking. Another internal conflict that Sarty faces is if he should run away from his father and his family in the end of the story. This is another conflict that he has with himself. He is afraid of leaving his family and of what might happen to him, but he doesn't want to be forced to continue to help his father and be forced to lie for him. The evidence for this is also what Sarty is thinking, printed in italics. This conflict is resolved by Sarty deciding on running away at the very end of the story. His father is going to burn down Major de Spain's house because he was going to be forced to give thirty bushels of corn to Major de Spain. Sarty's father is shot and killed in the end by Major de Spain, because Sarty warned him that his father was going to burn his house down. Sarty runs away to get away from his family and be on his own. I don't think that this conflict could have had a happier ending because either way, Sarty is in a bad position. Running away is probably the better solution anyway because Sarty is benefiting from it. An external conflict in "Barn Burning" is in the beginning, the conflict between the father, and society. The judge sentences the father to leave the country as punishment for burning down someone's barn. It is a conflict between the people whose buildings are being burned down, and the father. This conflict is resolved by Sarty's family being forced to leave the country and move away. The father encounters many other external conflicts as well. He has a conflict with Major de Spain. The father ruins one of Major de Spain's rugs, and for payment, he is forced to give bushels of corn to Major de Spain. The father attempts to resolve this conflict by burning down Major de Spain's house. This ultimately resolves in the father getting shot. Sarty warns Major de Spain, so Major de Spain shoots and kills the father. This conflict could have had a happier ending if the father had just decided to pay the bushels and not burn down any more houses, or if Sarty hadn't told Major de Spain, the father might still be alive. As can be seen,*

"Barn Burning" has many internal and external conflicts, none of which were resolved with a happy ending.

"The Catbird Seat" has many internal and external conflicts as well. The first conflict to arise is an external conflict between Mr. Martin and Mrs. Barrows. Mr. Martin sees Mrs. Barrows as a threat to his job at the office. She is new in the office, and has come in and fired people and started doing things her way. Mr. Martin doesn't want her to reorganize his filing department. She had already disrupted other people's systems, and he sees her as a threat. Also, Mr. Martin took an instant dislike to Mrs. Barrow. So Mr. Martin feels threatened, and is going to try to do something to get rid of Mrs. Barrows. This is how this conflict is resolved. In the end, Mrs. Barrows is removed from the office, and Mr. Martin's job is secure again. Mr. Martin succeeded with his plan. There isn't really a happier end to this conflict because either way, Mr. Martin or Mrs. Barrows is going to lose. This leads to the next conflict, which is an internal conflict with Mr. Martin. He has a conflict with himself on how to get rid of Mrs. Barrows. A piece of evidence supporting this is when Mr. Martin says "I demand the death penalty for this horrible person". He was planning on killing her, but that plan failed and he decided not to carry through. But another plan of his succeeded on getting Mrs. Barrows fired. This is how this conflict is resolved. Mr. Martin was always considered by everyone who know him to be a very reliable person with a good reputation. This works on his favor when Mrs. Barrows claims that he was at her house smoking and drinking, and saying that he was planning on killing their boss. He really did these things, but it was his plan to get rid of Mrs. Barrows. People thought that Mrs. Barrows went crazy, so she was fired. This is how this conflict was resolved. It is also expected that Mr. Martin will go back to his old self, now that his job is not in jeopardy. But if another situation like the previous one arose, he would probably devise another plan to secure his job. Again, there is not really a happier ending for this conflict. Theses are the main internal and external conflicts in "The Catbird Seat".

As can be seen, both "Barn Burning" and "The Catbird Seat" display many internal and external conflicts.

C.   The short story "Teenage Wasteland" by Anne Tyler, "The Rocking-Horse Winner" by D. H. Lawrence, and "A Good Man Is Hard To Find" by Flannery O'Conner all portray characters with questionable values and ethics. The Grandmother from "A Good Man Is Hard To Find," Cal from "Teenage Wasteland", and the mother from Rocking-Horse Winner" all display values and ethics that both mirror and differ from each other.

The mother in "The Rocking-Horse Winner" is a suitable example of selfishness and insensitivity. To give a direct example from the plot, she is not at all affected by the death of her young son. Though the direct cause of his death is unknown, it is implied that he died from overexertion. This exertion was brought on by the mother's constant desire for more money, as she had an appetite for buying frivolities. The boy, Paul, addressed his mother in the beginning of the story. He asks her about luck and what makes one lucky. His mother says that the ability to make money is what defines one as lucky. The mother paid little attention to the boy. To waive this negligence, Paul tells her:

"'Well, anyhow,' he said, stoutly, 'I'm a lucky person.'
'Why?' said the mother, with a sudden laugh.
He stared at her. He didn't even know why he had said it.
'God told me,' he asserted, brazening it out."

As one can see, the boy merely wanted the mother's attention. He tries again for attention, and Paul starts to gamble and makes a considerable sum of money. When he dies, it is given to his mother. The following excerpt from the part of Paul's death shows her ability to stick to her selfish and greedy values:

"I never told you, mother, that if I ride my horse, and get there, then I'm absolutely sure—oh, absolutely! Mother, did I ever tell you? I am lucky!'
'No, you never did,' said his mother."

A mother's selfishness and insensitivity are also characteristics of the tutor, Cal, from "Teenage Wasteland". A juvenile delinquent, Donny, is sent to the tutor because of failing grades and inappropriate behavior such as drinking and cutting classes at school. Cal gives Donny and his family the impression that he is a competent and mature teacher. However, the opposite becomes evident when Donny's friend, Miriam, states what occurs at Cal's house.

"'What a neat guy, and what a house! All those kids hanging out, like a club. And the stereo playing rock…gosh, he's not like a grown-up at all !'"

That gives evidence that Cal does not seem overly concerned with the children's academics or social behavior, but instead more about the money he earns in "tutoring". He improves their adolescent ability to socialize, but it will not help them later in life. More evidence comes after Donny stops seeing Cal:

"On the fifteenth of April, they entered Donny in a public school, and they stopped his tutoring sessions. Donny fought both decisions bitterly. Cal, surprisingly enough, did not object. He admitted he'd made no headway with Donny and said it was because Donny was emotionally disturbed." These values of greed and selfishness are much like the mother's in "The Rocking-Horse Winner".

The third character showing these values is the grandmother from "A Good Man Is Hard To Find". Throughout the story, she displays her selfish nature. The clearest example is at the end of the story, when the Misfit takes the lives of her family members. She does nothing that would save them, but instead makes every attempt to keep her own life. Specifically, she allows the Misfit to wear her son's shirt after he has killed him, and tells the Misfit that Jesus will save him. The following is an excerpt displaying her selfishness and cowardice:

"Jesus! the old lady cried. 'You've got good blood! I know you wouldn't shoot a lady! I know you come from nice people! Pray! Jesus, you ought not to shoot a lady! I'll give you all the money I've got!'"

This part in the story occurs after the family has met its demise, including the mother (who also was a lady). The grandmother has resorted to begging, even after she is the only one left. She did not try to stop the Misfit from murdering the rest of her family, yet she is selfishly and shamelessly begging for her own. These selfish values are found in the other characters, as well.

Though the mother, Cal, and the grandmother, all share the common values of selfishness, insensitivity, and greed, they also differ in their values. The mother from "The Rocking-Horse Winner" does not seem to have any moral values, which sets her aside form the other two characters. Every action she took seemed to imply that her family life had no importance to her. The beginning paragraph of the story discusses how she felt uncomfortable around her children, and almost feared them. Her main concern was money. Paul even tried to relieve her of this concern, but money still remained her first priority.

Cal is the sole character with values that seem the most unquestionable. Though he is depicted as a slacker and an underachiever, it is fair to assume that he cares about the children he tutors. Cal takes the time to thoroughly discuss Donny's academic and social problems with the family. He tunes in with the children well, which shows he does care about their current well-being. He is not, however, seriously considering how the slacking off could affect their future. Cal's values seem to be a bit shady. He wants to help the children, but the manner in which he goes about it could improve. The vital thing is that his heart is in the right place.

The grandmother lies in a medium between the other two characters' values. It is clear that there is not much to appreciate about this woman. Not only is she selfish, but she is a liar as well. At one point, she makes up the following story to avoid vacationing in Florida:

"'There was a secret panel in the house,' she said craftily, not telling the truth but wishing that she were, 'and the story went that all the family silver was hidden in it when Sherman came through but it was never found…'"

Despite these characteristics and values, she shows a more vulnerable side at the end that no other character did. She is obviously afraid that the Misfit will soon bring her to her end, and it starts to affect her. She mutters things about Jesus' ability to raise the dead and such, and begins to act less like such a sour old woman. The mother, who had a vulnerable side, but it was more similar to that of a spoiled child. The grandmother's was like an elderly lady, trying to meet her end with a shred of dignity.

The previous stories and their characters all had questionable values and ethics. They also had a deal of similarities and differences amongst those values. That, in turn, made them more lively characters and therefore valuable pieces to the stories.

The task of analyzing and evaluating the wide range of composing skills and writing conventions exhibited in these essays could tax even a seasoned English teacher. However, when they are viewed as emblems of students' overall learning process, they further illuminate the increasing gap between critical and passive learners that make up heterogeneous secondary English classes. From this standpoint, the deeper link between students' knowledge of literary conventions and basic writing skills, and between their literary knowledge and their ability to think critically become clearer. This specific task called on students to apply critical analysis to their interpretation of characters' internal conflicts in two separate stories. It also required them to develop similarities and differences across two works. Because of the range and degrees of writing problems displayed in the first two essays, it is easy to fixate on students' failure to master standard writing conventions. However, we are more concerned with what these essays tell us about the gap between how students are taught to learn literature, and how they need to learn this endangered discipline in order to acquire genuine knowledge and understanding.

A cursory reading of sample A could trigger an equally cursory judgment: this student simply fails to do the required task of comparing and contrasting the main internal conflicts in the two stories. However, the egregious incoherence of the entire paper suggests a more serious problem often whitewashed by both traditional and student-centered criteria for assessing writing. What this paper really reflects is a writer who cannot read for pre-established literary conventions, especially at the

10th grade level. This essay overwhelmingly mirrors the student's inability to read short stories intentionally and selectively by analyzing both characters' internal conflicts, and by comparing and contrasting two authors' different treatments. Reading as a complex process of deliberately applying a mental process like analysis to a specific literary element is unknown to him. We will never know whether this student reads literature, or anything else, outside school. However, his writing confirms that he cannot read fiction for the purpose of analyzing a single character's internal conflict, let alone comparing and contrasting two, because he lacks prerequisite literary knowledge and reading skills to do so. Specifically, he neither understands the literary convention of internal conflict, and the complex phases of the individual choice-making upon which it is built, nor how to apply analytic reasoning to his reading and writing about two main characters' internal conflicts. His attempt to analyze structural elements of information texts would surely devolve into similar incoherence. It would be senseless to penalize this student with a low grade for not applying thinking skills he does not have to a literary convention he does not understand. Yet this is what routinely goes on in high school. Even more illogically, these unqualified students pass from one grade to the next due to inflated grades and social promotions.

As this writer's incoherent analyses suggest, he lacks comprehension of the object about which he should be thinking, reading, and writing— the authors' literary convention for developing internal, not external, conflicts of the stories' main characters. His acritical reading producing only blurry fragments of both types of conflict, what transpires in writing are substandard sentences like, "Low self-confidence in himself, does not like any body around him who shows to be better or have more than his family" or "Sartoris loves his father no doubt about that but the main conflict dealing with interior had to do with his father. For the fact that he was very abuses to the family as will as himself." Through this incoherent word world, we can sense the student's inadequate content knowledge, his mixing of internal and external dilemmas, and his futile struggle to represent each conflict. His lack of necessary content knowledge nullifies the chance of logically analyzing the internal conflicts in both stories or comparing them with each other. Efforts to do so, however painstakingly made, turn out scrambled and distorted. Specifically, he fails to grasp this short story convention's underlying cause-effect pattern, its formalized movement from initial causes and motives, to building inner struggle, to a technical decision or turning point, and finally to various outcomes and consequences. Inadequate background knowledge triggers the vague and convoluted reasoning in which the student's thinking is mired: "Sartoris also didn't like or believe in what his father was doing to other people or the way he makes a living. The conflict between the father and other people was dealt with by dieing because his son had told on him and he was shot in the act." Similarly, missing content knowledge obscures his interpretation of the second story's internal conflict: "Most of the mother conflicts are interior conflicts.... The most problem she have is facing the fact that she tried as a mother therefore it caused all the problem above and more but it also caused exterior conflicts." Beyond this essay's excessive errors in word choice, grammar, sentence structure, and mechanics, what this disjointed writing emphatically conveys is that the student understands neither this genre's sequential formula for developing internal conflicts, nor how to read a story to extract this shared literary meaning. Why therefore should he be expected to compare and contrast in two separate stories a literary convention he is unable to discern and analyze in one?

In-depth analysis of this essay's syntactic flaws, including illogical sentences, missing transitions, and flagrant disagreement between main sentence parts will not eliminate or ameliorate this case of inadequate prior knowledge and learning skills. This student cannot make the required sense of these stories because he has been denied the learning conditions for connecting two critical thinking and reading skills with a complex, multi-step literary convention. Given the glaring discrepancy this essay exhibits between requisite prior knowledge/skills and the student's current knowledge/skills, it makes no sense to expect the student to read beyond the literal level for an artistic convention, or further for its metaphorical meaning. At the secondary level, such failed writing is often patent proof of the dead-end, acritical learning activities promoted by a student-centered, "feel-good" ideology and its preference for social skills over the academic knowledge and learning skills students need in preparation for the next grade. Yet to give the failed knowledge and reading on which this essay is predicated a failing grade would be as illogical as giving a student who cannot read a failing score on a grade-level reading comprehension test.

Regarding assessment, secondary writing teachers would most likely approach this piece as they would all other essays—at the level of discrete, measurable components such as rhetorical purpose, audience awareness, documentation, organization, sentence structure, and distinct classes of writing conventions. However, the deeper interrelated problems in knowing, thinking, and reading that underlie an essay's verbal surface are only superficially addressed, if not ignored altogether, by theorists of the student-centered approach to writing. These educators, in championing students' need to construct their own meanings, go to great lengths to emphasize the distinction between the process and the product of writing. Yet at the same time, they fail to acknowledge or clarify the specific critical thinking and reading skills students need to not simply make sense, but to make sense out of their academic sources in a continuum of specific and interrelated patterns. For example, students are taught to view and apply the writing process as if it were a series of chronological states, from rough draft to polished draft. Yet they are not, at the same time, intentionally taught to make integral connections between the consecutive stages of these process and the critical thinking skills of analysis, comparison/contrast, and synthesis that are expected throughout.

In addition, the specific critical thinking and reading skills presupposed by initial college learning tasks are routinely ignored by secondary programs that view and teach writing not as a vehicle for sharpening and managing academic learning skills, but as a static medium for communicating spontaneous responses on personally relevant literary topics. Student A's literary comparison/contrast, like any other required display of learning, is based on the assumption that he has the prerequisite knowledge and skills. However, we also suspect the student spent valuable classroom time writing comfortably and self-referentially in the personalized formats of free writing and journal entries before abruptly switching to reading and writing about literature for a broad audience. Thus the well-established practice of evaluating only the visible display of student writing, with its neatly compartmentalized and quantifiable features, unfairly masks the classroom practices that are equally responsible for student's fragmented and failed displays of learning. This practice especially countervails broader, learning-centered insights as offered by Link, when he states that "[a] student incapable of performing and applying these prerequisite operations can hardly be expected to perform the overall task. Clearly, if teachers fail to identify the specific source of the child's cognitive weaknesses, corrective actions in this area will suffer" (90).

In the case of writer A, there is no way to know whether corrective actions were taken to help this student understand how to apply critical analysis and comparison and contrast to reading and writing tasks. However, it is highly likely he was deprived of the pre-learning conditions necessary for reading and writing thoughtfully over many years of schooling. If student deficiencies in content knowledge and critical learning skills persist through 10th grade, they will likely continue throughout high school. Moreover, since this substandard essay was awarded a minimally passing score by the student teacher before submitting it to me as an end-of-quarter requirement, educators K-16 need to critically ponder the totality of substandard readings and writings slipping through secondary school's loose net of student-centered learning formats and assessment practices. Secondary programs that focus shortsightedly on the outer processes and measurable displays of learning, whether these involve reading, writing, speaking, listening, deny students the instruction and time-on-task for acquiring the knowledge and thinking skills that determine the genuine, immeasurable components of students' learning. The clutter of non-academic concerns with which secondary teachers, for over a decade, have had to align academic objectives like literary analysis, deprive students like writer A of time-consuming, structured in-class critical reading activities needed to apply patterns like classification, summary, analysis, and synthesis to their writing tasks. Where substandard source-based secondary writing is concerned, the student-centered learning ethos prevents weak students from developing the intellect-driven writing skills necessary for academic and life-long success. The over-emphasis on student-centered values at the secondary level deprives weak students of the learning-centered belief that "those who seem weakly disposed or who take to serious intellectual effort with difficulty need more of it rather than being switched to something less demanding or pressing" (Sizer 142).

Moving to sample B, it seems reasonable to assume that stronger thinking and reading skills drive this student's more proficient interpretation. Unlike the previous writer, whose inadequate literary background precludes meaningful analysis of either character's internal conflict, writer B's grasp of this artistic convention's cause-effect structure enables her to analyze several standard phases of the literary decision-making process. The application of analytic reasoning, however sketchy or incomplete, to a complex literary convention is the main strength of this essay. Competent analysis of any text, regardless of mode, involves purposeful reading for the smaller parts that make up abstract literary concepts and structures, as well as the main pattern linking these parts together. With literary analysis, the reader must be actively engaged in identifying the components of a specific convention, and in representing their implied relationship. To a degree, writer B Applies a more methodical and rehearsed habit of discerning and communicating the interconnected parts of literary conflict, from exposition to resolution.

However, bearing no immunity to flawed thinking and reading, she too resists the effort to think beyond the narrative surface and to link these conflicts intertextually through comparison and contrast, or extratextually with factors like the author's purpose or the stories' cultural contexts only implied by story line. We can only assume that these extended acts of interpretation exceed the more surface-bound thinking and writing practices instilled by her secondary experience.

After summarizing the first character's internal conflict, Sarty's dilemma over "whether or not to lie in court to protect his father, who burn barns and other buildings," she moves coherently through the exposition, the primary impetus for Sarty's conflict—his realization "that it is morally wrong to lie in court"; the complication—when "Sarty's father threatens to beat him if he doesn't lie in court"; and on to the technical climax or pivotal decision—that "Sarty would have told the truth in court if he was asked to testify." At this point, however, she abridges the full drama of Sarty's internal conflict by failing to explain the death of Sarty's father, the story's ironic dramatic climax. Instead she jumps directly to a vague and fragmented resolution, Sarty's exemption from having "to speak and defy his father." Yet despite substantial incoherence, her partial analysis reflects some understanding of the conventional formula by which short story writers develop a main character's pivotal decision. Even this immature level of conflict analysis can only be achieved by readers trained to notice this convention's standard literary phases, and to appreciate each author's unique variation of this literary norm for dramatizing private moral or ethical dilemmas. Thus already somewhat capable of applying analytic reasoning to a cause-effect literary convention, this student is, in a sense, rehearsing for the deeper structures and abstract concepts she will be continuously challenged to analyze in increasingly specialized academic texts.

However, bearing no immunity to failing to perform the required essay tasks, writer B resists thinking even more critically about two separate conflicts by inferring their deeper, intertextual similarities or differences. Literary analysis, the most fertile, accessible, and appealing form of critical analysis, has traditionally stimulated secondary students to broaden and clarify their understanding of shared abstract concepts, as well as intentional literary structures. Why is it then that this 10th grade writer, one who displays at least minimum competence in analytic reading and writing, fails to compare or contrast the internal conflicts in both stories; adamantly resists going beyond isolated source analysis by comparing and contrasting these separate conflicts? Why do these two narratives, with their potentially inspirational and thought-provoking webs of gripping parent-child conflict, fail to generate anything but two self-contained, mechanical analyses? Again, the answer to all these questions lies not in the outward displays of student writing, nor in a specific student's apparent deficiencies in knowledge and learning skills. Rather it lies in the broad, unnoticeable educational shift from content-driven to values-based education that prevents secondary teachers from facilitating students' development of a more critical and integrated learning process.

Nowhere is this educational shift more manifest or more corrosive than in the secondary sub-discipline of literature. In this pivotal area of knowledge and learning, this shift involves the unquestioned policy change from focusing on teaching students the literary conventions within each main genre, to focusing on teaching students how to connect literature with personal experiences and immediate interests. Secondary students, on the whole, are no longer capable of fluently synthesizing multiple short story writers' variations of a specific category of internal conflict, or several novelists' use of a similar point of view. This is primarily due to the pedagogical shift from the genre-based intertextual model to post-modern, student-centered approaches or processes for constructing "literary" meaning. Unfortunately, the long-range impacts of this increasingly acritical and non-literary approach to reading and writing about literature on secondary students' college preparatory learning skills have yet to be properly acknowledged or comprehensively studied. Nonetheless, those truly interested in the bigger picture projected by students' failed readings and writings are looking closely and critically at the non-literary approaches designed to impose this paradigm shift on the study of literature, further widening the gap between secondary teaching and students' critical learning needs. This can be confirmed by recent pedagogical texts that subordinate the student learning process to the behaviorist goal of meeting the student's total needs.

In introducing their book chapter, "More Than Great Books: Reader Response in a Whole Language Literature Class," the Stricklands firmly situate the meaningful content of literary interpretation outside of literature and squarely inside the reader's idiosyncratic associations and subjective views. They validate this approach, moreover, by unfairly pitting it against the narrow, author-based standpoint of new criticism: "This chapter will show teachers how to move out of the trap of instructing students in a way which privileges the memorizing of plot outlines and capsule critiques and move toward a classroom where readers are encouraged to respond on an affective level to a variety of works" (56). This either/or line of reasoning unfairly assumes that traditional literary instruction aims to teach students only arbitrary plots and preplanned essay formats divorced from their personal experience. It also assumes, more manipulatively, that the study of literary conventions, the structures that comprise the vast realm of verbal art, is somehow elitist, a way to honor "privileged" meanings deposited by "authoritative" authors. Such dichotomized thinking attracts even more strongly those old and new teachers who have been conditioned by the student-centered ethos of learning to believe that learning is only valid when made personally meaningful to increasingly troubled and distracted students. Thus this strategic appeal misleads readers and teachers to believe that out of these two extremes, author-based vs. reader-based, the latter is far more relevant to students' personal lives and habits of learning. This standpoint's circular reasoning eclipses the third and most relevant frame of reference from which to study literature—neither the reader's, nor the author's, but that of literature itself. Like many exclusive reader response proponents, the Strickland's success comes at the cost of suppressing the traditional and critical thought-generating genre-based model that has enriched the thinking skills of generations of students, while guiding secondary literary studies through most of the 20th century.

Ironically, this student-centered approach to literary interpretation often ends up restricting students' reading and writing about literature to simple plot summary. The ultimate goal of reading literature, as reader response proponents like the Stricklands reiterate, lies in the one-to-one connections students at varying developmental phases can make between a text's literal "story schema" and their personal identity, feelings, opinions, views, and experiences. So how then, we ask, has this fundamentally subjective and non-literary context with which a generation of readers has been conditioned to associate and construct literary meaning affected their development of literary understanding and critical thinking skills? If the instructional goals of secondary language arts teachers interviewed by the Stricklands are any valid measure of this pedagogical shift, two implicit conditions of this student-centered approach to reading and writing about literature presage continuing erosion of students' critical thinking and learning agendas, especially at the college level.

The most serious impact of this student-centered approach on students' learning process involves students actually selecting and controlling their own curricular objectives within a sub-discipline as broad and important as literature. In one district, a secondary teacher is praised not for teaching students *The Canterbury Tales'* role in the evolving short story genre, but for encouraging students to unconventionally "chose a tale to read, chose groups to work in, chose a mode to write in, and chose a strategy to use to retell their tale" (Strickland 41). Similarly, another secondary teacher is commended not for teaching students to critically analyze and interpret the innovative, satirical aspects of Hamlet's anti-heroic character, but for allowing students to "[choose] the mode of writing for their final exam, although all wrote on a theme of the play, comparing it with their own life experiences" (41). A third secondary teacher, confused over the obvious distinction between a literary topic and a literary genre, goes so far as to give her secondary students not only "the choice of topic or genre they wanted to write about, choice of novel they wanted to read…" but also "…the choice of how to go about responding to each other's interpretations of the text" (41). Additional anecdotal summaries in this and other pro-reader response texts repeatedly praise teachers for letting students concoct cross-modal and cross-genre displays of understanding of literary texts by retelling them from their subjective point of view; explaining how they affected their personal development; or transforming them into a different genre of their own making for which they, above all, receive personal validation.

Second, not only does the student-centered approach to literary study allow students to select which works to read, they delegate them the right to replace the study of literary genres with self-study that takes a myriad of forms. Aligned with the student-centered approach to learning literature is a hefty spate of time-consuming, self-expressive learning formats, from free-writing to various forms of journal writing, that invite students to pour spontaneous reactions to literary topics onto paper, free from the challenging and exhaustive standards for audience-based writing. These personal response writing formats, moreover, need not align with specific writing criteria or standards, nor with specific critical processes such as controlled analysis or synthesis. It is no wonder writers A and B fail to synthesize multiple views on a specific literary convention when they have also learned to associate literary analysis with painless, standardless personal response writing tasks. When students learn to connect the study of literature with personal preferences, feelings, interests, and needs, their innate literary imaginations, particularly their openness to the shared artistic conventions and standards that govern each genre, as well as their desire to tackle the challenges of thinking and writing critically about these literary concepts, become either suspended or permanently suppressed. Only students trained in closely analyzing and comparing and contrasting different authors' treatments of a shared genre convention can grasp the dual critical learning task the three 10th graders were required to write. Most will continue to produce exceptional personal response essays but weak to substandard literary essays because they have not been consistently taught the structural and conceptual conventions of each literary genre.

Besides this student-centered approach's increasing indifference to literary content, students' recently ordained right to choose "to read and write about what is important to them, what touches their lives, and what they need to learn about" (Strickland 42) factors strongly in the deterioration of literary knowledge at the secondary level. The drastic decline in college students' knowledge of the established literary conventions and artistic standards for each genre, and the related erosion in critical thinking skills for writing about literature, leads back to this student-centered imperative. Writer A's incoherent grasp of the short story convention of internal conflict development results, to a large degree, from deficient literary background. The resistance of both writers A and B to comparing/contrasting the internal conflicts in two short stories likewise would not have occurred with adequate instruction for applying this critical thinking skill within the broad context of short story elements and norms. Reader response approach, when unhinged from in-depth study of a specific genre, becomes a catalyst for the false learning objectives reflected in the above scenarios. When students control the literature curriculum, switching erratically from one genre to another, and from writing expressively about a literary character to writing transactionally about a formal literary convention for a wide audience, shallow, fragmented learning and a distorted view of literary mode itself are bound to result. Such intermixing of writing modes and cross-genre conventions by students who have no coherent grasp of these convention's genre-based meaning and function are the types of fractured learning conditions most likely responsible for writer A's and B's inability to analyze and/or synthesize a common short story convention. These students' literary essays, their inadequate exhibition of literary knowledge, need to be reassessed within these students' full learning context. Once secondary programs decide to do this, they can start to take issue with the failure of teachers, whether due to top-down policies or their own weak literary background, to motivate students to learn the dense sub-sets of artistic conventions and literary standards at the core of a literary discipline.

By contrast with A and B, model C reflects the writer's heightened skills in analyzing and synthesizing not two, but three short stories—competencies that can only be developed in classes emphasizing the intertextual or genre-based model for reading and writing about literature. This traditional paradigm provides students with the dense conceptual framework for understanding and synthesizing literary components across genre-specific works. Within the context of the short story genre, this student has learned to base the meaning of a short story's structures, elements, and devices on their relationship to a vast array of analogous elements in other short stories, ancient and modern. Her entire essay, in fact, is a testimony to her drive to write about literature, free from her narrow personal frame of reference. In her previous classes, she was most likely not compelled to read, write about, and understand literary concepts from her narrow adolescent perspective. Nor was her conception of imaginative literature constrained by new critical theory that situates literary meaning in the author's equally narrow and difficult-to-extract purpose. As her genuine literary analysis implies, she was free from these thought-constricting standpoints by teachers who were able to impart the knowledge of short story conventions upon which her critical reading and writing skills are predicated. Unfortunately, due to the continuing intermixing of opposing student-centered and knowledge-based agendas in the many secondary programs, students like writers A and B end up acquiring the substandard or minimal interpretive skills reflected by their essays.

Model C opens directly with a comparative thesis, focusing sharply on the "questionable values and ethics" of the central characters created by Tyler, Lawrence, and O'Connor. From the start, the genre-based teaching/learning model enables the student to situate symbiotic acts of reading and writing within the coherent, idea-expanding contexts of three different short story perspectives on the clash between self-centered values and abstract moral or ethical standards. Instead of restricting thought to superficial analyses of isolated conflicts, the inherently comparative thought mode of intertextual study both expands and interweaves this student's combined thinking, reading, and writing skills. As its overarching benefit, this discipline-based approach generates this student's implicit affirmation of the multiple perspectives the short story genre offers on a very precise category of internal conflict. Her organization and development of her three sub-topics, above all, reflect an atypical interest in and focus on these authors' different twists on the universal clash between individual and moral values. In fact, her focused, text-based analyses of all three main character's motivation issue from a simple desire to explore and affirm diverging views on this abstract concept with to we can all deeply relate. The openness to a plurality of views on common elements of human behavior, in fact, incites her critical efforts to recognize, document, analyze, and interpret all three characters' changing exhibitions of the self-centered trinity of selfishness, insensitivity, and greed. As a pluralistic thinker, she seeks to scrutinize, analyze, and creatively synthesize three characters' specific forms of selfishness, from the mother's "constant desire for more money, as she had an appetite for buying frivolities," to Cal's youthful preoccupation with both "the money he earns in 'tutoring'" and the recognition he gets from "all those kids hanging out" at his house, and finally to Grandmother's ironic failure to "stop the Misfit from murdering the rest of her family, [while]...selfishly and shamelessly begging for her own." While synthesizing three authors' variations on human selfishness, the student actively uses reading and writing to explore a few of the countless ways literary characters let self-centered values destroy deeper human bonds and ethical standards.

This capacity to recognize a plurality of views on any abstract component of the human condition becomes all the more significant against the backdrop of secondary practices hindering students from experiencing what Ricoeur calls literature's "disclosure of a possible way of looking at things, which is the genuine referential power of the text" (71). Many secondary students have never been empowered to use literature's multiple genre-based contexts, as does model C, for generating critical awareness of the exhaustive range of possibilities and variations for any abstract drive, value, or conflict. This high school sophomore's synthesis of the self-serving motives undermining three literary characters' ethical standards signals her educational good fortune. Her school-based and experience-based learning have together imparted the essential desire, knowledge, and skills needed to make sense out of literature's hypothetical perspectives. Other students remain less fortunate, as the struggle to think, read, and write critically about literature's artistic and metaphorical conflicts becomes a lost form of secondary currency.

A second critical benefit of the genre-based, intertextual approach to literary studies is the opportunity it affords students to recognize the complexities and ambiguities of what at first seem black and white issues. The knowledge students can gain from comparatively studying multiple short story conflicts can quickly transform into mature insights into previously unnoticed gray areas in their personal lives. This consciousness-expanding benefit is manifest in model C. Embedded as most are in an adolescent culture of self-centered, material gratification, secondary students today are unlikely to notice, let alone painstakingly interpret, the murky area between individual values and ethical standards conveyed by challenging short stories. Model C, however, does just that. With her thesis that all three characters "display opposing values and ethics that both mirror and differ from each other," she shares her anticipation of deeper conceptual ambiguity. As she explores and synthesizes each literary character's internal conflict, she continues to widen her grasp of the complexities and contradictions beyond these stories' literal façade of right vs. wrong. When compared with the mother's material obsession and insensitivity that indirectly causes Paul's death, Cal's disregard for "the children's academics or social behavior" greatly pales in degree of selfishness and disregard for others. Following her analysis of the third character, O'Connor's Grandmother, the student's broadened synthesis enables her to start to grasp the dark, inexplicable mystery at the heart of this literary conflict, and at the heart of human nature. At first, she first attributes Grandmother's unethical choices to overt traits of selfishness, insensitivity, and greed. Yet by keeping an open "literary" mind, she eventually senses this character's strange mix of shamelessness, cowardice, and religious hypocrisy (when she "allows the Misfit to wear her son's shirt after he has killed him, and tells the Misfit that Jesus will save him" and finally when she resorts to bribing him and begging for her own life), additional traits that continue to expand and complicate the meaning of this literary conflict.

Thus she moves close to naming the underlying fear of her own death that most shapes Grandmother's ambivalent character. By thinking comparatively about multiple short story conflicts, the writer becomes aware of the complexities underlying the not so simple conflict between individual and ethical values. For a 10th grader, this student exerts commendable effort to explore the wide-ranging factors and motives—from material obsession, to adolescent insecurity, religious hypocrisy, and fear of dying—that keep ethical conflicts, fictional and real, open to new views and meaning.

Model C does not stop with comparative analysis and synthesis of related literary conflicts. Despite unevenness in development, coherence, and writing conventions, the essay culminates even more thoughtfully with a brief but critical evaluation of the underlying ethics of three short story personalities. By intentionally synthesizing how all three "differ in their values," in fact, the student further connects these characters with her own ethical standards. For Lawrence's mother, the writer's indictment is clear: on the scale of ethical decision-making, she remains at the bottom, her obsession with money negating the possibility of "any moral values." The ethics of the other two, however, are viewed more ambivalently, as are their selfish motives. Perceptively, Cal is found to be considerably more ethical than the others, since despite being a "slacker and and underachiever"…"his heart is in the right place." As for O'Connor's infamous Grandmother, her ethical choices are open-mindedly evaluated as the most contradictory and difficult to judge. In the end, her selfishness and betrayal are balanced by both a "vulnerable side," a desperate fear of dying, and her twisted lady-like efforts to, as the student emphasizes, "meet her end with a shred of dignity." Here, from an astute 10th grader, are connections and insights that scratch away the thin veneer of artificial behavioral norms for a glimpse of what is and always will be the dark, unsettling human ambiguity—critical thinking about literature at its secondary best.

Because she has a much broader understanding of internal character conflicts, this student is able to identify and grapple with the difficult ethical conflicts that intrigue her and her readers alike. Strong background in the forms and conventions of the short story genre and a tight analytic focus enable her to avoid the organizational, developmental, grammar, and mechanical problems associated with the other model non-existent or weak literary knowledge. Most apparent is her ease in fully analyzing all relevant dimensions of a character's internal conflict.

The key point, however, is that the critical reading and writing processes reflected in this model would not have been possible without a strong literary background in short story elements and techniques, and a habit of reading for new and exciting variations each writer creates from a shared literary formula. All told, the student, in extending thought beyond the individual story lines, beyond the intertextual context of multiple stories, and toward deeper ethical standards, achieves a level of insight of which most 10th graders, and many junior and seniors as well, are incapable. From literary knowledge, to critical analysis and synthesis, and finally to interpretive writing, this comparative study represents, however jaggedly, a fully integrated display of student learning.

Suddenly public schools and state education departments are clamoring to make the objective, other-affirming, reflective source analyses and syntheses represented by our past and present student models the academic norm. While we applaud this shift, we are also aware that the education of critical thinkers and learners will not materialize overnight. Complex thinking processes can only evolve within dense, challenging, varied, and consistently provided reading contexts that have been and continue to be eliminated from high school history and English curricula. The integrated learning process reflected in model C was not learned quickly in the first year of college or even the last year of high school. Nor was it learned by reading watered-down social studies chapters; literature chosen solely for its degree of personal relevance; isolated data transmitted by unreliable internet sources; or by "reading nothing at all." The latter, which we take to mean the art of surf reading and surf writing, is now a popular route to high school graduation. We frequently hear the questions from concerned parents and educators: Is there a single factor that contributes substantially to the intellectual chasm separating the active reader/writer from the passive? Are the cultural and educational factors underlying the learning crisis so deeply rooted as to make them seem irreversible? Is there a single panacea that public education could apply in the next decade to reverse the crisis in learning? Because we do not aspire to the pessimist's or the cynic's closed mode of thought, we give a resounding "yes" to each of these penetrating questions. But before we try to answer these questions, we will evaluate the consequences of shallow content-instruction as revealed in more advanced college writing tasks.

Works Cited

Editor. "Core Knowledge Schools Take Root across the Country." *American Educator*. Winter 1996-1997: 4-7.

Freire, Paulo, and Ira Shor. "What Is the 'Dialogical Method' of Teaching?" *Journal of Education*. 169.3 Fall 1987: 11-31.

Freire, Paulo. "The Importance of the Act of Reading." *Journal of Education*. 165.1 Winter 1983: 5-11.

Link, Frances R. "Instrumental Enrichment: A Strategy for Cognitive and Academic Improvement." *Essays on the Intellect*. Ed. Frances R. Link. Alexandria, VA: ASCD, 1985. 89-106.

Ricoeur, Paul. *Interpretive Theory:Discourse and the Surplus of Meaning*. Fort Worth: Texas Christian Press, 1976.

Sizer, Theodore. *Horace's School: Redesigning the American High School*. Boston: Houghton Mifflin, 1992.

Stoddard, Thomas. "Gay Marriages: Make them Legal." *Current Issues and Enduring Questions*. 4th ed. Sylvan Barnet and Hugo Bedau. Boston: St. Martin's, 1996. 57-59.

Strickland, Kathleen, and James Strickland. *Uncovering the Curriculum: Whole Language in Secondary and Postsecondary Classrooms*. Portsmouth, NH: Boynton/Cook, 1993.

Chapter Four

The Proof Is in the Reading: In-Class Writing

Although all sorts of theoretical models can be used to illustrate the problems students have in thinking, and writing about what they think in the classroom, their actual writing can best serve to make our point. The following excerpts are from in-class essays randomly selected from several classes I've taught in composition, drama and Jewish-American literature over the past several years. We believe that they are an accurate reflection of the writing of these students since they wrote these essays as in-class themes for final examinations and had no opportunity to check their spelling, punctuation, grammar or word usage. The next section of this chapter will deal with prepared themes that students wrote in both of our classes.

In a sampling of essays by fifteen students from a variety of literature classes, the number of words used ranged from 245 to 542. Since students in such a test could choose to spend anywhere from ten minutes to one and half hours answering an essay question on an exam, such a variation might be explained by the amount of time each student chose to devote to the essay. What can be determined with more accuracy, however, is sentence length which is merely dividing the number of sentences by the number of words in the essay. Eliminating those either considerably under or over the median, we found that average sentence length among this group of students was about 16 1/2 words. Half of the sample were sixteen words long, the highest among the rest 18.5, the lowest 15 (To give you a sense of what a sixteen-word sentence looks like in mature writing, the last of those I've written above is seventeen words long, the rest from the beginning of this chapter average 37 words each.). The Best and Brightest of my students, however, average 31 words per sentence.

Along with sentence length, another factor that determines quality is the complexity of sentences; that is, the level of thought that goes into the making of the sentence including such factors as subordination and coordination of different components, the content of these components, and how they are combined to create a whole, complex thought. Here is an example of the opening of an essay which answers the rather straight-forward and simplistic question: If you were to choose a person you would most trust and least trust from the following, who would each be and why? Remember to illustrate from the plays in which these characters appear.

1. If I was to choose a character I would trust the most it would probably be Lena Younger from A Raisin in the Sun. 2. First of all, Lena Younger is an elderly, woman who obviously trusts her son. 3. I feel when people trust someone else it is easier to trust them. 4. Lena entrusts in her son, the insurance money, which could have been used to benefit the entire family. 5. Instead, she feels that she should give the money to her child and try to give him the benefit of the doubt and open his own liquer store.

Even allowing for the inaccuracies in spelling and the interpretation of the play, as well as factual inaccuracies—Lena does not want her son to open a liquor store and her intention was that the money benefit the entire family—the structure of the sentences are monotonously similar: subject, verb, object. The repetition of forms of the word "trust," five in five sentences, is reminiscent of the way in which students new to a language lean on a particular word of whose spelling and meaning they are certain.

Second, irrelevant details and observations clutter the opening sentences; that Lena Young is "an elderly woman" and that *"I feel when people trust someone else it is easier to trust them."* That Lena gave her son the insurance money could have been stated in the second sentence and not repeated in the fourth; moreover, the ideas in the last sentence could have been incorporated in the second as well: *"Lena is herself worthy of trust by allowing her son to have control of the insurance money, thus giving him the benefit of the doubt that he would use his judgement to serve the needs of the entire family."* A varied selection of words such as "giving" and "allowing," and substituting "serve the needs" for "benefit" would not only have avoided needless repetition, but have given the reader a fuller picture of Lena's trust of her son without fragmenting the ideas into short, choppy, and often irrelevant observations. But without the knowledge of such a vocabulary, the practice of syntactical flexibility, and the organizational skills necessary to put these diverse elements into a coherent whole, the student is unable to write meaty, interesting, varied sentences.

Compare that opening with a similarly worded question in which an imaginary meeting takes place between Tom Wingfield and Biff Loman. In this case, the student is a superior writer, that is, in comparison to most:

1. *Tom and Biff would make a very interesting mutual-support group.* 2. *Within a span of a few drinks (beer for Biff, bourbon for Tom), and an exchange of the facts of their stories, these two might well conclude that Willie and Amanda were made for each other.* 3. *Both would have seen their parents as trying to "pigeonhole" them into lives for which they had neither talent nor inclination.* 4. *They might see clear connections between the means of escape they found while they lived at home, as well as between the places they eventually found some satisfaction in later.* 5. *Tom, as a writer, would see the similarity between Biff's "wide open spaces" in the West and the "vast, trackless sea" where he found solace.*

The difference between the two opening paragraphs in these two essays is more than a matter of sentence length—18 wps for the first, 25 for the second—, complexity of syntax, and the errors in spelling, punctuation and usage far more evident in the first over the second paper. There is also a vast disparity in the choice of words, richness of vocabulary, and wealth of illustrations that mark the second passage as truly college-level writing.

While the first paper labors for five sentences on establishing one point which, as it turns out is incorrect in terms of Lena's real motive for giving her son the money, the second passage deals with a number of issues linking the two figures of Tom Wingfield and Biff Loman: their mutual distrust of their parents, their desire to escape from their environment, and even several brief quotes from the plays illustrating their aspirations. More important, the writer of the second passage was able to show a link between the two characters which was based upon a complex understanding of their personalities drawn from the texts, revealed in the playful suggestion that Tom would drink bourbon—a Southern drink—and Biff beer, derived from his working-class background. This playfulness, incidentally, this willingness to explore ideas and turn them around in different ways, is almost totally lacking in much student writing. For the most part, when it comes to exploring ideas, they are a humorless, and fearful, bunch.

This fear of language as a trap rather than a means of expression can be seen as well in the poverty-stricken vocabulary in which the first passage is written. As well as a repetition of forms of the word "trust," "benefit," and "money," forms of the verb "to feel" and "to give" are repeated among the ninety-one words used. The only words that might be considered above a sixth-grade vocabulary are "elderly" and "obviously" and that would be a stretch.

In the second passage, such words as "span," "inclination" and "solace," and quotes from the plays are included. Not only does the student report the details about the characters accurately, he imagines what they would drink based upon clues about their personalities in the text. There is little repetition of nouns or verbs; one sentence exhibits subordination and coordination of clauses; and an elegant phrasing "neither talent nor inclination" ends the excerpt.

An example of the unintended results of the high school "feel-good" approach to learning can be seen in the following passage. The question was similar to the ones already asked: From these groups of three characters choose those three whom you would either like least or most to invite to a party, and why or why not.

> *1. If I had a party, I would most definitely invite Col. Pickering and Nora but certainly would not want Higgins there. 2. I throw a pretty good party and there would be no time for ignorance or rudeness there, only, nice, respectful, easy to talk to, fun people! 3. I would invite Col. Pickering because he would probably pay me and my guests many compliments. 4. He is very intellectual and a good conversationalist. 5. I would not have to worry about him being rude to my guests or about entertaining him. 6. He would be very respectful and I'm sure my guests would call me the next day and tell me how great he was.*

Nothing in the passage reveals anything specific about Col. Pickering—who he is and how he behaves in *Pygmalion*—to justify the writer's confidence that "he is very intellectual and a good conversationalist." What one learns about the writer, however, is that she has a very high opinion of herself, loves to be flattered, and expects compliments from her friends the next day on the success of her choice of guests. Perhaps this is the way in which she was taught to have "self-esteem" in her writing in high school, but learning more about the writer than the subject of what is supposed to be an analytical essay is rather disheartening.

One of the randomly selected essays that I did not include in the calculations on sentence-length illustrates another problem in student thinking that is revealed in their writing: panic. The following sentence is ninety-seven words long, the longest of any in-class essay we selected. It is part of an answer to a similarly simplistic question used in these exams: Whom would you want to have as a neighbor from the following characters and why:

> *Walter on the other hand is the one that I would be able to handle the most if he were my neighbor, he seems like a strong man and one that means well and it shows in the end of the play where he changes, he speaks to the white man and says that his sister is going to be a doctor, he didn't seen to believe in her befor but he shows that he does now, he also realizes that he loves his wife and that moving into their home is whats right for his family.*

The frantic pace of the sentences, the complete disregard for logical punctuation, and the student's inability to make logical connections between the examples he chooses from the play and the point he is trying to make illustrate a mind in serious disarray. The most telling examples that would illustrate his point—the fact that Walter's father "earned" the right for his family to live in the house they've purchased in a white neighborhood, and the generational connection between him, his father and his son—are missing. But what is noteworthy about those examples he chose, one of which—that Walter loves his wife—is not even in the text, is that in the movie excerpt of the ending of *Raisin in the Sun* shown to the class, these two elements were demonstrated visually, especially the hug Walter gives his wife when the white man leaves. Although the writer of this passage saw that excerpt from the movie only once, and was supposed to have read key parts of the text several times, it was the visual rather than the textual cues that stayed with him the most. Incidentally, this particular student was scheduled to begin his student-teaching the following semester.

Another "frantic" response to the question, Whom would you invite to a party? is perhaps even more revealing:

If Torvald was my "date" for a party, or the reason rather why I would not like to invite him to one I would fear him to be prancing his date around like a showdog and after their "grand entrance" and after him showing them off-he suddenly makes the two of them leave so this grand skeptical which he made of his date could remain fresh and stick out in peoples mind as he did with Nora.

The writer was so uncontrolled that she did not even bother to cross out her false start when she erroneously began the sentence by calling her invited guest her "date," but somewhere in her panic she turned Torvald's date into "them." Inadvertently amusing as "skeptical" for "spectacle" might seem, it also reveals the extent of the lack of control of the writer who could have easily corrected the error had she looked again at the paper. But even more telling is the total lack of any clear antecedent referent in the last phrase of this "sentence." These are commonplace errors of an overwhelmed sixth grader, not, as was the case with this student, a graduating senior. This is one of the more vivid examples of the "chug it and puke it" school of learning. It's as if the lectures and discussions conducted, and essays that had already been written by her and her fellow students on *A Doll House* were so much garbage that had to be expunged from her mind as quickly as possible before she might be poisoned by them.

Occasionally, teachers receive on the internet or through regular mail a list of "bloopers" that students commit in their writing. Many of these, actually, are typographical errors that sound funny, some errors in logic, but they are often culled out of hundreds of student papers. The following, however, are examples from eight of the fifteen randomly selected papers we had chosen from recent classes. They were not culled or methodically selected:

1. *He is also worried about his nephew is was very sick and eventually died because of his sickness.*

2. *Things were not totally perfect....*

3. *She proves herself to be confident in herself dating men and living a fun exciting life.*

4. *He loved him, but I think only because he felt he had to love him because it was his father.*

5. *In the short story "Eli, the Fanatic" he was forced to change the Greenie. He took his suit away from him and that is all he had. That suit represented him.*

6. *All the men in her life had a powerful effect on her. When she got married, she was told she had to change her name. Then later on they decided to have a child. They could not decide what to name her.*

7. *Like the quote at the end from Lena referring to Walter doing the right thing at the end of the rainbow.*

8. *Now Jean on the other hand.*

The first of these is faulty not necessarily because the writer had carelessly left "is" in the sentence when it wasn't necessary, but that he felt he had to explain the cause of death which was self-evident. Also revealing in this sentence is the writer's lack of assurance that the antecedent was clear enough for the word "it" to be used as the pronoun for "sickness."

The second example, incidentally from a student who is generally a competent writer, illustrates the lack of awareness of the more subtle meanings of language. A more commonplace example is the inevitable modifier for "unique." But perhaps this expectation might be too high when the spelling of "woman" and "women" seems to be interchangeable these days in college writing.

The third illustration might not seem to be too egregious out of context other than the clumsiness of using "herself" redundantly in either instance. But in context, the student was asked to indicate some of the positive qualities of Beneatha Younger in *Raisin in the Sun*. "Dating men and having a fun exciting life" was certainly the least of them. The only specific reference to the play was that Beneatha was planning to elope to Nigeria, something that is a most remote possibility. But there is no reference to Beneatha's wanting to be a doctor or her advanced views on women's liberation or her agnosticism. It's as if the writer has only seen those very limited aspects of Beneatha's life, "dating men" and planning to "elope to Nigeria," aspects that might appeal to her personally, that seem to register at all in her recollection of the character.

In the fourth example, the first phrase is contradicted by the rest of the sentence and even then, there were clear indications in the story, "The Silver Crown," that the character in question actually hated his father. The conventional expectation that a child "must" love his father is foremost in the mind of the writer, even when the author of the piece, Bernard Malamud, quite deliberately worked *against* the conventional expectations of the reader.

In the fifth excerpt, the complete lack of clear pronoun reference— which "he" is referred to—obscures any vestige of coherence in this interpretation of a story that required a great deal more explanation in terms of the word "change."

In the next excerpt, the short, choppy sentences lead to the inadvertent humor of the non-sequitor between the second and third sentences. Had the writer simply combined the third with the fourth, some of the obscurity would have been eliminated. But many of these students don't seem to write in terms of units of logical thought patterns; they write in fragments which may or may not have a connection to each other but are the product of the plot-summary approach to any written work they have to do in literature. If they tell enough of the story, maybe something will make sense to the teacher.

The next excerpt is evidence of how little some students seem to retain of a precise quote even when they try to cite it. It's as if there is some kind of loose synapse in the area of textual memory that goes a little out of control every time they try to use it.

The quote to which the writer alludes when he *says "doing the right thing at the end of the rainbow"* was *"He finally come into his manhood today, didn't he? Kind of like a rainbow after the rain...."* It as if Dorothy from *The Wizard of Oz* and Spike Lee suddenly intruded into *Raisin in the Sun* with the resulting chaos. Since this passage was emphasized in class, particularly with the biblical allusion to Noah's flood and the "rainbow sign" from Black church tradition, it would be difficult to understand how the student could have muddled this passage so completely if we did not realize that he probably didn't understand what the allusion and the biblical passage indicated in the first place. He had a vague idea of what it was all about, but nothing definite, nothing logical, nothing coherent, as evidenced by the "end of the rainbow"…somewhere.

This bitter attempt at humor on the author's part is to try to mitigate the fact that the question most commonly chosen on these tests is the most "dumbed down" question I have been able to find in my thirty-five years of college teaching. It has been used more frequently in recent years because it seems to be the ONLY question that the majority of students appear to be able to answer, feeble as their attempts might seem. A few try to answer the more sophisticated questions offered as choice such as what are the cultural values dramatized by the Younger family in *Raisin in the Sun* or a comparison and contrast of Hedda Gabler and Miss Julie. These responses, too, are often disasters.

I saved example eight for last because it well illustrates another serious problem that students seem to have in college writing: a sense of audience. In this last case, the writer tries to adopt a conversational tone totally inappropriate to the nature of the audience for this essay. For the most part, these students write as if they are as determined to bore the reader and instructor and, perhaps, get out of attending class the rest of the semester, as they are to bore themselves. The lack of vitality in their writing, as well as the lack of content or coherence in what they write, reflects as much on their preparatory education in high school as on any one factor involving what used to be called native intelligence or the benefits of an intellectually stimulating home life. It seems that they are systematically taught—if there be system in it—in high school that writing is a boring, unpleasant and generally anxiety-ridden experience, that has no particular reader to whom their work is written, and no particular purpose except, perhaps, to communicate how one feels about the usual adolescent problems for which no context is made and no connections established with literature. That inspired moment in "Up the Down Staircase"—the movie, of course—in which Sandy Dennis "reaches" her pupils by asking them why the world they are living in is "the best of times" as well as "the worst of times" seems now a fond memory.

Recently, I have been teaching a summer course geared for the EOP (Educational Opportunity Program) students at our college, those who had such low grades and SAT scores and such economic deprivations that they would not have been able to attend our school without a remedial program. When I suggested that we begin the writing portion of the program by having them read Swift's "A Modest Proposal," a number of my colleagues doubted that I would have any success in "connecting" with the students. Not surprisingly, at least for me, confronted with first-rate prose, wit, and an interesting argument about the nature of poverty, all but a few of the students responded quite positively to the essay, actually getting Swift's irony. It wasn't as if they hadn't been capable of understanding such works in high school: they had never been given an opportunity to read them, or certainly not in a methodical, thorough, coherent way. But the class had only nine or ten students, not the usual thirty, and we met each day with adequate time for weekly conferences. We wonder what could be done with the "average" students we teach had we the opportunity to do so under such conditions.

If one were to notice a lack of "middle-level" student essays in these samples, we can only reply: there really aren't any. Students now seem, at least in their writing abilities, to fall between the highly competent and the inept; the merely competent seem far more rare than even the few brilliant students that at times lighten our loads and gladden our hearts.

Following, however, are very short essays written by students that might be considered below average, middle and high on the scale of writing proficiency:

A. *What is ironic about who owns the Cherry Orchard at the end of the play?*

What is ironic and typical about The Cherry Orchard is the change that occurs to the family. They were once very rich and in a high standing and now the ways have changed and they are just like ordinary people. They lost the Cherry Orchard and now are like everyone else.

B. *What does "mendacity" mean to Brick and Big Daddy?*

In **Cat on a Hot Tin Roof**, *Brick and Big Daddy use the word "mendacity." They define mendacity as a lie someone tells someone else to cover up something they know about that person.*

An example of this was toward the end of the play. Big Momma has just been told that Big Daddy is going to die from cancer. Gooper has just finished trying to get Big Momma to sign some papers giving him the right to decide how Big Daddy's inheritance will be given out. Big Daddy comes in and says there is a smell in the air, a smell of death. He asks everyone what is wrong and they tell him nothing, not knowing Brick has already told Big Daddy he is dying. He then asks Gooper what all the papers are for and he says nothing. Big Daddy then asks Brick if can smell the "mendacity" in the air. Brick answers yes, a lot of lies, a lot of lying going on. This shows that they define "mendacity" as lying to a person to keep him from knowing the truth about themselves.

C. *Write an imaginary dialogue from* **Oleanna** *between Carol as a caseworker and John who is on parole five years after he has lost his job and served his sentence for assaulting Carol.*

The dialogue would never happen. Even if the restraining order Carol had issued against John had run out within the five-year period, John, having learned that he will lose in any exchange of any kind with Carol, would demand another caseworker. Or, if you prefer a revenge plot. we could have **Oleanna ll**, *in which John goes along and lets Carol ruin him further, then gets her fired for knowingly accepting a case with a professional conflict of interest.*

The "A" passage simply does not answer the question. The point that had been made very explicitly in lecture and discussion about the play is that the irony of the ending is derived in part from the fact that Lopahin, who had been born a serf, became the new owner of the Cherry Orchard, dislodging the aristocratic Ranevsky family. Short and incorrect as the answer is, it repeats the idea that the family is "just like ordinary people." Moreover, in order to make meaning out of the statement that the family is "typical," the writer would have to describe briefly the unusual social situation in Russia at the turn of the century. The problem with this and so many other essays by the poor to mediocre students is that in the words of Gertrude Stein "there is no there there." Few if any references are made to specific incidents in the play or story or novel; everything is cast in the same grey focus.

Essay "B" is certainly better in that it is more accurate. But although this student was one of the better ones in this class, he seemed unable to show much mastery of expression in the way he illustrated his point from the text. The simple process of putting quotation marks around the word "nothing," rather than leaving the phrase ambiguous or misleading when Big Daddy asks the family what's wrong and then asks Gooper what is wrong seems beyond the linguistic capabilities of this student. He also does not seem able to describe this scene concisely and what might have been a vivid illustration becomes pedestrian, confusing, and boring.

The third example, "C," is, again, from the same writer who had provided the best writing in the previous comparisons. Alas, his is about the ONLY writing among the sample, and one of the very few among the students we have taught over the past five years, that can be considered a college-level writer. He is also a slightly more mature student, but even among older students, few we have found are writing with such proficiency.

In this case, he begins by showing independent thinking by stating "The dialogue would never happen." But then he goes on to present

several possibilities, including a "revenge plot," that he extrapolates
from the characteristics of the two figures in the play. What marks this
writing from that of all of the others in this sample is a confidence in
the use of language, and a playfulness of imagination in applying what
is known to what can be speculated on.

Student writing is not a pleasant subject for educators to discuss
because it can be so disheartening. In her book on the contemporary
American campus scene, *Bright College Years*, Anne Matthews devotes
less than a half dozen pages to discussing the actual learning process in
a book of over 270. What she has to say is alarming: that only 35 percent
of freshman have more than six hours of weekly homework down from
44 percent in 1987 (104), but that the way to develop the student's mind
in college is through "personal attention from faculty, a rich flexible
curriculum, and lots of involvement in campus life" (205). These latter
comments should be kept in mind for a later chapter because they provide part of the solution to the problem of improving student learning.
But in a book which tries to deal with so many aspects of the college
world: extra-curricular activities, dorm life, the professiorial scene, the
alumni, the viewpoint of the President of a college, the actual learning
process of the student is the one least focused on; perhaps because from
the viewpoint of most faculty it is the least understood.

Unfortunately, the consequences of this misunderstanding can be
seen in the following example of writing by a second-semester sophomore who had been given passing grades in all his courses through
three semesters:

I would pick Kreon as someon who I would want some quaities from. He
showed that He believed in the state over other things. Such as family At
first. But when he was thought to be wrong he switch his mind to help the
state. That showes me that He is not to good or even have to much pride to
realize when he had made a misteck.

Another reason was he showed a lot of strenge by not giving in at first to
family bonds. I feel as a leader one must not mix family withe the state. So

to me he showed how willing he was to take it. Eventhough he gave in at the end. It still take a man who truly believe in the rules of the state to be a great leader. Kreon would make a great president of the U.S.

The above is not the product of a poor, ghetto-school education or someone who has only been in this country for a few years. It's the result of twelve grade-school years of learning and more than three semesters of college instruction before anyone seemed to realize that this young man had severe learning problems which he had to deal with or he would fail. But since, apparently, he had been passed through the "system," he hadn't felt any necessity in getting help for his learning disability until I made apparent to him that he would fail the course without specialized help. Why it had taken that long for his problems to be addressed is one more example of how inept the grade school system seems to be in dealing with writing, reading and thinking skills of students who are simply passed from one grade to another, mastering their social skills and feeling "good" about themselves.

Granted, there are many factors that might contribute to such abysmal performances by students besides those we have already discussed: test phobia is certainly one of them. It should follow, then, that given the time and opportunity to write and revise a theme paper, students should be able to do a better job of writing. And, in fact, there are more positive examples from a randomly selected group of outside papers than we found in those written in class. The following opening paragraph, while not as stylistically attractive as the best model I have presented, seems, at least, to have substance and indicates the capacity for the student to analyze:

The treatment of the "lowest" class of people in Russian and American society is strongly different despite that fact that both were considered slaves and then were freed. But freedom for Russian serfs led to potential opportunity where in the case of freed Blacks in America led to more frustration. This contrast can be seen in comparing Lopkhin's purchase of the cherry orchard and Walter Lee Younger's purchase of a house in a White neighborhood.

All the necessary factors in developing a sound paper are exhibited here with an interesting and arguable thesis, a sound point of comparison, and a well-chosen point of contrast to demonstrate the distinctions between Russian feudal serfdom and chattle slavery.

More typical, however, is the opening paragraph of a comparison between spouses in *A Doll House* and *A Raisin in the Sun*:

Husband-wife relationships have changed almost as much as has the role of women over the past century, as in the relationship between Nora and Helmer **in A Doll House** *and with Walter and Ruth in* **A Raisin in the Sun.** *Both marriages reflect change in husband-wife relationships to one another due to change in society.*

In this second example, the writer never identifies what is meant by the word "change" through modifying its meaning in terms of husband-wife relationships or social change. The concept of change is modified in the next paragraph, somewhat, Though the fundamental idea, the thesis of the essay, is never clearly explained or defined throughout the paper. There is a maddening vagueness in the opening paragraph with the repetition of the words "relationships" and "change." Rather than express the point of comparison between the two pairs of spouses, the writer can only use the vague connective "and with," not even introducing the concept of "comparison" in the thesis paragraph. The writer seems to have no definite sense of what she is comparing or what she means by "change" in the comparison. And this is what is most distressing about this kind of writing: it does not indicate any active thinking. The writer is passively trying to cope with the material she has been given; she shows no skill or understanding of how to shape it and form it and direct it toward an interesting or original idea. And this is after having gone through two drafts and two conferences with the instructor!

Even in some papers that have promising starts, most often students fail to provide adequate evidence to support their assertions. In the use of quotes, many are uncertain of what constitutes an appropriate quote; or if they find one, how to excerpt the section most relevant to illustrating their point; or if they can accomplish this task, how to present the quote so that it is intergrated into the text and is grammatically consistent with the language of the words surrounding it. The whole process of using quotes is a painful and uncertain one; once found, the quote is dropped in the lap of the reader without much if any analysis of its meaning beyond its initial use as an illustration. This timidity in interpreting quotes is another indication of how unfamiliar language is with so many of these students: it is a dangerous and treacherous beast that can entrap and fool you if you try to become too familiar with it. Best have as little to do with it and it might eventually leave you alone.

Still, the occasional essay that shows the writer to have a fluency, a sense of control over language, is a joy to read and proves that it is still possible for students to learn how to write and think:

During the last century, dramatic roles for women often mirrored the various changes that occurred in society as women sought to extricate themselves from the constraints of a patriarchal mold, which was suffocating their spirit.

Man having devised a system of patriarchy which increased their own empowerment became reluctant to give up their over-valued status. Women would need help in gaining their release from the legal and social structures which ensured their debased and devalued status. Recognizing the injustices inherent in a patriarchal society, artists, writers and playwrights reached out to address some of these cruel double standards with their work.

Ideologically focused as these introductory paragraphs are, they are also clear, concise, and complex. They are written with zest and energy as if the writer felt that someone was really interested in what she had to say. This is missing from all but a handful of essays we read each year, and we believe, reveals the soul-deadening or superficially self-congratulatory way in which students are taught what writing is supposedly about. The next three chapters will develop our reasoning on how to best ameliorate the secondary learning crisis. We will also provide compelling solutions to the serious writing problems experienced by today's college students.

Work Cited

Matthews, Anne. *Bright College Years*. New York: Simon and Schuster, 1997.

Chapter Five

A Plan for Resuscitating the Secondary Student's Mind

Susie B., along with twenty other first-year students, waits restlessly for me on the first day of her course, Academic Writing I. As I enter the classroom, she watches me guardedly. She shows none of the outward signs—vitality, anticipation, and curiosity—teachers hope to see in new students. Instead her vacant stare and strained posture signal deep unease over this course's rigorous academic reading and writing assignments. For a number of years, I have become a sounding board for first-day college writing anxieties. After my detailed overview of the course requirements and syllabus, students' worries burst from confinement. How much reading will we be expected to do outside of class? How long will we need to spend on each reading? What if I have difficulty understanding the reading sources? How long will we have to work on our essays? Will we get help with our writing problems? Will we be able to revise? How many times? What about my terrible spelling and grammar that never improved throughout high school? And there are bigger questions that are the subtext of those they ask: Do I have the skills needed to succeed in this course? Will I be able to pass this course the first time? With each fear-laden question, students nervously grope for validation and closure to a course that has barely begun.

Unfortunately, both legitimate and illegitimate experts who ponder the crisis in thinking and learning fail to analyze the full secondary context in which these college writing anxieties have been systematically instilled. Each year, secondary students are required to write in seemingly opposing modes, the expressive and the transactional, with no understanding of the connection between the two. On the one hand, their first-day anxieties reflect years of frustration over secondary school's prescribed doses of formal writing tasks. Having grown up conditioned to meeting departmental, district, and state writing standards, secondary students automatically view school-based writing as a vehicle for achieving standardized writing outcomes—fixed numbers and lengths of essays, fixed organizational patterns and writing conventions for each grade level. Consequently, they associate college writing with the same discrete features and immutable patterns of their school writing tasks.

On the other hand, since the early 80's secondary learners have had to mentally zigzag between the view of writing as test and the postmodern reconception of writing as personal expression and self-enhancement. During high school, classroom writing is often a vehicle for meeting an educational goal far removed from college learning objectives: the advancement of students' total psychic development at the cost of their intellectual growth. Under the mantle of behavior modification programs designed to build self-esteem, cooperative behavior, and multicultural awareness, secondary students receive ample opportunities to write in the mode that best accommodates their need for self-expression and self-glorification, the expressive mode. However, the over-emphasis on "expressive" genres—journal entries, free-writing, and reader responses to literature that foster expression of personal opinions, transient interests, and social experiences in informal and often sub-literate prose—reduces the time and instruction students need to develop competence and skills in transactional or audience-based writing. As a result, first-year college students lack adequate knowledge of the primary writing mode for building knowledge across the college disciplines. The secondary writing history of most students boils down to a frustrating flip-flop between writing to display imposed writing standards and writing to self-express. As long as secondary writing tasks remain torn between these antithetical goals, students' fundamental college learning skill, students' ability to write meaningfully about reading sources will remain stunted and severed from their natural growth as writers.

Pulled between these contrary views, secondary students are denied adequate opportunities to understand and practice the transactional writing skills that will help them advance in an academic discipline. As students begin college, their most serious learning deficiency is their inability to think and write critically about required academic reading sources. In short, this means they are unaccustomed to thinking about how source authors think. This is a daunting task for students who cannot explain their own thought processes and who mistake analysis for an external formula for organizing an essay rather than a set of related elements they must actively read for and communicate to an audience.

Having gone through high school accustomed to writing for themselves or for their writing assessors, they have little training in using writing to analyze the multiple intentions of the authors they read; their own intentions in writing about particular sources; and the intentions of the implied audience reading their analysis. Put another way, they have no background in using writing to think: to think about how source authors make sense, to think about the different kinds of sense they can make out of the sources they read, and to think about how to communicate their understanding of a source to an audience. Students' ability to think, read, and write critically about other writers' thinking is a far from a realized secondary outcome. The majority of first-year students require extensive practice in shifting from expressive, self-referential writing to transactional or audience-based writing. Their tightly packed secondary curriculum made no room for adequately learning the underlying concepts and surface conventions that make up this social and contributory writing mode. When they begin their first academic writing course, they also reveal no grasp of the developmental link between the personal and public writing modes. When we consider the stab of inadequacy experienced by many on the first day of class, their stress and anxiety are completely understandable.

Inadequately prepared to think and write critically about challenging reading sources, many incoming college students view college writing tasks as a serious threat to their academic success. They are now expected to apply the critical thinking processes of analysis, evaluation, comparison/contrast, synthesis, and argumentation to a variety of discipline-based texts and writing tasks. They can no longer comfortably "write about" personal experiences or existing knowledge; rather they must "write for" an audience that demands much more than the writer's personal views and experiences on a topic or issue. College-level expository synthesis of the current causes of homelessness, for example, can provide a knowledge-hungry audience with in-depth analysis and evaluation of three or more writers' causal reasoning, as well as comparison and contrast of these writers' supporting reasons and evidence. In this case, the synthesis writer's dominant goal in writing is to give a real-life audience a more informed perspective on a set of underlying causes and, in turn, to make a verbal transaction of broad social impact. Multiple source synthesis, a staple of academic research, also requires students to incorporate prior critical thinking skills of source summary and analysis, thus applying the recursive and expanding nature of critical thinking to source material. Fewer and fewer entering students are prepared to achieve this level of critical writing. The degree and ways in which students are suddenly expected to critically read and write about other writers' complex ideas and positions send many into a state of denial. These students cling to the hope that a well-written summary and or jazzed up personal response will pass for single source analysis, comparison/contrast of two sources, or multiple source synthesis. Still others with practice in applying their innate thinking skills of analysis,

evaluation, or synthesis to academic sources are hampered in communicating more critical readings by a deficient vocabulary.

In voicing first-day anxieties, what my academic writing students
most reveal is failure to understand the process and nature of "making a
verbal transaction with" an audience. Most unexpected is the academic
audience's insistence that the writers they read also be critical thinkers
and readers. These intellectual dimensions of academic writing are
mind-boggling to students who were oblivious to them throughout
high school. With the exception of formal high school literary analysis
and comparison/contrast essays, students' initial source-based writing
seldom penetrates textual surfaces. For the most part, they remain
locked in a shallow mode of "writing about" or retelling what they have
read. As source writers, they do well summarizing one or several
sources' main ideas. Nevertheless, they come to college generally lacking
the disposition and skills for delving beneath non-fiction texts and
developing insights into broader sociocultural issues. That such transactional writing could also create a knowledge-building dialogue with
an audience is beyond their grasp. Rare was my student who on the first
day of Academic Writing II requested to use his writing to explore new
forms of homelessness due to recent "downsizing" or the student who
assertively shared newly-made connections between her active reading
and the causes of adolescent violence. Such critical writers make up a
small percentage of first-year students to whom academic writing is an
empowering and transforming intellectual act. Sadly, most beginning
students relegate college writing to a long dreaded learning task they
have thus far managed to postpone and now merely hope to "get
through." Rare is the entering student who views writing as a self-
directed and self-expanding learning tool.

Dishearteningly, they come late to the bridge between college writing and their development as thinkers and learners. Despite the time
and instructional resources dedicated to making secondary writing
more student-centered by integrating this skill with reader response,

multicultural topics, and various behavioral outcomes, high school did not prepare Susie B. for the increasingly challenging, student-directed source-based reading and writing tasks that dominant college learning. By the worry on her face, the uncertainty in her voice, and the questions she does not ask, I can tell she is beginning a journey into a strange and intimidating intellectual land.

The ongoing decline in both secondary and college learning skills has been repeatedly emphasized in our preceding chapters. We have drawn on the written words of students for proof of the startling reading and writing deficiencies with which so many begin college. In doing so, we have sought to clarify the broader educational causes of the anxieties and inadequacies with which many students begin college. There is no shortage of learning problems besetting the new college-bound. However, secondary students' view of writing as test is a key factor in the learning crisis that still begs closer analysis and scrutiny. Small problems like first day jitters over the surface features of their writing and big ones like the shocking realization that their writing is disconnected from their thinking are deeply rooted in students' ingrained secondary notion of the prescriptive nature of academic writing. This perception, therefore, must be factored into the current thinking and learning crisis so comprehensive solutions can be proposed. The deeply embedded concept of school writing has long concerned theorists and practitioners dedicated to shaping and imparting a more active, transformative view of writing at all levels of learning. As a key piece in our evolving portrait of the thinking crisis, it sheds additional light on the gap between how secondary students are taught and how they need to learn to read and write if they are to become critical thinkers and knowledge-builders across the academic disciplines.

School Learning, School Writing, and Acritical Thinking

The contradictory concepts of student-centered learning and school writing are instilled in tandem throughout secondary school. Concurrent with learning that writing can be a liberating and rule-free form of self-expression, secondary students habitually view writing as a test, an end-paper to be graded. Susie B., in fact, could have been any one of the secondary students during my secondary career whose writing, in the long run, was measured quantifiably rather than qualitatively. As formal writers, she and her classmates learned their primary job was not to develop their minds, but to produce a required number of essay tasks every marking period (every 10 weeks) and as part of closed-ended unit tests and year-end comprehensive exams. In fact, her English teachers and her classmates were continually pressured to teach and learn an arbitrary number of formal essays, each with an arbitrary set of criteria; consequently, her teachers lacked the time to adequately teach students to critically read, analyze, and evaluate non-literary texts. Within such a regime of writing norms, students' writing is ultimately reduced to a coefficient of x, x being the number and types of essays—expository, narrative, descriptive, persuasive, or literary—mandated for each marking period and included in comprehensive unit and course exams. Knowledge of writing, long diluted by affective goals and activities described in chapter two, is further stunted by impersonal per course writing outcomes and quotas students are required to fulfill.

Throughout my secondary teaching career in two different school districts, my secondary English students, with the exception of those taking 12th grade Research Writing or Advanced Placement English, were required to produce two of more out-of-class essays per marking period. Thus by the end of a year-long course, they wrote, on average, 10. Also factored into students' mandatory school writing assignments were in-class essays that were part of unit tests on specific genres, individual works, or thematic units. My 9th grade students, for example, were required to demonstrate proficiency in analyzing short story elements like dominant character traits or the link between setting and theme, as part of their summative test on this genre. 12th grade Humanities students were required to display their understanding of advanced literary concepts by analyzing, comparing and contrasting, and synthesizing full-length works. Even the least mathematically inclined can appreciate the extensive time and effort secondary English teachers must spend thoughtfully reading, commenting on, and evaluating up to 12 times the number of students' out-of-class essays, as well as "test" essays written to show on-the-spot mastery of specific learning objectives throughout the school year. Today, rising secondary enrollments further compound this oppressive "learning" condition. While 90 to 120 students constituted an average secondary teaching load from the mid-80's to mid-90's, the average student load now reaches as high as 150 students in increasingly overcrowded and outdated schools. This makes the English teacher's task of reading and evaluating fixed numbers and forms of essays even more grueling and impersonal.

When juxtaposed with these depersonalized testing conditions, pedagogy designed to improve students' read-to-write skills exists in principle only. The process approach to writing, for instance, can enable students to realign this dual learning skill with specific critical thinking processes as they work through the various phases of writing from initial focusing and planning to final revising and self-editing. However, the relentless standardization of secondary writing reduces the writing process to a series of isolated mechanical steps rather than an integrated thinking-reading-writing process. When teachers and students must comply with arbitrary writing objectives, they cannot also be expected to effectively teach the individualized, self-reflective, and integrated pedagogy that recent theorists intend and secondary students deserve the writing process approach to be. Guiding even the average class load of 100 English students through the phases of planning, drafting, revising, and editing 10 essay per year would bring the teacher's total readings and evaluations per year to well over 3,000. Secondary schools may claim they embrace the process approach to writing, but their rigid imposition of standardized writing norms and testing conditions debunks such claims.

Obviously, an integrated approach to writing that instructs and guides students through a multiple draft process for aligning writing with the development of critical thinking skills and content knowledge is negated by a system that mandates external writing outcomes. No two students, let alone an entire English class, can equally benefit from the writing process and its related practices of writing workshop, conferencing, and mini-lessons designed to meet students' individual writing needs—not, that is, as long as excessive and arbitrary numbers of writing tasks are required. From the start of any process writing task, students' individual writing strengths and weaknesses, particularly the degree to which they can incorporate reading material into informative, persuasive, or literary essays, should dictate the number and level of revisions needed. At present, secondary English teachers need all the support they can get in helping students uniformly build minimum college entry-level skills of objective source analysis, evaluation, and synthesis. Until secondary language arts teachers are guaranteed the time and instructional resources students need to make these crucial learning connections, their writing will remain in a state of perpetual catch-up.

Despite its grounding in the belief that each student's writing process is unique, recursive, and contingent on individual needs, the process approach is often subsumed within an antithetical top-down, outcome-driven, factory learning model. Too many secondary schools that proclaim allegiance to the process approach simultaneously mandate essay totals and formats, and timed writing tests. For example, New York State's Comprehensive Regents Examination in English requires students to write essays of several different types, each of which must now adhere to predetermined standards of composition, critical thinking skills, and multiple language skills. While students are given more time to write these test essays, as well as directions so explicit they could eliminate the need for critical planning and thinking, these newly integrated writing tasks are still essentially timed, closed-ended tests. However, the bigger questions for us remain unasked and unanswered: Have these students had adequate opportunities to develop the content knowledge, especially the writing concepts, implicit in these transactional essay tasks or the critical reading and writing skills on which college literary and academic source analysis depend? Have their teachers been adequately prepared to teach an integrated approach to writing, one that combines multiple language skills with students' critical thinking skills and content knowledge? And is any writing test ever a valid measure of a student's writing aptitudes?

The incongruous yoking of students' individual writing process with educational bureaucrat's educational testing agenda continues to restrict their development of the complex and integrated skill we boil down to academic writing. Writing as any form of exit-exam fails to meet the affective or cognitive learning needs of student writers. Not only do standardized writing tests negate the personal commitment students need to bring to audience-based writing, they deny students the time and means to connect writing with critical thinking and reading, as well as new content knowledge. Regardless of how much preparation students have been given, writing tests nullify the open-ended and recursive nature of the writing process. The message to students is clear: although you have spent much time learning to plan your essays in multiple drafts, and learning to reflect on and painstakingly revise and edit the multiple phases and dimensions of your writing, you are now required to undo all that you have been taught about how we evolve as genuine and thoughtful writers. When secondary students must constantly use writing as test, they are unlikely to connect writing with serious agendas like developing broader and denser discipline-based concepts. They inevitably associate formal writing tasks, the kind they expect in college, with mastery of standardized forms and conventions, and with the attainment of grades that signal eligibility to pass on to the next one. Why should we expect them to associate college writing with anything more empowering as they begin their first academic writing course?

In sum, we find that the gap between secondary students' writing and critical thinking skills, particularly when analyzing and synthesizing ideas from sources, results neither from limited verbal aptitudes as pseudo-experts contend nor from unwillingness to learn. To the contrary, the widening gap between students' thinking and language skills results largely from the conflicting affective and academic programs in which they learn. Their writing especially ends up only as squeezed and fragmented as the programs in which they are forced to learn. Affective learning outcomes, as mentioned before, demand so much classroom time that students cannot build the integrated language, thinking, and knowledge-building skills for holistic writing tasks that are genuinely their own. Most entering college students come from secondary English programs that link writing antithetically with self-expression and standardized objectives. Yet when learning skills as important as critical reading and writing are subsumed within a supermarket of competing agendas, students are robbed of the time, incentive, and active learning upon which successful college writing is predicated. In fact, the dominant secondary agenda, the drive to socialize and psychologize the academic curriculum increasingly results in disconnected, dead-end activities. These projects in turn displace students' development of socially and intellectually useful tasks that would better prepare them for the challenges of a college discipline. Finally, the opposing secondary goals of student well-being and standardized assessment prevent the classroom teacher from integrating students' thinking, language, and knowledge-building skills so they can become holistic, self-directed learners before entering college.

Essential Teaching and Learning Conditions for English Language Arts

Secondary education's continuing emphasis on time-consuming affective goals and standardized assessments has serious educational and ethical effects on student achievement. From the perspective of how students need to learn reading and writing—our primary concern—this marriage of opposites impedes teachers from giving all students ample time to sequentially integrate critical reading and writing skills with content knowledge. The disconnection of critical thinking skills from meaningful reading, writing, speaking, and listening tasks is the biggest cause of the achievement gap in secondary English programs today. Ethically speaking, this bureaucratically induced mismatch deprives poor minority students of the critical literacy skills needed to succeed in college from the start.

While most secondary schools rank the development of critical thinking high on their published mission statements, they fail to adequately define this intellectual goal, or to establish and support instructional methods for helping students actively develop it. Paying lip service to this pivotal learning tool is the norm. Conversely, schools fail to require English and social studies teachers, those most responsible for critical reading and writing skills, to be competent in teaching these interrelated learning processes. From district to district, secondary students receive glaringly inconsistent instruction, modeling, and guided practice in applying different critical thinking patterns to challenging content texts and related writing tasks. Due to this overlooked gap, only proficient, self-directed, and fortunate readers can confidently apply internalized patterns of analysis, comparison and contrast, and synthesis to their first-year academic sources.

Whether students are prepared or not, their first college writing course requires them to build essays around critical thought processes by which they must make different kinds of sense out of academic sources. What many college teachers themselves are unprepared for is the double sledgehammer effect that academic writing tasks have on the majority of first-year students. Suddenly, students are confronted with a mode of writing, the transactional, whose purpose is to communicate ideas and information carefully gleaned from academic sources to a diverse academic audience. This writing jeopardy doubles when they realize they can no longer use writing to passively cover a source's main ideas. Without warning, they must shift to thinking long, hard, and according to distinct critical thinking patterns about discipline-based concepts, social issues, and historical events, many lacking clear connection with their lives. They must attempt an intimidating source-based mode of writing, one that involves decoding other writers' technical and abstract vocabularies and struggling to apply a specific critical thought process. On top of these new feats, students must be able to replace conflicting habits of personal and formulaic writing with the standards of an audience interested in neither. The purpose and principles of academic writing could not be more alien to the post-secondary learner. It is little wonder Susie B. looks stressed when first introduced to the sea change called academic writing.

Ironically, the concept of the critical and reflective learner is touted as a major goal of books dedicated to revising writing pedagogy to accommodate adolescents' personal experience and interests. These revisionists uphold the popular student-centered view of learning, the myth that teachers need to adjust both teaching and learning formats to meet students' total individual needs rather than their total learning needs. Their texts celebrate the success stories of secondary students who became "hooked on" reading after discovering the personal relevances of required fictional and non-fictional texts. These narratives involve excerpts from student writing illustrating the use of writing to personalize literature by altering artistic elements of literary works to suit personal taste, describing personal experiences similar to those of literary or historical figures they studied, and expressing a wide range of personal connections with textbooks, literature, films, and videos. However, these classroom testimonials clash with our first-year students' initial efforts to summarize, analyze, and evaluate a college-level academic text. The assumption that personally relevant reading and writing tasks generate life-long readers of the views of others is sharply undercut by the reading deficiencies and blocks of first-year students whose fractured writing programs squeezed out their development of critical reading and writing skills.

This brings us to another contradiction. While many language arts practitioners and theorists continue to promote secondary students' ability and right to use writing to "make sense" out of their personal worlds, these experts often betray a superficial understanding of the complex, recursive, and individual nature of the critical thinking process. Volumes of popular "reconception of writing" books being marketed refer redundantly and generically to personal writers' new-found sense-making expertise while failing to provide valid evidence that students intentionally applied specific thinking patterns to reading and writing tasks. Crucial pre-college patterns of analysis, comparison and contrast, and synthesis are seldom identified, modeled, examined, evaluated, or clearly connected to expressive or transactional writing tasks. As we will later illustrate, the homogenized concept of "making sense" revealed in these texts promotes teachers' and students' misconception of the critical thinking process as an all-purpose ability to draw conclusions and ignorance of the conceptual differences between expressive and transactional writing.

Of all secondary subjects, the teaching and learning of English has the greatest bearing on the uniformity and degree of students' literacy skills at graduation. The main goal of the twenty-first-century English language arts program, therefore, must be the establishment and maintenance of a holistic curriculum, one that offers all students consistent and sequential integration of the severed components of learning: critical thinking skills, language skills, and knowledge of the main sub-categories of English—language, composition, and literature. This premise is the philosophical bedrock upon which the four essential secondary teaching and learning conditions we are proposing, in this chapter and the next two, must be built. By grounding the language arts curriculum in this theoretical model, secondary English programs can begin the arduous but essential work of reconnecting students' thinking, language, and knowledge-building processes. If this belief fails to buttress English programs, students will continue arriving at college without the intellectual framework on which to build not just an advanced knowledge of their chosen discipline, but the cross-disciplinary learning skills and attitudes for creating a better world. Educators K-16 should heed the words of Theodore Sizer who roots his vision in the mind-driven secondary model, especially when he reminds us that "the school's central focus must be on the intellect, on helping each young citizen learn to use his or her mind resourcefully and well. Other enterprises, however worthy, that conflict with this goal must yield" (*Horace's School* 142).

Shifting From a Fragmented to an Integrated Approach to Teaching and Learning

In writing this book, we are trying to clarify the broader classroom and cultural contexts that program and constrain student learning today. We have tried to emphasize, from the student-learner perspective, not just the welter of conflicting approaches to teaching and learning with which students must cope, but also the corrosive effect a jumbled learning model has on their attitudes toward learning and ability to learn. The argument launched by many whole language theorists illustrates the degree to which dualistic conceptions of learning as either student-centered or teacher-centered, behavior-based or knowledge-based continue to fragment and restrict the learning potential of secondary students.

From the beginning, whole language proponents claimed that students are more apt to achieve optimal development of reading, writing, speaking, and listening by actively applying these skills to appropriate content-based texts. Throughout my career as a secondary English teacher and whole language advocate, I designed students' learning formats so they could inductively learn their academic objectives—from language, to composition, to literary concepts—within grade-level reading texts and their own writing tasks. For years, I never questioned the efficacy of helping students acquire and develop their language skills within a challenging and, for the most part, established literature curriculum for each grade-level. From my whole language standpoint, Charles Dickens' *A Tale of Two Cities* became one of many stimulating and shared literary contexts in which ninth graders could discover and understand literary conventions, language devices, grammar and vocabulary principles, writing concepts, and life-concepts relevant to their developmental level. Just as important, this detail-packed historical novel provided an invigorating panorama of characters and events, conflicts and themes which students could examine on literal and critical levels through guided reading, journal writing, class discussions, and oral presentations. Here their ticket to learning was applying their developing language and thinking skills to the expanding pool of literary elements and historical data forming their conceptual knowledge base. The *what* and the *how* of learning were intrinsically linked.

Each day, students actively explored a key literary convention by finding, analyzing, and comparing its use in relevant passages; each day, they discovered new character traits or new dimensions of an emerging conflict; each day, they developed a broader view of a literary concept, whether the art of descriptive writing or the functions of metaphor. The key to their success was a whole language approach in which they were given time to identity, analyze, compare, and contrast a specific element in relevant passages. Their close reading and analysis of selective passages in turn became the prime catalyst for linking and expanding literary knowledge, language arts, and thinking skills. In providing guided textual analysis, I and my colleagues were implementing the main tenet of the whole language approach: enrich students' understanding of a content objective by inviting them to apply, ideally, all four language skills. Via this instructional approach, students could became conscious of using their own thought processes to learn new literary concepts, while applying the cumulative power of developing listening and speaking, reading and writing activities. By providing students countless variations of this "whole learning" approach, I hoped to instill an integrated, self-directed learning model, students' ticket to academic success and life-long learning.

From another standpoint, however, proponents of a radical version of the whole language approach completely ignore students' need to build an interrelated set of critical thinking skills—skills like analysis, comparison/contrast, and synthesis—by consistent application to content-driven reading and writing tasks across the secondary curriculum. Recent books on whole language methodology go so far as to support the dismantling of a core English curriculum in favor of a student-selected reading and writing curriculum. Amidst inflated notions of equating secondary learning with self-exploration and self-betterment, student-centered as opposed to learning-centered whole language advocates dismiss the role that dense conceptual areas—Greek mythology, short story and novel genre, American and British literature, sentence structure and parts of speech, to cite only a few—play in students' overall learning process.

The Stricklands epitomize the shift of many whole language proponents from an integrated to a fragmented learning model. They reflect this radical change when they argue that whole language has become not so much a way for students to learn English as a "philosophy of instruction in which learners actively engage with their teachers, their classmates, and their environment in order to create their curriculum" (Kathleen and James Strickland 7). As a result of this reconception, the thinking and knowledge components of the English curriculum are replaced by a romantic focus on a student-directed learning model. Content knowledge is replaced by subjective views and transient adolescent interests. Bolstering this drastically altered model is the untested assumption that secondary students should still be using language to express personal needs and make personal sense out of self-chosen reading and writing tasks. By stretching student-centered learning to unprecedented curricular extremes, this version of whole language joins a host of "quick-fixes" for building students' self-esteem and other affective goals.

When subjected to this approach, secondary students cannot consistently apply critical thinking or language skills to a sequential and shared knowledge base of literary concepts, genres, periods, and themes. They especially cannot if they all decide to read and write about books representing different genres or a hodge-podge of writing modes and tasks, not to mention varying purposes, topics, vocabularies, levels of meaning, and audiences Dishearteningly, this altered version of a potentially cogent approach to secondary language learning will most likely end up perpetuating the shallow, self-centered reading and writing habits many students now struggle to overcome at the undergraduate level and about which increasing learning theorists and classroom teachers express alarm. By contrast, in a recent article Hirsch underlines what most builds literacy in the early grades, "according to the ablest researchers: providing an explicit, coherent, and carefully cumulative approach to a broad range of knowledge and language" ("Making Better" 7). Shouldn't it be the charge of secondary schools to guarantee students this same integrated model designed to meet the needs of disadvantaged and advantaged students alike?

The major problem lies not with the whole language approach per se. This movement began as an important step, especially at the secondary level, in creating the integrated teaching and learning conditions that increasingly disadvantaged students need to progress in all dimensions of learning, not just language development. Unfortunately, due to gradual distortion and misapplication by educators and administrators alike, the whole-language approach I now read about in books and journal articles has more to do with reaffirming public school's allegiance to students' total well-being than with meeting the total learning needs of increasingly heterogeneous, print-resistant, apathetic, and borderline illiterate secondary students. Any learning model that overemphasizes the fulfillment of individual needs and wants to the degree that it allows students and teachers to make up their own reading and writing curriculum denies students the time, instruction, and incentive to think, read, and write critically about a shared content area, whether it be literature, language, or composition. The adverse effects of such ersatz trends on disadvantaged students are too numerous to detail here. All the same, to prepare all students for the intellectual demands of future academic and work worlds, secondary educators are obligated to place the holistic learning model at the center of not just language arts, but all academic disciplines.

In his 1984 study, *Horace's Compromise: The Dilemma of the American High School,* Theodore Sizer concluded that due to the combined distractions, rigid scheduling, fragmented curriculum, and inconsistent teaching styles, high school is like "an academic supermarket. The purpose of going to school is to pick things up, in an organized and predictable way, the faster the better" ("What High School Is" 27). However, the ongoing tug-of-war between student-centered and test-centered agendas or, put another way, between accommodating the total needs of the student and the standards set by educational bureaucrats has by now severed students' intellectual development from their school learning to a much greater degree than it did over a decade and a half ago when students, less affected by television and passive/receptive technologies, grew up in environments more likely to stimulate active, thought-provoking habits of reading and writing, listening and speaking. Unfortunately, many students who enter college have never read an entire novel, written a full-length research paper; or experienced the joy of discussing books they love and ideas that inspire with friends and family members. Few were encouraged by friends and family to be active and broad readers. And few enjoyed reading experiences parallel to my son's in the early 80's.

For Jim, the initial reading of Salinger's *The Catcher In The Rye* during adolescence led to a life-long habit of synthesizing a creative writer's unique perspective on a life-concept with his own self-knowledge. With each subsequent reading, he understood deeper implications and levels of Holden Caufield's awakening to the corruption of the adult society. Luckily, he learned early on that a literary work could become much more than a plot one cursorily skims and just as quickly forgets. As a result of his continual re-readings, he learned that a book can transform into a context of ideas always there to give the active reader, who seeks to continually replenish his or her knowledge, an expanded view of the worlds beyond the self.

This early active reading experience, fueled by our lively discussions about Holden, the narrator, and the ever-skeptical "Holden" in my son and other adolescents, did not produce a literary scholar. However, it did create the symbiotic connection between intellectual development and reflective reading that continues to recharge my son's desire to learn in school, at home, at work and at play. No price can be placed on a child's discovery that reading, often and widely, is the most accessible and powerful generator of life-long critical thinking, knowledge-building, and communicating skills. Blessed with this awakening during early adolescence, my son went on to achieve his Masters in Special Education and continues to be a critical learner who gives top priority to understanding and meeting his family's and his students' total learning needs.

Today, unfortunately, the majority of secondary students have not grown up in extended families that model reading, repeatedly and broadly; they have not internalized or valued reading as the most cogent vehicle for broadening their understanding of common human dilemmas, experiences, and concepts; for expanding and enriching personal perspectives; and for stimulating reasoning and communicating skills. To substantially offset the current thinking and learning crisis, therefore, educators and policy makers, from elementary to graduate school, must move beyond trumpeting to actively shaping critical secondary thinkers, readers, and writers. By adopting a holistic learning-centered model, those who shape and implement secondary English curriculum, policies, and standards can begin to reverse students' shocking lack of preparation for their intellectually demanding, discipline-centered college reading and writing tasks.

The lack of a comprehensive and integrated learning model across the secondary curriculum also adversely affects a major link in the K-16 learning continuum—the student-teaching experience. As both the culminating display of how one generation has learned to learn and the starting point for the next, the student-teaching experience can signal replication or innovation, stasis or change. Having taught high school students throughout the now decades-long erosion in thinking and language skills, I am frustrated whenever my student teachers revert to the same fractured approaches to teaching and learning that stymied their generation's intellectual growth. Like fate, the severed contexts from which teachers teach and students learn can be mechanically reproduced from one generation of students to the next generation of teachers.

Current English student-teachers are under increased pressure to overplay the personal relevance of lessons while simultaneously teaching the rigorous language arts standards now mandated at state and district levels. Their defense mechanism for coping with this split agenda is inevitable. Average English student-teachers today have adequate, but far from complete, understanding of the broad English content areas of language, literature, and composition. Nervous about the content objectives and related language arts standards they need to teach, many compensate by weighting lessons down with attention-getting and student-appeasing activities. While this defense separates the affective and cognitive dimensions of students' learning, it helps student teachers mask and/or cope with varying forms and degrees of content deficiency or instructional anxiety.

This generation of student-teachers, in fact, spends excess energy and talent devising novel ways to make content objectives not just personally relevant, but entertaining enough to satisfy media-addicted, image-craving secondary students. Whenever the opposing poles of the fractured learning model for simultaneously meeting individual needs and standardized objectives cannot be linked, student teachers resort to artificial stimulators. Unfortunately, activities that focus solely on entertaining and engaging students result in little to no new knowledge. Learning theorists and seasoned practitioners in all disciplines agree that the strongest lesson motivator is one which unites affective and cognitive needs by inviting students to display their relevant prior knowledge to which a new learning objective can be linked. Not surprisingly, those preparing to teach today often distort and misapply this bedrock learning principle. Over the past year, I've observed 7-12 English lessons in which the initial prior knowledge-eliciting phase was replaced by "fun" but unrelated reaction sessions. My first formal observation of a student-teacher can bluntly mirror the long-range consequences, on students and teachers, of secondary education's deeply ingrained "balance of opposites" view of how students should learn.

A recent lesson I observed illustrates the deep imprint this self-perpetuating model has on student teachers. To personally involve 9th graders with their short story unit theme of perseverance in the face of adversity, one student teacher began by appealing to the adolescent fascination with entertainment and sports celebrities with a display of glossy magazine images of current favorites. Inevitably, the planned cue-setting phase veered off track. On the one hand, it gave students equal opportunity to sort through private storehouses of celebrity tidbits and flaunt "bits and pieces" of their icons' lives. Lasting almost ten minutes, this lively large group-share session satisfied the lesson criteria for student motivation and engagement. In addition, self-esteem, cooperation, and respect for others' views seemed equally distributed among the class. On the other hand, few student responses had any connection with the lesson's short-range objective, the short story's unique view or theme on the abstract concept of perseverance. In this case, students' random exhibition of star trivia became an end in itself rather than a bridge to understanding the difficult and often oversimplified convention of literary theme. As a learning hook, it failed to establish explicit links between the story's theme and students' relevant prior knowledge of the concept of perseverance or the convention of theme. This popular opening strategy thus substantially reduced the time students needed for genuine understanding, via guided application of language and thinking skills, of a complex literary convention.

What suffered most was students' need for guided analysis—involving reading, speaking, and writing—of the specific literary elements related to perseverance and the coherent view of this concept that unfolds throughout the story. After spending several minutes settling the class down and quieting potential disrupters following the lively opening response session, the teacher briefly summarized the adversities these celebrities had courageously overcome or learned to cope with. Then with less than half the period remaining, approximately 15 minutes, students were rushed through a collaborative activity in which they discussed, wrote, and presented varying and undocumented inferences of the particular story's view of perseverance. Inevitably, with no clear learning task or outcomes, students lost interest, and the need for constant monitoring and reminders minimized the teacher's ability to productively interact with groups. Initial time and energy spent generating students' collective, spontaneously generated trivia on cultural icons prevented students from building a critical and integrated understanding of literary theme.

In this case, the winner in the learning triad was language. All students spoke, listened, wrote, and read; however, they thought little about their learning objective. Time dedicated to emotionally charging students at the beginning of the lesson cut into the time and instructional strategies, particularly effective questioning techniques and guided analysis of relevant passages, needed to think, read, write, and speak about an underlying theme that could not be more important to middle school students. The resulting display of new learning was only as fragmented and shallow as not so much the student teacher's lopsided lesson planning, as her ingrained perception of the teaching and learning process.

This lesson mirrors the pervasive impact of public education's split affective/academic learning model on the upcoming generation of teachers. From my supervisory vantage point, the most serious effect this learning paradigm had on my student teacher was readily apparent. Conditioned by her own schooling to overplay a lesson's emotional and personal appeal, she dodged the chance to create just as appealing but intellectually challenging strategies for helping students build in-depth and connected knowledge of the objective. A lesson that succeeds in teaching secondary students to critically read literature for a specific convention, analyze its literal and artistic meaning in context, and contemplate its metaphorical implications cannot afford extraneous motivational ploys. Yet over a period of 12 years, present-day student teachers develop an unquestioned connection between daily lessons and their own interests and needs. Out of habit, many view dedicating a third of a lesson to generating students' personal views and spontaneous associations as a prerequisite for learning. From my student teacher's perspective, she was replicating an ingrained practice, an immutable component in her fixed view of the teaching and learning process.

Secondary English education student-teachers currently invest a great deal of time, effort, and creativity trying to make lessons on clear content objectives personally and culturally appealing to adolescents. Ironically, in doing so they deprive increasingly print-resistant and weak readers and writers of guided in-class intellectual engagement with content objectives. For disadvantaged students, the English classroom is often the only venue where they can practice integrating the three components of their learning process, especially their thinking skills. However, the time teachers spend meeting students' own culturally ingrained needs to socialize, self-gratify or "have fun" drastically diminishes the time, incentive, and effort needed to recognize, take charge of, and link critical thinking skills with developing language skills and content knowledge.

Because of this pervasive and implicit belief, new student teachers tend to skim over or superficially "cover" a lesson's main literary concept, failing to present it comprehensively, visually, and analytically so students can grasp its full range of grade-appropriate functions and examine each in-context of the work. Extensive feedback and remediation from cooperating teachers and supervisors can provide student teachers with the rationale and techniques for internally motivating students to learn content knowledge. However, it will take the concerted effort of educators K-16 to even begin reorienting the next generation of English teachers toward the integrated and holistic learning process in which their daily lesson plans need to be anchored.

What my student-teacher's 9th grade English class needed from the start was a tightly focused and coherently implemented lesson on what should be an "easy sell" for this grade level: the theme of the often whitewashed benefits that result from an individual's struggles to achieve a worthy goal. Analyzing and comparing and contrasting relevant examples of this theme in previously read short stories could have lured students from the start into the inductive process of determining the author's deeper message and scrutinize and analyze, through close reading and collaborative discussions, the multiple motives leading to characters' decisions.

Starting with a no-frills opener, he elicited students' prior experience applying analytic reasoning to school or job-related problems. His carefully planned questions quickly elicited practical and academic uses of this thinking skill, from learning to get along with employees, to deciding what college to attend, to inferring an author's underlying intention. This internal motivation taking less than five minutes, it triggered student awareness and ownership of their active learning goal: analyzing the many complex motivations driving each main character's' key decision. Armed with this critical awareness and guided by the teacher's graphic organizer on internal and external motivation, students spent the remaining two-thirds of the class collaboratively analyzing the contradictory elements motivating their assigned character. To close, each group presented a documented analysis of a broad range of factors contributing to their character's critical decision. Finally, the class as a whole discussed how their learning activity enhanced their knowledge of not just Shakespearean motivation, but human motivation in general. The homework, developed for independent application, asked students to compose a thorough analysis of equally broad and conflicting factors leading to a critical decision of their own. In this lesson, the often-severed dimensions of personal and literary, content and process could not have been more in synch.

Instead of neglecting the thinking component of students' learning agenda, this student teacher singled out critical analysis ahead of time as the lesson's long-range driving force. In doing so, he made an acute paradigm shift—away from perpetuating students' view of learning as a passive process by which the teacher magically provides equal doses of affective and academic components and toward empowering students to view learning as a life-long process by which they actively apply critical thinking and language skills to perseverance. Inviting students to jump into the text and try to figure out the unique light a particular story sheds on perseverance is more apt to generate analytic and abstract thinking than any degree of personal appeals. An integrated learning process would give middle school students the intellectual stimulation and broader perspective for scrutinizing and evaluating concepts like being a celebrity and material success, instead of perpetuating their passive displays of received opinion.

The learning-centered English teacher moves beyond the secondary model that caters to students' self-centered needs and standardized educational requirements, further severing their affective and cognitive drives. Transcending this dualistic model of teaching and learning, this teacher designs even the introduction to a lesson objective, whether a literary, vocabulary, grammatical, or syntactic concept, so students can simultaneously grasp and affirm its personal and intellectual relevance. The goal here is to adjust the lesson, especially the problematic element of student motivation, so it reunites secondary students' frequently divorced personal and academic drives into a single, coherent learning process. The surest and quickest route to accomplish this, and needless to say the most controversial, is to make students' discovery and application of their innate critical thinking skills both the impetus and the long range goal of their learning.

To illustrate how easy and natural this principle can be in practice, a student-teacher of mine recently demonstrated an uncommon strategy for motivating recalcitrant 10th graders to become active, critical readers of Shakespeare's *Julius Caesar*. He did not begin the lesson with routine pitches to students' spontaneous views and opinions on this brilliant drama of the human condition. He especially did not take time trying to win students over with an opening act that conjured up analogies between the play's complex human conflicts and students' watered-down adolescent versions. Rather his only motivational ploy, aimed at students' complete learning needs, was to encourage them to build knowledge of discipline-based concepts. As his lesson confirmed, the time dedicated to relating a key thinking skill like literary analysis to students' personal academic agendas goes a long way to reducing the gap between teaching and learning.

What this student teacher avoided during his lesson is equally important. In focusing his opening on the process of analytic thinking and reading, he rose above the pedagogical trap of balancing affective and academic goals that stymies the instructional potential of teachers and the learning potential of students. Instead he made students' long-range critical thinking the key impetus for both his teaching and their learning. He did so knowing that students must be able to think critically about a literary concept for any content objective to build new knowledge.

The first step secondary schools must take to heal the gap between students' thinking and learning is a philosophical one. They must focus on the total learning needs of students and support the curricular and pedagogical changes necessary for meeting them. By fostering an integrated learning process that allows secondary students to consistently link content knowledge with developing language and thinking skills, secondary English programs will best prepare students for self-directed college learning tasks. Educational policy makers hold a power of which many are unaware. This is the power to perpetuate the top-down model in which students' learning is stunted by conflicting imposed goals, or to replace it with a truly student-centered model that evenly nurtures the internal components of students' learning process.

Creating Partnerships Between Secondary and English Education Programs

By now, the crisis in student thinking has become not just a thorn in the side of secondary education, but a virus that weakens college students' academic achievements and development of life-long learning skills. Any effective solution to the widening gap between teaching and learning demands the collaborative effort of all players on the educational team. We have consistently advocated an approach to secondary learning that joins high standards of content knowledge and language arts with critical thinking skills. The adoption of this integrated model would have two important long-range benefits at the college level: secondary students would be better prepared to apply the full range of prerequisite skills and knowledge across the college disciplines, thus achieving higher levels of undergraduate success; also, English education majors would have the prerequisite skills and knowledge for achieving the advanced, comprehensive knowledge their undergraduate courses are designed to instill. These desired outcomes remain educational pipedreams as long as a critical link in the learning continuum is missing—the establishment of working partnerships between secondary English and secondary English education programs.

From our perspective, the combined resolve and expertise of secondary English and English education faculty would be a powerful force in reducing the widening gap between New York State secondary graduation standards and college-level entry standards. The inability of many SUNY-Cortland first-year writing students to organize, analyze, and communicate source information and ideas is a long-range consequence of this missing link. Recently, the AFT's higher education program drafted "First Principles: A Commonsense Agenda for Higher Education," which advocates long-term partnerships across the K through college curriculum. As one of its goals, this report urged higher education to become..." a full partner in K-12 reform, working closely with the schools to raise high school curriculum, graduation and college entry standards" ("Putting Our" 11). We only hope that the NYS Department of Education will create the necessary policies for establishing these learning partnerships.

Secondary and higher education programs have too long operated as separate decision-making bodies. In a discipline as essential to students' development of long-term language and thinking skills as English, the shift from curricular-setting entities to partnerships in learning is imperative. At best, these alliances would enable secondary and college programs to uniformly implement an integrated learning model for grades 7-16. Until these coordinating links are established, the discontinuity between secondary and undergraduate English standards will continue; furthermore, promises to raise students' academic standards at either level will remain empty rhetoric. It is time that secondary and teacher education programs work together to establish coherent standards.

Currently, secondary teacher education programs are undergoing wholesale curricular and pedagogical changes to meet new state and national teacher education standards. English education programs, however, are saddled with a far more pressing obligation. A prime force in determining secondary literacy, they must assure candidates are more than proficient in teaching language and thinking skills 7-12. Active vocabulary-building skills; active, directed, and critical reading skills; grammatical and syntactic concepts and how to teach them directly and inductively; phonology and morphology; and the three writing modes and related features: advanced knowledge of these and other literacy-related areas must become required content for secondary English candidates. These preparatory programs are instrumental in resuscitating secondary students' pre-college thinking and language skills. Their charge moves far beyond the confines of state or national standards/assessment movements.

SUNY-Cortland's newly revised major in secondary English education, now called the Bachelor of Arts in Adolescence Education, English 7-12, provisionally certifies undergraduates to teach 7-12. After taking the prerequisite number of general education courses, program candidates must take a minimum of eleven required English courses (35 hours), two additional advanced-level English electives (6 hours), and 32-33 hours of professional courses in education, methods of teaching English language arts and literature, and psychology. They should be well prepared to use their beginning practice to significantly increase students' language and thinking skills and overall academic achievement. This expectation seems all the more reasonable since candidates must maintain a *2.75* grade point average in English courses to qualify for student teaching during the senior year. Unfortunately, the shallow and disconnected knowledge of literature, composition, and grammar and the weak language and thinking skills with which a growing number of elementary and secondary education majors begin college limit not only their academic success, but their effectiveness in teaching reading and writing to seriously deficient students.

Students planning to teach English now enter college with a diminished knowledge of literature, composition, and grammar, as well as inferior language skills, compared to their predecessors. What is less apparent is that secondary programs' failure to guarantee mastery of specific standards for each of these content areas is due, in turn, to the failure of state education departments to publish and hold individual schools accountable for teaching clear, uniform, and sequential content objectives in all three areas. Due to inconsistent state-wide 7-12 content standards, deficiencies in pre-college critical thinking, reading, and writing skills go undetected in secondary school's carefully masked student-centered reward system. Among this system's common practices are reteaching and retesting so that all students can pass when they are ready to try (mastery learning), issuing incompletes to irresponsible learners, inflating grades, tolerating excessive absenteeism, and replacing earned promotions with social promotions. Because of the normalization of these anti-learning practices, students come to college with more serious problems than the comma splices, sentence fragments, and substandard diction about which college teachers complain. While surface conventions can be quickly improved, college students can never fully compensate for the lost learning skills or deep gaps in content knowledge for which they were rewarded in high school.

The most publicized impact of inadequate secondary knowledge, beyond the obvious fact that college admission standards for education majors in any academic discipline have progressively declined, is the greatly reduced value now placed on the high school diploma by students, teachers, and employers. In 1998, a Public Agenda poll showed that based on a survey of 250 employers, 250 college professors, 700 teachers, 700 parents, and 700 middle-school students, 76 percent "of professors and 63 percent of employers say a diploma is no guarantee a student has learned the basics." ("High School" 3A). The first two groups, moreover, agreed (77%) that the grammar and spelling skills of high school graduates were "poor" or "fair." By contrast, the poll found that a smaller percent of teachers (26%) and parents (32%) had "serious doubts" about students' basic English skills (*Ithaca Journal* 3A). There is no lack of either quantitative and qualitative data confirming students' deteriorating knowledge of literature, composition, and language, as well as their poor college-preparatory reading and writing skills.

Students comprising the sample populations of endless studies and surveys on deteriorating English skills come to college assuming they are not expected to know as much as previous generations. Thus what high schools ultimately fail to prepare students for is the startling realization that their secondary English background is woefully inadequate for college work. While undergraduate admission standards may have dropped, the required academic thinking, reading, and writing tasks have not been made proportionately easier. Both a stab of disappointment and a seed of resentment underlie the anxiety students display in their first-year writing courses. The most traumatic change many experience is the sudden shift from feeling okay about their overall high school records to the painful realization that it did not adequately prepare them for the cumulative reading and writing tasks required across the college disciplines.

When we factor in the discrepancy between secondary students' achievement in English at graduation and the higher standards set by teacher education programs, the problem of teacher preparation intensifies. Many education majors spend four years struggling to achieve and maintain competency in their discipline. The struggle is even harder for students who transfer from two-year colleges since many must make up additional prerequisites. In the meantime, experts on K-16 representing opposing views remain locked in the circular, no-win argument over who or what is most responsible for declining thinking, reading, and writing skills K-12. The bottom line, however, is clear. As long as secondary schools establish vague and non-sequential language, literature, and composition goals and teacher education programs place disproportionate value on the development of pedagogical attitudes and skills, the erosion of future English teachers' content knowledge and related thinking and language skills will continue. The key here is mutual consensus—at the secondary, college, and state levels—as to the grade-specific content knowledge secondary English students must master, The big problem is that the development of increasingly advanced content knowledge for students and students teachers is not a public education priority.

At the college level, the most obvious effect of inadequate teacher preparation is the extensive remediation that goes on in required courses to compensate for students' inconsistent and weak secondary background. For years, remedial courses in basic English and math skills were standard fare at most two- and four-year colleges. These "crash" courses in basic reading, writing, and math skills that should have been mastered in high school have been higher education's instant remedy for a far-reaching and complex learning crisis. While arguments continue nationwide over the efficacy and cost of remedial education at the college level, what is overlooked is the invisible and gradual incorporation of this 'basic' approach to learning in required undergraduate courses.

To illustrate, students taking Grammar and the Writing Process, a prerequisite course for student teaching, often require extensive remediation in basic grammatical concepts such as parts of speech, sentence parts, phrases, and clauses that at one time were taught and learned well by 9th grade. The increasing time secondary English majors need for such "catch-up" work in this advanced course points to two missing knowledge links. The first involves students' deficient prior knowledge of essential language concepts. Students who fail to understand the fundamental sentence structure concepts of coordination and subordination lack the basis upon which to build advanced concepts of coherence, variety, balance, and emphasis. This content gap, invariably, stunts their future instructional range. The extra time and effort undergraduates spend learning and applying basic concepts of sentence structure mean reduced time developing the advanced concepts and related teaching methods the course is designed to teach. Those strugglers who manage to pass this increasingly difficult course with a C+ will continue to suffer from the cumulative effect of a grammatical gap

long into their teaching career. Many novice teachers, themselves
deprived of a coherent, sequential, and developmental approach to
grammar instruction, sadly remain in a permanent "catch up" mode.
Ironically, instead of fixing the obvious problem, policy makers shift the
focus to professional development and other band-aid approaches to
improving subject knowledge.

Likewise, insufficient knowledge of basic concepts of nouns, number,
and ownership equates with repeated errors in apostrophe use. Simple
mechanical errors, however, can spell disaster for new English teachers.
During undergraduate writing intensive courses, students frequently
complain of never learning the grammatical concepts underlying conventions of apostrophe and comma use. While they did well on high
school essays, many claim recurring mechanical errors went unmarked
and unconnected to relevant concepts. Thus how can prospective teachers be expected to achieve the more advanced, in-depth knowledge that
upper-level methods courses are tailored to teach? Especially when they
must spend an inordinate amount of time learning the underlying concepts upon which a required methods course like Grammar and the
Writing Process should build, not teach from scratch? Even more problematic, how can they adequately develop pedagogical skills when still
struggling to learn the concepts they must teach?

Deficient prior knowledge of composition concepts is the second
missing link shortchanging students' achievement in Teaching Writing,
another prerequisite for student teaching. Students enrolled in this
course often lack prior knowledge of the fundamental composing concepts upon which the course is designed to build. Published goals
include research-supported instructional strategies, curriculum planning, and assessment techniques for teaching writing 7-12. Yet these too
are watered-down by students' inadequate prior knowledge of rhetorical
purpose, organizational structure, audience, level of language, and other
writing fundamentals. Low achievement in this course is again synonymous with missing content knowledge. There is no time for "teaching

from scratch" in a course where students must quickly link proficient personal and public writing models with a broad range of up-to-date theory and methods for both teaching and assessing writing. Extra time forfeited to learning essential composing concepts and related skills cuts deeply into the time needed to achieve the course's advanced goals.

To illustrate, extensive instruction and modeling of the criteria for writing a synthesis of existing literature on a chosen educational issue is aimed at helping secondary English students compose this crucial genre of academic writing. Yet several students were so preoccupied with revising and improving habitual writing problems, particularly in sentence combining, transitions, and spelling and mechanical errors that they could not concentrate on the task's critical thinking and research-related criteria. Their synthesis goal alone required them to carefully research, select, analyze, incorporate, document, and interrelate up-to-date sources on common aspects of the relevant writing issue like portfolio assessment they were researching. Those struggling to master basic writing concepts and skills, let alone the difficult critical thinking skill of source synthesis, were in trouble from the start. There is no valid reason why secondary students have not learned to recognize in models and apply to their own writing the fundamental concepts of rhetorical purpose, structure, language level, and audience awareness form, and how these differ in personal and public writing by the time they enroll in their first academic writing course. Needless to say, adequate and sequential instruction in basic language and composition concepts would make a world of difference in every English education major's academic outlook and achievement.

The dominant goal of both courses, the development of varied methods for teaching in-depth knowledge of grade-appropriate concepts and skills, is seriously undermined by shallow and fragmented secondary learning. When students begin their teaching practicum, they should be unconditionally ready to apply what they learned about modeling, graphic organizers, questioning techniques, collaborative group strategies, deductive vs. inductive approaches, and myriad other new teaching approaches. They should not be worried about the level, depth, and quality of the content knowledge, whether advanced concepts or basic skills, that drives their selection and use of methodology. Yet content-weak undergraduates whose academic achievement is constantly interrupted by remedial "catch-ups" are all the more susceptible to the student-centered pedagogy of the entertaining and engaging activity-based lesson.

In one case, a student teacher's literary background most likely lacked in-depth knowledge of Shakespearean extended metaphor. To begin his lesson on this complex figurative device, he had students find examples of simple metaphor in Act I of *Macbeth* and listed these on the chalkboard. Next he organized students into groups and instructed each to interpret the function of an extended metaphor in an assigned passage. However, he provided no instruction—deductive or inductive, verbal or visual—on the literary objective of extended metaphor that in this play is one of Shakespeare's richest and most cogent conventions for capturing the depth, range, and ambivalence of Macbeth's tragic character. In groups, students exhibited many outward benefits of collaborative learning pedagogy such as guided reading, cooperation, alternate views, multiple language skills, and kinesthetics for added variation. By contrast, they received no new knowledge of the unique features and form of Shakespearean extended metaphor, experienced none of the excitement of grappling with the contradictory insights into human power that this device's multiple levels and associations can generate, and displayed none of the signs of a holistic learning process. But this was not just a case of student-teacher instructional failure. Within the deeper educational cause/effect framework, this non-lesson is a glaring reminder of a K-16 educational system that tolerates inconsistencies between secondary teaching practices and teacher preparation goals and ethics.

Both seasoned secondary and practice teachers succumb to the activity-based lesson model. The former group does so because for decades school policy, at district and state levels, has pressured teachers to align collaborative and inductive or discovery learning formats with the teaching of content objectives. After spending many years designing and formatting collaborative projects and discovery lessons at all levels and a few years inventing more "authentic" ways to assess learning, even experienced English teachers inadvertently shift their priority from effective ways to teach new content knowledge to exciting ways students can come together and display their learning. The "what" of learning is often eclipsed by the new activity and assessment culture. As for practice teachers, they enter a school's culture as visitors whose role is to "take in" what they see and hear. Their visitor status makes it difficult to infer that what is being taught is not new knowledge but fancy ways to show what is already known; simply put, to realize when genuine teaching does not occur. Both groups must reconsider the ethics involved in every instructional choice; they should consider one educator's wise reminder that the methods and activities teachers devise are ultimately "but a path or a tool in the labor of genuine learning" Reed 48).

Unfortunately, novice teachers schooled with a superficial concept of their own learning process are easily misled into using pedagogy as both new knowledge and a vehicle for building new knowledge. When experienced and beginning teachers display confusion over their main responsibility in the classroom, it is a wake-up call for restoring and maintaining an integrated secondary curriculum, especially in English language arts.

Toward this end, higher education should set seek innovative and "authentic" ways to improve teacher preparatory programs. The first step should involve making exit standards tougher for those enrolled in secondary teaching programs. Calls for arts-and-science programs to demand more comprehensive, in-depth knowledge of core subjects like English, history, math, and science flood educational publications. However, those advocating this position concentrate almost exclusively on the progressive watering-down of core subjects over the past decade. From this narrow perspective, they fail to recognize the deeper cycle of inadequate secondary preparation and compensatory college remediation fueling declining undergraduate content knowledge, higher college drop-out rates, and other learning problems college students should not have to cope with. Equally myopic is the proposal to require teaching candidates in all states to pass more rigorous subject-area competency exams to be provisionally certified. Over4eliance on state-by-state standardized exams will not reduce weak teacher preparation. It will only increase students' subjection to more untested tests and inconsistent testing criteria on anything from basic literacy skills to advanced knowledge of literary works and concepts.

Higher education-based proposals for extending, diversifying, and enriching the student teaching experience is another well-intended but shallow panacea for the deeper causes and effects of undergraduate subject deficiency. Catherine Emihovich, associate professor in SUNY-Buffalo's Graduate School of Education, represents this skin-deep solution to the 7-16 thinking and learning crisis. She recommends extending the student teacher-cooperating teacher relationship to five months to allow for joint research projects that explore topics such as "increasing student motivation, seeking better ways of assessing learning or developing more effective teaching strategies. In this way, the teacher and student jointly reflect on specific topics related to improving teaching and learning, and the student has a unique opportunity to learn more about the classroom, the school and the community prior to student teaching" (Emihovich 9). Such joint research projects could provide the content-rich novice teacher with a doubly powerful opportunity: first, to become a more reflective practitioner who learns early to expand her knowledge by collaborating with experienced teachers; second, to get an early start advancing her own research interests and professional development. Such a liaison is unlikely to provide what a growing number of student teachers in English and other disciplines need most—a denser and broader grasp of the content knowledge they will be responsible for imparting. Like other digressive measures, it cannot reduce or recover the learning lost during four years of fragmented secondary instruction.

Also representing the graduate perspective on the thinking and learning crisis is the newly formed Cohort in Education Program, an exciting partnership between the Southern Connecticut State University's graduate school of education and the New Haven Federation of Teachers. This partnership's aim is to better meet the urban education needs of students enrolled in the two-year graduate program. Its three specific objectives are: "courses tailored to the needs of teachers working in an urban school system; collaboration among the participants; and insight into the academic reforms taking place in the city's public schools" ("The Stuff of'" 6). This collaborative model could surely enhance secondary English graduate students' understanding of more effective ways to teach inner-city students. The flip side is that its narrow focus also excludes a long-range remedy for the cross-demographic problem of weak subject knowledge at the crossroad between high school and college. Currently, the need for millions of new provisionally certified teachers is undercut by the inadequate secondary education many receive. Given this paradox, graduate education programs' most incisive long-range goal would be to build partnerships with secondary programs that guarantee students an integrated learning process and clearly defined academic standards for graduation. Another higher education solution focuses on professional development programs to ensure that provisionally certified teachers meet subject and pedagogical standards. This panacea also side steps the problem of inadequate secondary content knowledge that, in a field as comprehensive as English, can severely restrict undergraduates' crucial knowledge-building phase.

We believe that an integrated model for learning English, one that sequentially connects students' expanding conceptual knowledge with developing thinking and language skills, will shape "whole" English learners rather than "whole" high school students. When grounded in this theoretical base, partnerships between high schools and English education programs can establish, revise, and maintain the coherent discipline-based standards students must meet for graduation and for acceptance into college preparatory programs. No logic supports the current practice of allowing students to enter secondary education programs with lower achievement levels than those entering other academic programs. Nor does it make sense to perpetuate the current system in which the academic standards for secondary English programs are determined in isolation from those set by teacher preparation programs.

Following is a preliminary list of the functions these English education partnerships could provide in their capacity as joint academic gatekeepers:

#1: Form satellite programs consisting of a geographic cluster of secondary schools and a university/college teaching hub which collaboratively set the English standards for high school graduation and for acceptance into the English education program.

#2: Establish a time-line for raising the academic standards of high school graduates and for correlating these with academic standards set admitting first-year college students.

#3: Establish grade-specific 7-12 standards for critical thinking, reading, and writing and for content areas of language, literature, and composition so students are ready for college-level reading and writing tasks and have prerequisite discipline-based conceptual knowledge.

#4: Read, discuss, and meet to evaluate new research-supported theory of teaching and learning English language arts and meet periodically to collaboratively realign predetermined standards with theory and practice.

English education programs can start right now by establishing and rigorously maintaining integrated English standards. To create effective partnerships, members must develop a sequential and comprehensive enough 7-16 curriculum to meet students' full learning needs. The above steps aim to build English studies K-16 around a coherent intellectual framework that compel students to consistently build interdependent content knowledge, language arts, and thinking skill. In other words, they will help to reconnect the long-severed relationship between how students learn and how teachers teach. English education programs are now responsible for setting specific and high standards for resuscitating and integrating the long-fragmented components of English.

Works Cited

Emihovich, Catherine. "New Ways to Teach Tomorrow's Teachers." *New York Teachers.* 11 May 1998: 9.

"High School Grads Can't Spell or Write, Say Employers, Profs." *Ithaca Journal.* 9 Jan.1998: 3A.

HirschJr., E.D. "Making Better Use of the Literacy Time Block." *American Educator.* Summer 2001:4+.

"Putting Our First Principles First." *AFT On Campus* 17.2 Oct. 1997: 11.

Sizer,Theodore. *Horace's School: Redesigning the American High School.* Boston: Houghton Mifflin, 1992.

"What High School Is." *Rereading America: Cultural Contexts for Critical Thinking and Writing.* 3rd ed. Ed. Gary Colombo et al. Boston: Saint Martin's, 1995.20-30.

Strickland, Kathleen, and James Strickland. *Uncovering the Curriculum.* Portsmouth, NH: Boynton/Cook, 1993.

"The Stuff of Revolution." *AFT On Campus.* 18.3. Nov.1998: 6.

Chapter Six

The Missing Art of Moving Students from Personal to Public Writing

The Need to Realign Practice and Theory for a More Integrated Writing Process

In previous chapters, we have emphasized the shallow, conflicting, disconnected ways secondary students are compelled to learn. These combined learning problems specifically characterize the ways secondary students are compelled to learn writing and literature. As for writing, they learn no comprehensive knowledge of the underlying rhetorical features of writing; these include the writer's dominant mode or purpose, frame of reference, thought process, and audience; yet these are all deeper concepts that need to inform academic writing tasks. For the most part, they are led to view writing antithetically as a test or way to display pre-established writing standards, and as a vehicle for unevaluated self-expression, but not as a means to communicate the sense they make out of what they read to an implied audience. When students begin college, they have acquired the simplistic notion that writing is a language skill, separate from active reading, needed to express personal views and demonstrate content knowledge. Writing for them also means learning how to apply ironclad formulas to required essay tasks and exams, not a multi-dimensional process of reconstructing and communicating the various meanings and thought processes implicit in what they read. For most, writing remains cut off from the active thinking and reading that prepares them for college work.

Two out of three essential ingredients for developing new knowledge at the secondary level, a coherent body of facts, skills, procedures, and concepts about writing with which to link new writing concepts, and students' critical thinking skills are not consistently linked with their school writing skills. Or these learning components are missing altogether as students are swept along in the rapid, mechanical secondary assembly line of writing informative, persuasive, analytic, or descriptive essays for grades. For only rare secondary students is writing synonymous with the integrated process of understanding what writing means and thinking, reading, and writing critically upon which their academic success depends. These more connected learners include those fortunate enough to take advanced writing courses that introduce them to the rhetorical concepts of writing modes, the range of purposes a writer can have within each mode, and the nature and needs of the writer's audience, especially when communicating another writer's meaning. The majority must wait until introductory and advanced college writing courses to benefit belatedly from a holistic, integrated, and mature concept of writing as a body of knowledge in itself, as well as a thinking and language skill.

New York State Department of Education's *Learning Standards for English Language Arts,* in formulating its writing outcomes for high school graduates, reflects the shallow curriculum required for secondary writers. According to the document's 1996 revised edition, by graduation students are required to use written language: "to acquire and transmit information" (4); "for literary response [involving] presenting interpretations, analyses, and reactions to the content and language of a text" (8); "for critical analysis and evaluation" (12); and "for social interaction

[that] requires using written messages to establish, maintain, and enhance personal relationships with others" (16). Unfortunately, what is missing in this set of long-term writing goals is an implicit vision, a guiding theory on how students learn to conceptualize and distinguish among a variety of writing tasks as they prepare for college. While the first goal is both worthy and practical, it is far from reality. High school graduates are generally unprepared to use writing, as they begin college, "to acquire and transmit information" because they are not taught the fundamental differences between the communication or transactional mode, on one hand, and the expressive or self-writing mode on the other. In first-year writing courses, students' most common weaknesses include the inability to adjust word choice, sentence structure, and content for the purpose of communicating the ideas they read to an audience with demanding criteria. Since secondary writing assignments and writing tests are not grounded in students' understanding of the three dominant modes or purposes of written language, the majority are unprepared to adjust their dominant writing purpose, frame of reference, and thought process for a demanding academic audience when they begin college. At the same time, they struggle unnecessarily to align their writing conventions with the critical thought processes of analysis, comparison/contrast, and synthesis that form the intellectual backbone of introductory academic reading and writing tasks, and also the basis for complex evaluative, argumentative, and research tasks required by specific disciplines.

To implement the final goal, using writing "to enhance personal relationships with others," the document recommends students spend time using "electronic forms" of writing, as well as personal notes and letters that entertain and interest the recipient" (16). Obviously another example of public education's long-standing effort to rigidly align academic and behavioral outcomes, this goal neither requires nor guarantees the integration of knowledge, thinking skills, and language facility that could give secondary students a head-start as academic writers. The key question raised by this goal is, will these real-life, personally meaningful forms of discourse impart the writing concepts and skills students need to master college writing tasks, and, later, the precise technical writings tasks demanded in their workplaces? Here the extremely vague standard, using writing "for social interaction," is associated with informal tasks that require none of the specific knowledge and skills demanded by the heightened purposes of academic writing and by its demanding audience. Thus it is another way secondary students are distracted from preparing for the challenging concepts, forms, skills, and conventions that make up academic writing.

The lesson here is that New York State graduating seniors will not be prepared for academic writing until they have a more complete grasp of the discipline of writing, and can apply the critical thinking skills of summary, analysis, comparison/contrast and synthesis to meaningful reading and writing tasks. These four goals typify the vague, incomplete, and even irrelevant standards set by state education departments and local districts across the country which fail to guarantee secondary students the minimal knowledge, thinking, and reading skills to succeed in introductory college writing courses. These students uniformly lack knowledge of the deeper rhetorical concepts embedded in academic writing, and the ability to bring their critical thinking in line with their reading and writing tasks. However, there is one sure way to reduce the gap between what secondary students need to understand about writing and what they actually learn. The concepts of the expressive, transactional, and poetic uses of writing must be systemically taught, integrated with critical thinking and reading skills, and applied to all three writing modes at each grade level.

Secondary students are capable and deserving of acquiring a more comprehensive and reflective view of their three innate modes or uses of writing. To do so, they need generous opportunities to analyze and compare/contrast the underlying attributes that link their expressive, transactional, and poetic uses of written language. Currently, school writing assignments and exam essays are divorced from James Britton's integrated theory that students develop the three main uses of writing in conjunction with their maturing listening, speaking, reading, and thinking skills. Britton's concept of the three predominant functions of writing, however, will empower students to understand, take charge of, and feel committed to their full range of built-in writing aptitudes. Secondary rhetorical education can only begin when teachers are themselves prepared and willing to offer students the conceptual knowledge and related skills that enable them to distinguish personal writing from transactional and poetic. Unfortunately, an imposed grocery list of traditional rhetorical patterns—expository, persuasive, descriptive, narrative, etc.—continues to mold students' concept of writing and stifle their control. This pervasive system of preconceived writing forms prevents teachers and students from apprehending an organic, holistic, and student-driven view of writing. Missing conceptual knowledge of the three modes often results in writing that is unacceptable simply because students have not learned to analyze the common elements linking each mode and explain how each must change when shifting from personal to transactional writing, or from personal to poetic mode. Once secondary students acquire a more comprehensive view of their natural writing territories, their academic writing experience will be a liberation rather than a constant struggle to get by. After all, shouldn't this be the long-range preparatory goal of the secondary English program?

How Missing Knowledge of Writing Affects College Writing Tasks

When students begin college, their ability to read and write successfully across the academic curriculum has already been diminished by inadequate instruction in critical thinking and writing concepts, two main components of learning to write. During high school, Susie B. never learned that analysis is a built-in thought process she must actively apply to non-fiction and literary sources. The combination of her failure to read enough so that applying a thought process like analysis to sources becomes automatic, and her teachers' failure to encourage her in-depth analysis of underlying concepts or structures largely accounts for this learning gap. But her more fundamental and serious learning deficiency is that she never consciously thought about writing as a body of information and concepts upon which to progressively build new knowledge and understanding. No math teacher would teach trigonometry to a student who has not first learned to master the basic principles of algebra or geometry. However, secondary English teachers regularly expect students to write transactional pieces, such as informative and persuasive essays, without first teaching them the information and concepts shaping the transactional mode, and how this use of writing differs from the expressive and poetic. In doing so, teachers violate a key principle of knowledge-building, that "in order to comprehend incoming information, the learner must initially 'build his own meaning' by linking old information to new information" (Marzano 5). Consequently, most high school students arrive at college with no general knowledge of academic/source-based writing, and no knowledge of the specific attributes that distinguish academic writing from other transactional forms, including the formulaic writing tasks required in high school. While this knowledge is considered non-essential for secondary success, it is implicit in writing tasks required across the college disciplines.

The theory of the three developmental modes or linguistic uses of written language, first posited by James Britton in his seminal 1970 study, *Language and Learning,* and continually expanded and reinforced in his later works, has long under-girded writing curricula at the undergraduate and graduate levels. What Britton believed is what language arts experts now overwhelmingly advocate: students' writing develops in conjunction with their interrelated language and thinking skills. By 2000, there is no lack of studies acknowledging and supporting Britton's theory that students begin to write in the expressive or self-referential mode in which they use writing mainly to express subjective feelings and views. As their thinking expands outward toward the objective and imaginary worlds, so does their writing. They start to shift their use of writing toward the transactional mode when they become capable of inductive-deductive reasoning and communicating ideas to an external audience. By contrast, when their interest veers toward the creative potential of language itself, they begin to enter the poetic or literary mode.

The distinction of Britton's theory is his emphasis on the writer's developmental stages of using writing to refer to increasingly depersonalized frames of reference. In the first stage of writing, the expressive mode, language is used to refer predominantly to personal or subjective realities. As the writer's experience, thought processes, and use of language mature, writing starts to evolve along two different trajectories: toward increasingly objective meaning as the writer internalizes the world beyond the self (the transactional mode); and along a second path toward language and its potential to create rich, alogical categories of figurative meaning (the poetic mode). Based on this landmark theory, as Zemelman and Daniels point out, schools begin to develop literate writers…"by accepting and celebrating [children's] expressive language and then [by providing] occasions that invite students to grow toward the transactional and the poetic, to extend their language range" (Zemelman and Daniels 74). If secondary teachers consistently practiced this theory, and gave students guided practice in stretching their writing outward, along the transactional and literary paths, more literate writers would come to college prepared to confidently and proficiently construct meaning in these two modes.

The fact that many students come to college unable to write at a minimal level of effectiveness in the transactional mode bears considerable irony. Educators across the P-16 curriculum have widely voiced support for Britton's developmental theory of writing modes, and its underlying assumption that students can and need to diversify their writing so it evenly spans all three major functions by commencement. Yet despite broad support for this language-based theory of writing, first-year college students still lack thorough understanding of how to write transactionally, to communicate meaning—in this case, the many meanings they must glean from academic texts—to a public audience. By contrast, they are prepared to write according to ready-made patterns, discrete features, and iron-clad conventions. They are ready to write to reproduce what Marzano noted almost ten years ago: the "traditional modes of discourse (e.g., narration, description, exposition, argumentation, and poetry) which by the 1970's had devolved to static structures taught as ends in themselves rather than as active ways of exploring ideas" (79).

Most graduating seniors fail to understand and take charge of their full writing potential; to direct and develop it in all three modes, exercising the full range of their innate writing purposes and needs. When secondary programs fixate students on the outward forms and features of writing, forcing them to write in a modeless context so to speak, they rob them of the knowledge and skills they need for college writing. Knoblaugh and Brannon provide a fitting analogy for this writing-to-learn crisis when they insist that writing students are being misled to think that "a knowledge of the features leads to an ability to compose 'persuasive essays'—which is like asking someone to bake a cake by pointing to a finished cake and explaining that it is devil's food rather than angel and two-layered rather than three" (29). Due to many agendas considered more relevant than a learning-centered theory grounded in students' evolving uses of writing, secondary students are excluded from learning what it means to write for three vital human functions—to express the self, to communicate meaning to others, and to create verbal worlds. Most to the point, until they grasp the rhetorical principles linking all three modes, their potential as transactional writers will remain stunted. They will arrive at college lacking the transactional range and maturity for thinking, reading, and writing critically about increasingly difficult discipline-based sources.

We have suggested an array of factors contributing to the serious decline in students' writing skills, from watered-down reading curriculum, to the disappearance of critical thinking/reading/writing skills, to added-on behavioral outcomes disguised as learning goals, to diminishing teacher knowledge. Regardless of the causes of this learning crisis, students arrive at college confused about what it means to write successfully in the transactional mode. This is most unfortunate. Whether writing teachers and theorists approve or not, academic writing, situated squarely in the transactional mode, dominates and will continue to dominate discipline-building college writing tasks. As a major form of source-based writing, academic writing is highly transactional in its fundamental aim to communicate to academic audiences the ideas and thought processes of other writers. It is perhaps the most difficult transactional genre, since it compels students to write simultaneously from several unfamiliar frames of reference: the internal thought process by which they intend to construct source meaning; the source and its literal and implied contexts; and the purposes and needs of their readers.

College students will make these interconnected transactions countless times as they progress in their discipline, writing summaries, critical responses, analyses, evaluations, comparisons and contrasts, and syntheses of fictional and non-fiction texts, as well as their own source-based arguments and research projects. The transactional nature and premise of academic writing has not changed over the decades, nor has its alliance with critical thinking, reading, and writing skills. What has changed is that high school graduates no longer have the prerequisite knowledge of writing concepts and reading skills for academic writing as did prior generations who grew up thinking, reading, and writing critically about sources. To us, it all leads back to students' inherent reading deficiency—their lack of training in closely reading texts for a multitude of literary and non-literary meanings. Addressing this crisis, Berthoff emphatically reminds language arts educators that "Close reading is closely linked to literacy, thought of as what we want to assure in our students, namely, the capacity to construct and construe, to apprehend, develop, and control meanings" (672). Sadly, college students are no longer trained to read texts closely and actively for genuine literacy; or, from a Brittonian perspective, to appreciate, grapple with, and understand other writers' dominant purpose, meaning, and ways of thinking about the world.

Diving into the Transactional Mode: Making a Case for an Integrated Approach to the Teaching and Learning of Secondary Writing

Students enrolled in my recent Academic Writing I sections arrived, as those in previous semesters, with no prior knowledge of the principles underlying the transactional mode of writing and its relationship to the expressive and poetic. In fact, they had no initial grasp of the three different purposes and frames of reference that govern all acts of writing. This missing background knowledge can lead to months of frustration and disappointment, an academic catch-22, for beginning college writers. It leaves most shockingly unprepared for the course's challenging objective: learning to summarize, analyze, and compare/contrast academic sources for a public audience seeking to understand other writers' main ideas, supporting details, structural elements, and key concepts.

Fortunately, the course also comes equipped with a built-in measure for addressing students' deficient knowledge of writing. Their first required essay is an objective response to an academic source. To start, this task invites students to use their writing for an expressive purpose: to describe an experience, from their subjective frame of reference and in their personal voice, that relates to an issue of broad significance which they have already read about and discussed. This initial task allows them to briefly prolong their expressive role as both writer and audience of their own writing. In a short time, however, they must abruptly switch from expressive to transactional mode. To do so, they must significantly alter their personal response so it simultaneously acknowledges two external frames of reference: that of the source author with which they must now align their personal response, and that of the implied public audience to whom they are communicating this new connection. If adequate learning conditions are provided, students' initial personal response can create an inductive format in which they can discover the key rhetorical differences between expressive and transactional writing and be ready to write in the "academic" mode. In other words, they can acquire the missing link of "old information" upon which to build genuine understanding of academic writing's multiple frames of reference—the internal thought process by which they will reconstruct the source; the source author's purpose in writing; and the audience's purpose in reading. Armed with this rhetorical knowledge, they can at least dive smoothly into their new role as public writer.

Many advocates of the personal response essay view this as a necessary cushion against the complex, anxiety-provoking task of writing about academic sources for a public audience. Many reason, moreover, that frequent respites in students' true comfort zone of expressive writing, the self-exploratory mode that for many secondary students is almost synonymous with writing, will help build their confidence as writers as they journey into the rigors of transactional writing. Indeed, the personal response essay, as its name implies, meets all the criteria for expressive writing, allowing students to focus freely on developing private thoughts and feelings, unhampered by what other writers think or what a real-life audience needs to know. However, secondary programs do not intentionally teach students the rationale and the mechanics for shifting their writing from a subjective to an objective frame of reference. Thus, we have found, when first-year students start right out learning the principles and techniques for framing their subjective responses in context of an informed author's view, they get a head-start making the essential academic transition into writing both from and for external frames of reference.

The objective source response essay requires students to develop a "critical" personal response to a wide range of discipline-based essays, from philosophical to sociological, literary to historical, in which they have strong personal stakes. They still develop their personal experiences and views. However, they now do so in the dual external contexts of another writer's ideas, views, and claims, and an implied audience's need for information and logic. My recent class, for example, used writing to objectively respond to brief argumentative essays on the causes of homelessness; the effects of high-tech crime-fighting devices on individual privacy rights; the benefits of abolishing mandatory school attendance policies; the questionable ethics of new reproductive technologies; and the ways students' view of college life has changed over two decades. These transactional pieces involved broad social issues to which they could personally respond before starting to collectively analyze deeper concepts and structure. What initially motivated groups to choose one source over another was the strong personal relevance of the topic. Their quick choices, in fact, confirmed Britton's premise that all writing, regardless of its dominant mode, issues from an expressive matrix, the writer's evolving pool of personal experiences, feelings, beliefs, interests, and views. Students' success on this transitional task, however, depended on two factors: their willingness to transcend personal stakes in the issue, and their effort to compose an objective response whose meaning grows out of and is enriched by another writer's intellectual frame of reference.

Students began this transitional writing task in expressive mode. Unconcerned with their source author's meaning to start, they were free to write about personal experiences and opinions, as long as these related to the main source issue. As they often did in high school, they unleashed personal thoughts and memories in the flood of words and welter of feelings that typify expressive writing. They wrote spontaneously about whatever came to mind, uninhibited by the arbitrary forms, rules, and conventions governing public writing.

When we ask students to shift from personal to source-based/public writing, it is crucial that we, as educators, intentionally prepare them, cognitively and affectively, for this college learning skill. Assuming students are prepared to make what for many is a huge intellectual and technical leap can prove self-defeating for college teachers and students alike. The writing teacher's lesson planning, therefore, should involve careful scrutiny of the many challenges posed by, what is for most, the daunting task of suddenly reading and writing critically about academic sources. The pivotal assumption underlying the assignment of academic writing tasks is that students are actually prepared to coherently shift their writing from their personal frame of reference to that of an unknown source author. Yet when one considers the lack of prior experience students have critically analyzing or synthesizing elements of informative texts, it should not be difficult to imagine the cognitive overload the shift to source-based writing imposes on first-year college students. Many have never written a page in an effort to go beyond the author's literal meaning and analyze deeper structures, concepts, and conventions. Their history of writing about literature often boils down to a pot-pourri of personal responses and opinions, at the cost of ignoring the rich array of techniques authors use to create different kinds of meaning.

Yet at college students are suddenly expected to analyze a source author's deeper meanings, conceptual as well as structural. The challenging skills required by a source-based response essay alone are many. These include reading selectively for source ideas to which students can link personal responses; coherently incorporating, fairly representing, and accurately documenting these source ideas; developing thought-provoking inferences on these ideas based on prior knowledge and the source itself; and establishing clear connections between personal responses and the author's views (similarity, contrast, example, change, cause, effect, and so on). As students realign their subjective responses—their charged memories, strong opinions, and ambivalent feelings—with an author's frame of reference, they start to relinquish biased views and unfounded generalizations. Their reward for doing so, they quickly learn, is the new knowledge they create by synthesizing personal experience with an author's broader perspective. However, as they also discover, this reconstruction phase often entails drastic revision of initial personal responses so they smoothly dovetail with an author's specific points.

For many students, the other major transition required for source-based writing, the shift from self-writing to audience-based writing, is equally difficult. This shift assumes students will be able to identify specific expressive writing habits and features they must now either eliminate altogether or considerably sophisticate out of respect for their public audience's need for coherent organization, well-developed subtopics, and appropriate diction. When teachers assign students any source-based writing task, they assume they are prepared to acknowledge a public audience, apply the technical skills and conventions expected by this implied readership, and actively evaluate and revise their own writing process to accommodate this second external frame of reference. Thus from the start, first-year writers are placed in a double jeopardy that remains invisible to both secondary and college teachers who take for granted they have the prerequisite knowledge—the rhetorical concepts, the active and critical reading skills, and the audience-based writing conventions—for initial academic writing tasks.

Therefore, it made a great deal more sense to invite students not to reinforce ingrained habits and attitudes of self-writing, but to quickly learn the rhetorical principles for converting expressive writing into the academic tasks they'd be required to write for the next four years. This classroom opportunity is crucial for beginning college students. It will continue to be until all high school students are uniformly taught the concept of the three dominant uses of writing, and practical strategies for shifting from expressive to transactional writing. Unfortunately, first-year college students have only a few weeks to adjust personal writing content and style for source-based and audience-based tasks. Thus it was all the more important that I adjusted the teaching of the source response essay to facilitate their outward shift from private to public writing, as well as their inward shift from passive to active learning of the sub-concepts, the rhetorical principles informing and distinguishing these two modes. The least I could do was help students like Susie B. acquire the missing content knowledge needed to dive, competently and confidently, into academic writing.

To nudge students into academic writing, I designed a preliminary activity to help them discover and think critically about the four rhetorical concepts underlying their own expressive writing. Also sparking this activity's creation was students' urgent need to understand how the internal and external features of personal writing relate to those of source-based writing in a positive rather than negative, and potentially inhibiting, light. They could best meet both of these learning goals by analyzing the rhetorical elements of their freshly written personal responses and then using these as an index from which to compare and contrast the same elements of academic writing. To begin this process of self-assessment, the following questioning guide launched students into the first phase of their transition from expressive to source-based writing. It did so by compelling them, as they worked in pairs, to identify and define the common rhetorical elements in each other's expressive response. This set of probes weaned them away from the powerful but unreflective spontaneity of personal writing, and oriented them toward the more critical and controlled frame-of-mind essential for academic writing:

1. Why does a writer choose to write in the expressive mode in the first place? What is the dominant use or function of expressive writing that will govern all of its other attributes?

2. What is the expressive writer's dominant point of reference? In other words, what broad category of meaning does the expressive

writer create? To what general area of experience does the expressive writer refer? Why?

3. What dominant thought process does the writer apply when writing expressively? Why?

4. Who is the expressive writer's audience? How does this audience impact the writer's dominant frame of reference (meaning), thought process, and writing conventions?

Many reputable texts for teaching academic writing across the curriculum repeatedly emphasize the importance of the three separate purposes that intersect in academic writing: the student's purpose in writing about a source; the source author's purpose for writing; and the audience's purpose in reading one writer's response to another writer's text. These texts include Mary Lynch Kennedy and Hadley Smith's popular writing-across-the-curriculum texts that encourage students to think critically about these interwoven purposes. However, we designed the above questions to also focus students more sharply on, and become critically conscious of, a writer's initial choice of one of three dominant functions of writing—the expressive, transactional, or poetic. We felt this was essential, since Britton's concept of the three modes of writing is not integrally or cumulatively taught in secondary English programs.

After drafting their expressive responses to their source issue, students worked in groups applying all four questions to their own and each other's drafts. These questions triggered individual reflection and collaborative discussion on the different uses of written language. They especially helped students view expressive writing more objectively as one of three main functions of writing, and to internalize the key changes they would have to make when called on to write about academic texts for a public audience. By applying these questions to their expressive responses, students were able to contemplate the common rhetorical elements that shape expressive writing. They also began to understand the negative effect that the initial choice of expressive writing has on the writer's frame of reference or meaning, thought process, and audience awareness—rhetorical features they could now critically examine in their expressive writing or that of others. In fact, the views they set forth while discussing and analyzing these four rhetorical features echoed some or Britton's points on the same. Following is a comparison/contrast of their views and Britton's on these elements:

Expressive Mode

Expressive writing is used primarily to explore, clarify, and give meaningful shape to our personal views and experiences. This dominant use or function of written language, in turn, frees the writer from the need to conform to preestablished, imposed rules and conventions of language. By contrast, expressive writing is the first stage of writing that helps writers explore their personal thoughts and feelings about their immediate experiences and surroundings; their reactions to events or issues that directly affect them. Even if these ideas make little sense to other people, it is a way to help writers get their thoughts down on paper and better understand themselves.

Students' views on the function of expressive writing focused mainly on this mode's ability to fulfill their need for unregulated self-expression. Britton, by contrast, claims that expressive writing functions primarily as "written-down-speech":

> Its function in one sense is a way to be with. To be with people. To explore the relationship. To extend the togetherness of situations. It's the language of all ordinary face-to-face speech. So it's our means of coming together with other people out of our essential separateness. But it's also the language in which we first-draft most of our important ideas. In other words, most of the important things that there are in the world were probably first discussed in expressive speech with somebody who was in the context …and its the form of language by which most strongly we influence each other (*Language* 97).

Intriguingly, his correlation of expressive writing with spoken language supports the writer's fundamental need to use this mode not so much to give shape to personal views as to frame them within an assumed dialogue, a trial communication of sorts. Also, by equating expressive writing with the initial drafting of "our most important ideas," he further suggests that the flushing out of personal thoughts is all the more powerful and influential because writers are free to assume that whomever they are writing for knows what they are talking about. Thus Britton strongly links expressive writing with the spontaneous "togetherness" of spoken language, on the one hand, and the liberating assumption that the listener understands the writer's immediate context or situation, on the other. His cogent insights valorize expressive writing as the true starting point, the natural rehearsal phase, for any writing task. Britton's expressive theory provides secondary teachers the missing frame of reference from which students can critically analyze their expressive writing. It can guide students out of their main writing dilemma, their difficulty in shifting from the closed, assumed, immediate, spontaneous, and personal context of "written-down-speech," to the wide-open, logical, impersonal, and abstract terrain of academic writing. However, teachers' main challenge is to guide students into source-based writing while sustaining the spontaneity and vigor Nancie Atwell refers to as "first-draft chat, not polished pieces of writing" (178).

Expressive Meaning

Expressive meaning is essentially subjective; the writer focuses on what he or she knows and feels based on personal experiences and direct observations. Once the writer decides to write expressively, the subject of written language—that to which it refers—automatically becomes the subjective realities in which the writer is involved. These include a rich tapestry of feelings, ideas, memories, aspirations, and judgments to which the writer needs to give shape. By using language to express these subjective elements, writers can understand themselves. Since expressive mode enables writers to "see" more clearly their thoughts about their personal world, it can become a powerful tool for building self-awareness, self-assessment, and overall maturation.

Students' ideas closely meshed with Britton's definition of the referential function of expressive writing as "language close to the self; language that is not called upon to go very far away from the speaker. The prototype for linguists is the exclamation. You know, the noise you make when you drop the hammer on your toe. And if you are by yourself it's purely expressive. In other words, merely vents your feelings" (*Language* 96). To Britton, the venting of spontaneous feelings seems to be the referent and meaning of expressive writing. Therefore, by helping students recognize the developmental and cathartic value of their expressive writing, their verbal exclamation marks that are crucial in their growth as writers, secondary teachers can facilitate their natural progression from writing themselves to writing the world.

Expressive Thought Process

The thought process of the expressive writer tends to be rambling and incoherent, as it primarily needs to make sense to the writer. Because meaning is created within the writer's personal frame of reference, and the act of written expression matters in itself, the writer need not be concerned with the organizational criteria and the writing conventions that are crucial when communicating meaning to a broader audience. Expressive thought flows more spontaneously from the inside out, from the writer's feelings to the words on the paper. Expressive writing also frees the writer from the need to be logical or to move back and forth between inductive and deductive reasoning. This inherent freedom from logical thinking is ameliorative as well. It allows the writer to think and write spontaneously and also according to alternate patterns such as association, opposition, comparison, or substitution (i.e., metaphorical thought). These patterns help writers make original connections, not previously recognized, among subjective elements. Students, obviously, focused on the alogical and creative thought processes triggered by expressive writing.

Britton, staying true to theory, brings his fundamental equation of expressive writing and spoken language to bear on his view of the writer's thought process. Paramount to him is that the expressive writer, like the oral speaker, assumes "that the hearer is interested in the speaker as well as in the topic. In fact if I had to tie myself to one thing about the expressive I'd say that that was the most characteristic.... It's relaxed and loosely structured because it follows the contours of the speaker's preoccupations" (*Language* 96). Britton, thus, reminds educators of the power and attraction expressive mode holds for young writers. It appeals strongly to their need for spontaneous expression, gushing self-preoccupations, and rambling thinking. It appeals just as powerfully to their freedom to assume that who they are and what they have to say is interesting and valid; to be exempt from the ingrained anxieties and inhibitions they associate with writing for a public audience, let alone a specialized academic audience. These fears are dispelled by the liberating anonymity of the expressive writer's ghost audience. What Britton would most likely suggest is that secondary and college teachers discover creative ways, in line with students' inherent needs for validation and ownership, to lead them into academic read-to-write tasks, without kindling audience fright.

Expressive Audience

Finally, according to students, the expressive writer's main audience is the writer's self. From their perspective, self-writing has a restraining effect on the writer's development as an individual and a writer. While they believed expressive writing creates a vehicle for scrutinizing and expanding personal views and opinions, they had no experience acting as an audience or examiner of their own writing or using this mode to reevaluate and broaden personal views. Nor had they learned to perceive expressive writing as a distinct and natural phase in their growth as effective communicators. To them, self-writing meant developing self-awareness and self-understanding in isolation and also freedom from others anxious to evaluate, correct, and red-pen their written work.

On this element, the students' view was a long way from Britton's dynamic view of expressive writing as a chatty dialogue with oneself; a trial-run with an implied but familiar audience; or an impromptu rehearsal for the mature business of communicating and making written transactions with an objective and impersonal audience. Here again, Britton provides unconventional but valid reasons for guiding secondary students to reconceptualize expressive writing as the cornerstone of all their writing; as the "matrix from which will develop transactional and poetic writing, as well as the more mature forms of the expressive" (*Language* 64).

The following chart provides an additional self-assessment guide that helped students conceptualize how the pivotal choice of writing expressively governs the other internal features of their writing—frame of reference or meaning, thought process, and audience. They were starting to view these four components of writing, moreover, as a set of interrelated features which they alone choose, control, and integrate in order to successfully shift from expressive to transactional writing:

Why Write?

- the fundamental decision to use writing for self-expression

Write About What?

- the impact the initial choice has on the writer's construction of meaning

Think How?

- the impact this choice has on the writer's thought process

Write for Whom?

- the impact the initial choice has on the writer's sense of audience

The immediate knowledge students gained from thinking critically about their initial expressive writing pieces was the concept of choosing to write from a personal frame of reference in the first place. Previously, they had not viewed self-writing as an intentional choice. Instead, it was a vehicle for getting personal thoughts, responses, and feelings down on paper as quickly as possible. They had no opportunity in high school to reflect on the valid reasons why writers choose to write in the expressive mode, from a self-centered point of view, or to define and analyze the kind of meaning they can actively construct in this mode. They also brought to this class no broader awareness that choosing to write expressively automatically means choosing not to write factually, logically, objectively, and according to the conventions of a public audience seeking to be informed or convinced. For the most part, journal entries and personal responses to literature and non-fiction works were ways to record spontaneous reactions to literary or real experiences of strong personal relevance; or to brainstorm a pool of associations or related ideas in preparation for a formal and graded writing task. Prior to this class, my students did not view expressive writing as an integral and preliminary step in their growth as transactional writers; a natural starting point from which to understand the complex ways their use of language must change as they shift from personal to source-based writing.

Having grappled with and analyzed the internal, self-directed elements of their expressive writing, students were ready to begin the transition from expressive to transactional mode. Upon this transitional and intellectual step students' success as academic writers depends. The crucial role of the instructor in walking them through the internal and interrelated changes they must make in their writing, as they shift from subjective to objective frames of reference, cannot be underestimated. Unless students are actively and critically involved in their shift from personal to public writing—a shift that involves rigorous scrutiny and readjustment of personal writing choices too often taken for granted—they will be unable to execute an informed and controlled dive into the rigorous, student-driven forms of academic writing.

The next phase of students' self-directed transition into academic writing involved contrasting their expressive responses to a journal article with objective source responses written by prior first-year students. For first-year writers, this particular connection made sense.

Since academic writing, a major transactional genre, is driven by the writer's built-in, recursive thought processes—objective response, summary, analysis/evaluation, comparison/contrast, synthesis, argument, and hypothesis—the most reasonable task for the fledgling academic writer is, as explained earlier, the objective source response essay. This is the second phase of their metamorphosis into academic writers capable of viewing personal writing from the standpoint of objectivity and logic at the heart of academic writing. Inevitably, this meant altering the four initial questions to challenge students, still working in shared-topic groups, to think critically and comparatively about their personal responses from the multiple standpoints of source-based writing.

The following directions and questioning guide facilitated students' conversion of spontaneous personal responses to objective responses that were more aligned with their new transactional role, their author's purpose, and their new audience's purpose. Unlike the initial guide, this prodded students to analyze how the writer changed his or her dominant use of written language, frame of reference, thought process, and audience awareness in an effort to write transactionally rather than expressively.

The Main Conceptual Changes in Shifting from Personal Response to Source-Based Response

Directions: You have just described a personal experience that relates to a controversial source issue. Your have written this, moreover, in the Expressive or self-referential mode. Your next task is to decide how to turn this personal response into a transactional piece that is no longer written from your personal standpoint, but rather from two external frames of reference: the views and ideas of your source author on your shared issue, and the writing standards expected by your public audience. As you respond to the following questions, develop a set of guidelines for adjusting your dominant use of language, your meaning or frame of reference, your main thought process, and your sense of audience as you convert your expressive piece into a more objective and informative source response:

1. What major change will the dominant purpose or mode of written language undergo when the writer decides to shift from personal to objective source response, a gateway into transactional writing?

2. What major change does meaning or frame of reference undergo when the writer decides to shift from personal to objective source response?

3. What major change does the dominant thought process undergo when the writer decides to shift from personal to objective source response?

4. How does the writer's concept of audience change when shifting from personal to objective source response?

By applying these questions, in groups, to their chosen essay, students were able to formulate general guidelines for transforming personal responses into source-based and reader-accommodating responses. After discussing the first question, they unanimously agreed that changing their dominant use of writing from an expressive to a transactional function would be difficult. At first, this overarching shift presented a double bind; they must now subordinate their personal point of view to a source author's frame of reference, and also to their audience's need for context and conventions. However, after examining additional models of audience-based response writing, they realized this pivotal change was not so much about forfeiting their personal view on an issue as about exchanging it for a powerful, self-expanding use of writing: to communicate an idea of broad social relevance to a real-life audience. By paying close attention to the sticking point, the different reasons why writers write in the first place, students began assimilating Britton's principle that both expressive and transactional writers choose to write in a "participant" mode. They understood that the "need to act and decide characterizes the participant role—to act and decide in response to the social demands of human co-existence" (*Language* 105). They also realized an important distinction that Britton points out in another work: The expressive writer aims to "further his own development" and "structure his own experience" by exploring personal knowledge, whereas the developing transactional writer uses language to organize increasingly "impersonal, objective, socially approved bodies of common knowledge" that evolve into "areas of shared curiosity" (*Prospect* 77). The students finally understood that while both modes involve writing for established purposes, it is the realities they seek to organize that vastly differ.

This point led directly into students' discussion of the second question, and their subsequent realization that the frame of reference of transactional writing, regardless of personal appeal, must now be presented thoroughly enough to affect a broad range of readers, and concretely enough to convince them of its relevance. They understood that their meaning, to achieve such a complex transaction, must be generalizable or applicable to multiple readers. In other words, they made the critical leap from viewing writing as self-exploration to viewing it as an instrument of potentially strong public impact. As a result, students became more receptive to the changes they must make when writing transactionally. Grounded in their first task as transactional writers, both emotionally and intellectually, they looked forward to constructing the more impersonal and objective meanings that grow out of an informed writer's reasoning process. They were eager to write from an alternate viewpoint, the key precondition for objective source response.

Critical analysis of objective source response models also clarified the major change in thought process required when writing for an audience. The use of models particularly helped students realize that choosing to write to transact means choosing to think logically and coherently, and according to specific thought processes, as opposed to spontaneously and randomly from jumbled feelings, memories, and attitudes. From their objective analysis of models, in fact, a transactional concept of thought process emerged. Their new notion of writing-to-think meant organizing their response so it makes sense to their readers, allowing them to connect new ideas with their prior knowledge. For this source-based task, their altered notion also involved transforming a personal example into a suitable illustration of a source author's main idea or claim. Many students, unaccustomed to reading for underlying concepts and thought processes, had trouble inferring the deductive-inductive, general to specific, pattern embedded in the objective response models examined in class. However, having intentionally analyzed and internalized this overarching thought process, students were ready to reconstruct their source response on the intellectual basis supporting academic writing. Their growth as an academic writer would continue with the next task, writing various types of source summaries, and culminate with the publication of an original discipline-based research project in their final year.

Most encouraging was students' eagerness to take on a new dual role as gleaners and communicators of shared knowledge. Having already shifted from "writing for self" to "writing for others," they were prepared to assume a proactive and transactional view of the fourth, and perhaps most misconceived, rhetorical element, the choice of writing conventions. In smooth but rapid fashion, they had internalized the transactional writer's dominant and interrelated choices of language use, meaning, and thought process. However, to stay within a writer-driven framework, their fourth shift also meant apprehending the deeper relationship between the source meaning they reconstruct and the external forms they must selectively use for effective communication. Already they had embraced several concomitants: that readers needed thorough and coherent background information on any given issue or concept; that carefully chosen and controlled thought processes go hand-in-hand with choosing to write for a public audience. The remaining objective to complete basic training—in this case, mastery of minimal transactional competency—involved reconceiving public writing standards (for diction, usage, sentence structure, punctuation, mechanics, etc.) as the culmination as opposed to the sticking point of their initial into transactional writing.

Students' eagerness to write transactionally was due largely to their active analysis of the four interrelated choices that link all expressive and transactional writing tasks. Despite the constraints of a crammed and tight timeframe, we avoided presenting the potentially daunting element of audience expectations as an externally imposed norm, a fixed and immovable tenet of writing. High on our agenda was the need to avert the cycle of writing fear and repeated errors that result whenever students learn source-based writing from the outside in. Constant invitations to conceptualize writing as transactional in mode and spirit spurred students to view writing conventions as an integral set of choices they make and control. Only when students have the opportunity to simulate these four developmental and interconnected shifts from expressive to transactional writing, can they be sparked into shaping their unique transactional persona and the broad communal consciousness upon which success in this mode depends. If first-year college students can make these internal changes in record time, over the course of a single semester, think of the amazing progress along the transactional trajectory secondary students are capable of making in four years.

After contrasting subjective source responses with more objective versions whose dominant function was to make a complex transaction—to link a personal experience with another writer's abstract reasoning and to communicate this original synthesis to an audience—my class reclaimed the missing conceptual knowledge essential for beginning academic writing. They now understood the four rhetorical elements, the crucial choices, that ultimately determine whether one is writing in the expressive or transactional, the private or public, the experienced or read worlds. They could articulate the crucial distinctions between "writing for" themselves and "writing from" another author's frame of reference. It is this internal writing concept that puts young writers in charge of rather than at the mercy of academic writing tasks. At the same time, the students had a simple and useful rubric, a comparison-contrast index, to ensure a smooth dive into the self-directed and highly intro-spective read-to-write tasks required across the disciplines. Sooner than anticipated, they were prepared to write in the source-based genre by which they would progressively construct knowledge in their chosen dis-cipline. They were, in fact, anxious to build on this new knowledge; to try out their multifaceted role as critical readers, active reformulators, and effective communicators of other writers' meaning. They were ready, affectively and cognitively, to "morph" into full transactional mode by composing a source-based and audience-based response.

Following are excerpts from two revised response essays. While both are products of the multiple draft approach to writing, more impor-tantly they mirror a budding awareness and appreciation of the new frames of reference from which academic writers must learn to write. Overall, these excerpts reflect students' strategic effort to convert per-sonal writing—specifically, the dominant use of language, frame of ref-erence, thought process, and audience awareness—to effective source-based writing. Opportunity to compare and contrast expressive and transactional models for these internal components generated stu-dents' rudimentary grasp of their self-directed pathway from expressive to transactional writing, the missing conceptual framework for source-based writing at the secondary level. Just as necessary, self-reflective instruments like concept developers, self-assessment guides, peer-edit-ing rubrics, and one-to-one student/teacher conferences provided stu-dents vital feedback and focus for infusing personal responses with transactional function, meaning, thought process, and audience. These student models, moreover, were selected only in part for meeting stan-dards-based criteria for organization, development, and a host of writ-ing conventions. The central achievement they represent is first-year writers' internalization, at varying degrees of sophistication, of key internal changes they must enact and control in order to shift from expressive to any form of transactional writing. As this project irrefutably confirms, writing process theory and practice, in isolation from students' natural developmental writing path, fails to offset the shallow and disconnected knowledge of expressive and transactional writing with which students begin building discipline-based knowledge.

The first excerpt is analyzed in sections to highlight the specific skills the writer needed to apply to achieve each of the four internal changes. The second is presented intact to capture this first-year student's enhanced fluency, and experience, in critically reading and writing about texts for the purpose of expanding prior knowledge of a specific, discipline-centered issue or concept. Following each excerpt is an analysis of the specific internal changes, the neglected features representing growth toward transactional writing.

Of all the skills expected of first-year writers, apprehending, acknowledging, and thoroughly representing a source writer's point of view is by far the most difficult due to lack of training in critically reading texts from another writer's frame of reference. The built-in assumption that secondary students need to use writing predominantly for self-exploration and self-validation has, unfortunately, greatly reduced both motivation and the time needed to explore the specific thought processes, the lines of reasoning, of other writers. Ironically, it is also assumed that the academic writing teacher will somehow magically disentangle first-year students from the web of unfounded assumptions about how adolescents should and should not learn, especially to write. On the other hand, when students are intentionally taught the underlying principles distinguishing transactional from expressive writing, many go overboard in trying to achieve source-based writing criterion. The following excerpt reflects a first student's commendable effort to write about the issue of mandatory school attendance policies predominantly from the viewpoint of author and SUNY-Cortland Distinguished Service Professor of History, Roger Sipher:

Another main point that the author argues is that in high schools during the '70s, many students did not receive the grades that they deserve. As Sipher states, "At the point when students could legally quit, most choose to remain since they know they are likely to be allowed to graduate whether they do acceptable work or not" (128). He argues this point because there was a great deal of injustice in schools then; students were graduating whether they deserved to or not. In fact, the author believes that the grades many high school students received then did not always represent their actual academic achievement. Moreover, this point is important to him because it puts the students who truly deserve to graduate on the same academic level as the students who did not genuinely earn their graduation. Thus a major goal of the author's is "for grades to show what they are supposed to: how well a student is learning" (129). He hopes that by abolishing the mandatory attendance policy in American schools, grades will once again represent academic achievement, and letter grades will regain their meaning, a meaning that continues to be lost in high schools today.

Analysis: When students grasp the overriding distinction between expressive and academic writing, the difference between choosing to write about self versus choosing to write about objective realities, including another writer's thought processes, the second related shift from subjective to source-based meaning becomes challenging yet manageable, as Amy's response supports. In fact, the spontaneity normally associated with expressive writing permeates this excerpt. Besides electing to subordinate her views to Sipher's, a strategy often lambasted by champions of prolonging the personal, she struggles valiantly to represent the larger context surrounding his view. In fact, she delights in the interplay she creates between her acknowledgment of Sipher's main idea and the inferences she automatically draws about his thought processes as she links his main claim with related ideas in his text. A convention easily overlooked, Amy's use of simple present tense action

verbs to represent what source authors do, further reflects her willingness to subordinate personal views to authorial intent. This usage also
confirms growing awareness of the timeless significance that another
writer's construction of meaning has to a community of readers in
which she plays a small but significant part. In other words, she is not
simply communicating Sipher's argumentative stance; she is actively
integrating it with relevant context so that her readers can better comprehend his unique frame of reference. Quite effectively, she has constructed the dual connection, between writer and source author and
writer and audience, that forms the backbone of academic writing.

The faster students can willingly cede the dominant point of view to
a source author, the more likely they are to develop the broadened perspective required for academic writing, and all forms of public writing,
for that matter. Most importantly, as the above transactional excerpt
suggests, Amy now uses writing to explore a writer's key concept or idea
within the context of the entire essay. The passage captures the dynamic
process by which the source-based writer first focuses on and reads for
an author's main point, then endeavors to connect this idea with related
ideas in the text. Her use of writing clearly transcends personal needs
and interests; it now reflects a critical reading process of reading back
over a text numerous times, reading recursively, each time discovering a
new dimension or extended meaning of another writer's main idea.

As a source-based response writer, moreover, Amy is free to develop
whatever connections she chooses to make between an author's abstract
reasoning and the text as a whole. Based on her personal experience and
views, she is motivated to elaborate on the underlying values and broad
secondary trends informing Sipher's belief that most students "choose
to remain [in school] since they know they are likely to be allowed to
graduate whether they do acceptable work or not." Her use of writing to
clarify a writer's specific reasoning and related ideas signals considerable growth along the trajectory from expressive to transactional writing. Without realizing it, her writing becomes a way to prepare herself

for the challenging read-to-write tasks ahead. These include writing-to-learn tasks like synthesizing multiple source views on a discipline-based concept or issue or objectively analyzing and evaluating an author's argumentative structure that will become commonplace as she advances in her field of study. Needless to say, in an age when declining literacy coexists with an increasingly standardized, visual, and consumer-based adolescent ethos, nothing could be more valuable than guiding high school students through integrated learning activities like critically reading for and objectively responding to a source author's main idea or claim. Secondary programs need to make the art of critically examining and communicating an author's key concept, within overt and covert contexts alike, a pivotal long-range graduation goal.

Having successfully internalized and applied the first required shift from a subjective to an external frame of reference, Amy automatically converts her personal experience into more objective, applicable meaning. Having done so, she executes the second necessary shift to the transactional mode:

I can relate to Sipher's argument because the same situation occurred at the high school I attended. On many occasions, students who played on athletic teams received unfair treatment and passing grades that were not earned. For example, a student in my sociology class used to receive unusually high grades on his report card. This would not have been conspicuous, but the student, Greg, did not study for any of the tests or complete homework assignments; when he did attend class, which was rarely, he did not participate. On the other hand, most other students, including myself, did not miss a day of class, participated a great deal, always studied for tests, and did fairly well on them. I could not understand why Greg received higher report card grades than I, when I put so much more effort into the class. One day, I overheard a conversation between him and the sociology teacher. Greg was explaining that he was not going to be able to hand in an assignment because he had baseball practice after school, and would not have time. Consequently, the teacher gave him a week extension on the assignment, and

told him, "Don't worry about it, just keep up the good work out on the field."
Devastated by this, I realized how Greg, the captain of the baseball team, had
acquired his grades so far. There would be no reason to confront the teacher
since he would most likely deny any accusations I would make. Unfairly,
Greg ended up graduating with honors, and received acknowledgment for
having the highest class average in the sociology class.

Analysis: When I asked the students to objectively respond to their source author's general stand or purpose, I could have assumed they understood the deeper rhetorical elements implied by this seemingly simple writing task. By the time Amy wrote her final draft, however, the preceding critical reading tasks and group activities enabled her to internalize the three initial changes that ensure a successful shift from personal to source-based writing. Using questions 1 and 2 as her revising prompts, Amy intentionally altered her personal response, first by clearly linking it with the author's purpose and second by transforming it into the more objective and coherent piece of information her audience needs. While the above excerpt does not completely transcend personal views, as a whole Amy redirects her writing to convey the broader, more factual context missing in her personal response. In doing so, she transforms personal memory into valid evidence to support Sipher's main claim.

Drawing on her new knowledge of what it means to write from another writer's frame of reference, Amy also realized this meant not just acknowledging the author's unique ideas and views, but creating a new link between her personal experience and an author's stand on a widespread educational issue. She realized she needed to interlock disparate frames of reference, hers and Sipher's, in a meaningful way. In addition, she recognized it was now up to her to decide how and why to take this critical "transactional" step. Her topic sentence, emphasizing that the "same situation occurred" to her, connects her disturbing first-hand classroom experience with Sipher's much earlier causal reasoning. With this thoughtfully constructed synthesis, Amy executes the difficult second transactional shift to a source-based frame of reference.

Outwardly, this new connection involves a tangible shift from passive to active learning; from superficially skimming a text for literal meaning and personal associations, to actively and selectively reading to discover new and unfamiliar dimensions of subjective reality. An observer could see Amy intentionally marking her text for the author's ideas that best correlate with her own first-hand experience. The intangible transformation in her thinking process is even more significant. She no longer reads the text for expected self-validating ideas. Instead she intentionally reads Sipher's brief piece to infer his abstract reasoning process that both incorporates and empowers her isolated experience. This synthesis of concrete and abstract thinking on one hand, of personal viewpoint and an expert's far-seeing generalization, heralds the first-year student's readiness for the difficult task of interpreting academic sources according to increasingly complex and recursive critical thinking/reading/writing patterns. Amy and her classmates will soon be required to analyze and evaluate the underlying concepts and structures of single sources; synthesize multiple source views on common points; argue positions based on inductive-deductive logic; and hypothesize relationships between independent and dependent variables relevant to their discipline.

What Britton calls "the marriage of the process of composing in written language to that of reading" (*Language* 159) enables Amy to fuse personal knowledge with an unknown writer's deeper causal reasoning process. And by doing so, she achieves the third shift in her rapid evolution as a communicator and public writer. As the above excerpt also suggests, she has internalized the public writer's implicit goal of constructing objective rather than subjective meaning. The distinction between the two is as difficult to teach today's print-resistant students as it is for them to learn. For undermining the reciprocal teaching and learning of this missing epistemological shift are the false motives and unearned rewards with which many secondary students associate school writing. These include receiving inflated grades for voicing and writing personal response without any awareness of their divorce from logic and reason. Discouragingly, the typical high school graduate has not learned to actively use the reading-writing connection to internalize the abstract reasoning of others or, just as important, to use these informed generalizations to enrich and expand their experiential and academic knowledge.

By contrast, Amy transforms her subjective view of Greg into more concrete, communicable form. Transcending personal opinion, her newly detailed account of Greg's actions adds both immediacy and validity to the author's generalization about mandatory attendance policies. She initially chose to read this essay for the familiar; for whatever corresponded with her schooling experience. However, she now smoothly shifts to reading and writing from an external frame of reference, an intellectual context capable of suffusing her personal account with a communal perspective and standards of logic. What equally matters about this fledgling transaction in writing, therefore, is her revision of Greg's behavior from Sipher's inductive-deductive reasoning process. She moves beyond her initial subjective opinion on one student's unearned graduation to an objective account that places Greg's dishonesty within a larger educational context. The act of reading from an author's contextual frame generates not only Amy's more detailed and comprehensive report, but also the development of her own intellectual frame of reference. By deliberately constructing more objective meaning, she indirectly raises a number of tangential issues—gender bias, favoritism, and grade rigging, for example. On the one hand, she reconstructs personal experience from another's brief but mind-altering context; on the other hand, she stretches her own frame of reference to include details and ideas that speak more potently to her audience. Overall, her struggle to situate a narrow personal response within another writer's conceptual framework and causal reasoning underscores the importance of teaching secondary students early on the transactional principles underlying this crucial shift. There is no legitimate reason why teachers should not be able to stretch the time spent teaching standardized personal response, informative, and persuasive essays to include the art of shifting from expressive to source-based writing years before students plan to enter college.

Just as implicit in Amy's more objective account of unearned academic achievement is her fourth successful shift—the shift from personal to public writing conventions. One of the most widespread and hard-to-break self-writing habits, first-year students' misuse of the second person pronoun, "you," to refer to a public audience, is absent. Nowhere does she deviate from her objective point of view by incongruously referring to her implied, real-life academic audience as "you." But then again, such inappropriate point of view shifts point back to the first-year writer's missing knowledge of the different frames of reference, thought processes, and audiences that distinguish personal from source-based writing. Since Amy has learned to recognize and apply these internal changes to her own writing, it is likely she will continue to do so in the future. She especially understands the external contexts "from which" and "for whom" she is now writing; her writing skills and conventions can only improve when connected with rather than isolated from the underlying rhetorical principles upon which academic/source-based writing tasks are predicated.

Also absent in the above excerpt is the first year student's expressive habit of mixing source-based writing with jarring personal opinions and levels of diction. Like many of her classmates, Amy struggles to communicate a source author's point of view to a broad public audience; she understands her purpose as a source-based writer and how to accomplish it. She has developed this reflective stance, moreover, because she has been offered what I.A. Richards refers to as "*assisted invitations* to attempt to find out just what [she is] trying to do and thereby how to do it" (ctd. in Berthoff, *Forming* 2). Above all, she has had the chance to understand the key concept underlying academic and other forms of transactional writing, the idea that her writing must function "as a verbal transaction, a means of getting something done through language—whether it be asking or giving information, instructing or persuading" (Britton, *Language* 124). Armed with this conceptual knowledge, she can redirect her writing to integrate prior knowledge with new source meaning while simultaneously applying writing conventions needed to convey this knowledge-building synthesis to a public audience.

Almost automatically, Amy incorporates in her writing many of the audience-based standards applied by her source author, conventions students are more apt to master when motivated to read and write critically about non-fiction texts dealing with personally relevant social issues. Amy's ample use of logical transitions between ideas further confirms the power of writing from a public writer's frame of reference. Additionally, her use of concrete nouns, precise action verbs, and active as opposed to passive voice are part of an integrated learning process by which students adjust reading, writing, and speaking skills to expand conceptual knowledge. When students have the opportunity to analyze, evaluate, and apply the fundamental principles of transactional writing, they develop the conceptual framework that validates and motivates them to use writing conventions—diction level, mechanics, usage, punctuation, and sentence structure—modeled by writers who have themselves long internalized public writing norms. Or as Britton would say, they learn to view public writing conventions positively as an integral component in the process of using writing to "get something done" in the world.

Overall, Amy's "transactional" version of her experience with Greg evinces numerous, beneath-the-surface benefits of reconceiving her role as an academic writer. She now chooses not to use writing to vent her feelings and thoughts about a personal matter; not to write about herself for herself. Instead she chooses to use writing for self-expansion. Britton characterizes the pivotal choice of the transactional, regardless of what form it takes, as the writer's decision to make "explicit reference to the outside world. The personal features that are not relevant are omitted, and more of the context is filled in for somebody who is not in it already, not face to face sharing the same situations and event" (*Language* 106). Thus the secondary student's self-directed plan to read and write about the worlds beyond the self cannot be overestimated. It enables Amy to reexamine and rewrite personal experience and views from an unfamiliar author's position on mandatory school attendance policies and from the previously unconsidered values, beliefs, concepts, and facts that inform this position. It also invites her to render it more factually and objectively so others can relate to and build on this accumulating pool of knowledge. Having made the outer world of ideas and facts her dominant frame of reference and assumed the responsibilities of writing in the "getting something done" mode, Amy automatically makes the surface changes that culminate her shift to source-based and informative writing.

Her readers learn the effects a mandatory attendance policy had on one secondary student's study habits, homework, and attendance in a specific class; the unfair discrepancy that existed between student effort and grades; and additional factors responsible for this single case of rigged grades and undeserved graduation. Having carefully reexamined previously unnoticed aspects of Greg's case, she provides a more in-depth analysis of the issue so her audience can make their own relevant associations. Her initial private view achieves a more representative status due to her fundamental transactional choice to link it with another writer's ideas and a real-life audience's standards. Ultimately, Amy's reconstructed source response reflects a learning process in which the skills and conventions of public writing evolve in conjunction with the knowledge of the underlying principles of transactional writing. That in itself is a hefty accomplishment for the average first-year student with little to no experience adjusting personal experience to the standards of logic and writing underpinning written communication. Her successful shift to transactional mode confirms the benefits of a sequential and integrated approach to academic writing across the 7-16 curriculum.

A second student's objective source response essay is equally telling. The following excerpt reflects not only the writer's internalization of four key transitions first-year students must make from self-based to audience-based writing, but also his heightened fluency in reading for and writing about an author's meaning at the start of college. Without prior experience with critical read-to-write tasks, Andy would not have chosen to respond to a political science professor's linguistically and conceptually challenging argument that new reproductive technologies exploit and dehumanize women. He was one of only two students out of 17 who chose to critically read and objectively respond to Jean Bethke Elshtain's essay, "Technology as Destiny," in which the author argues her own standpoint while representing the views of two opposing groups. The following excerpt constitutes the body of Andy's self-directed, audience-based response to Elshtain's argument:

According to Elshtain, "Feminists have sorted themselves out into three major conflicting positions on the matter of reproductive technology and its mind-boggling implications"(174). She goes on to fully explain the positions of the pro-interventionists, anti-interventionists, and those who believe in a mix of both. Based on her representation of these views, Elshtain would agree that these groups would differ widely on the outcome of my brother's conception in distinctly different ways, had certain reproductive technologies had been available. From her perspective, the pro-interventionists would have approved of the use of reproductive technology to not only determine whether my brother would be born normal, but to also exterminate him if he were not. According to this group, an imperfect human has no reason to live (174). This of course does not seem to fit with the fact that Matthew now leads a so-called normal life. The anti-interventionists, on the other hand, would claim that there is no valid reason to use technology that intervenes in any way with the natural reproductive process. By contrast, they believe that using this technology is just another way for those with power—in this case doctors—to control who lives and who does not (175). This view would not have worked in Matthew's favor.

However, anti-interventionists also advocate censoring of all manipulation of human choice and reproduction. Therefore, they would have condemned my mother's use of technology to even determine whether her child would be born healthy, had she wished to do so. Elshtain, herself a member of this group, claims that all new reproductive technology is an extreme intrusion into the human body ( ). As she insists, these technologies leave nothing untouched, and there is nothing that they will not do. From her anti-interventionist position, it is difficult to imagine Matthew's brain cells being used to cure Parkinson's disease for someone that no one in the family will ever meet. Finally, the most popular group, the one that acknowledges some validity for both sides of this controversial issue, argues that it is ultimately the parents' right to make any reproductive choice. Nevertheless, in my brother's case, they would most likely argue that some of the more intrusive technologies should not be used (177). This view also would have worked in my brother's favor since it leaves these ethical choices up to the parents.

Amy and Andy, typical first-year students, are nervous initiates into the empowering task of objective source response. They both chose to rewrite a piece of their personal world from another writer's frame of reference. Yet their responses differ significantly in the connection each makes between their prior knowledge of a common issue and a source author's extended view; they also reflect different ways to link old and new, or personal and personal and public, knowledge. Amy's new knowledge of Sipher's position on mandatory attendance policies compels her to convert a first-hand experience into a more objective and representative version of unearned graduation. Her revised transactional piece reflects the expanded perspective first-year writers achieve when they synthesize isolated personal experience with an author's line of reasoning and a public audience's general knowledge. Moreover, having transformed her private experience with Greg into supporting evidence for another writer's claim, Amy's writing takes a sharp rhetorical turn. With this critical decision to frame personal ideas within an author's intellectual framework, Amy not only shifts from expressive to transactional uses of writing, but she learns, hands-on, the contributory role private knowledge plays when intention-ally yoked to the broader issues and diverging positions shaping her gener-ation's social conscience. She is now using writing to conduct what Berthoff poignantly calls "the continuing audit of meaning that is at the heart of learning to write critically" (*Forming* 27).

By contrast, Andy's synthesis reflects a more complex relationship with multiple source views, and a more recursive process of self-reflec-tion and self-expansion. Unlike Amy, he moves smoothly back and forth between multiple positions on a volatile social issue and his own dynamically changing perspective. He synthesizes his view with not one but three different positions on the ethics of reproductive technologies. Prior to this verbal transaction, Andy had no knowledge of the special interest groups classified by Elshtain; no awareness of the power each has to alter the value of a child's life. Instead of generating a supporting example as in Amy's case, Elshtain's wider-ranging multiple frame of reference sparks Andy's gritty speculation about a brother's worth from diverging standpoints. It compels him, moreover, to pose several hypo-thetical realities, each further complicating his view of his brother's worth, or any child's, when measured by conflicting belief systems. Hence, his revised response mirrors the process of actively reconceiving prior knowledge from multiple standpoints representing the totality of views on reproductive freedom and choice. For Amy, rewriting personal experience from a new vantage point means synthesizing it with one writer's compatible framework of beliefs and information. She does not change her preexisting stand on the disadvantages of mandatory atten-dance policies; instead she uses the source to validate her opinion. For Andy, source-based writing initiates sweeping internal and external changes in his new role as an academic writer. He synthesizes multiple views; adds breadth and depth to his concept of reproductive responsi-bility; raises open-ended questions, and suggests jarring implications. From his reader's perspective, he has used writing incisively to extend and inflame the debate over an issue central to our human condition.

Andy's transactional use of written language is exciting because as he synthesizes multiple views, he alters his prior concept of reproductive freedom while rattling his audience's. He uses writing to communicate, and also to acknowledge, clarify, and speculate about previously unknown views on the ethics of technologically-induced reproductive choices. Prior to this source-based writing task, he took for granted the value of his brother's life, never considering the latest technologies that offer choices where there once were none. Before this critical read-to-write task, the realization that the unconditional value he attaches to his brother's life is, from another standpoint, a burden never occurred to him. Before this active learning activity, he lacked knowledge of the latest technologies, the options like artificial insemination and sex-selection they make possible, and the opposing positions that have evolved into powerful moral, political, or economic agendas. Writing from Elshtain's multiple frame of reference, however, compels him to apprehend a plurality of views on reproductive choice; to grapple with previously unconsidered assumptions and reasons. While undergoing this concept expansion, he finds himself reasoning abstractly about his brother's life from varying belief systems. Clearly, Andy's outward shift to transactional writing parallels a substantial intellectual shake-up and maturation process. The intentional linking of alternate perspectives permanently stretches and blurs a once clear-cut category of human responsibility.

Andy's excerpt provides a further rationale for teaching students to objectively and critically read and write from the perspectives of non-fiction writers long before they arrive at college. Undergraduate achievement depends on this integrated skill, the dual ability to critically interpret and effectively communicate the deeper levels of meaning in informative and persuasive texts. Andy's revised response reveals the intellectual and ethical benefits students reap from reading and writing critically about discipline-based concepts. It reflects, above all, the underappreciated role of the oversimplified source-based writing genre in shaping future transactional writers, abstract thinkers, and ethical beings. From this brief student excerpt emanates a wealth of insight into the value of encouraging students to transcend the fractured confines of school-based writing, and to think, read, and write critically and transactionally about shared life-concepts from multiple perspectives for multiple readers.

By the end of this holistic process of writing, metawriting, and revising, my students accomplished more than an objective source response essay; more than an intentional verbal transaction. Their finished pieces conveyed their new knowledge of the rhetorical choices and concepts underpinning expressive and transactional writing. They now viewed both modes of writing as sets of interlocking choices writers make and control regarding their dominant use of writing, their frame of reference or meaning, their main thought process, and their relationship with their implied audience. Having learned to identify and evaluate these related choices in their own expressive drafts, they were able to grasp the purpose, benefits, and limits of expressive writing. They also had a clear point of reference from which to gauge their transformation into knowledgeable and effective communicators of others' meaning. Permeating students' revised responses was their new respect for and commitment to academic/source-based writing. Only from this expanded concept of the expressive to transactional writing trajectory can students continually build their skills in acknowledging and representing, analyzing and evaluating, and dialogically illuminating the human themes that bind us together.

All told, students' revised responses confirmed their new knowledge of and responsibility for their rhetorical craft. They understood the pivotal language decisions they needed to make, modify, and control when shifting back and forth between expressive and the transactional modes of writing. By the end of a intense four-week workshop, they exchanged their narrow conceptualization for the open-ended, constantly expanding world of academic thinking and learning. Having grasped the obscured or altogether scuttled tenets of expressive and transactional writing, their future passages from one mode to the other would seem as natural, integrated, and challenging as any genuine life-transition.

From Britton's perspective, there is no valid reason why the rhetorical principles governing students' growth from personal to academic writing should not be taught sequentially throughout middle and high school, if not much earlier. A key sticking point, however, is that many secondary programs inadvertently create roadblocks to students' developmental pathway from expressive and transactional writing, blurring the different language uses and choices with which students need to associate these two writing modes. Hampered by time and packed curricula, and also by increasing emphasis on writing-to-test, many programs sever students' expressive writing acts, including free writing and journal response, from their development as public thinkers and writers. But when expressive writing is divorced from the functional and public use of writing, regardless of cause, students lack the prerequisite knowledge and dispositions to become reflective and effective writers across the academic disciplines.

Until students receive uniform and sequential education in shifting among all three modes of writing, their ability to read the written texts of others for their varying levels of meaning and purposes, a learning skill implied by all forms of academic writing, will be deficient. In addition, they will be deprived of the conceptual base needed to understand and apply the full gamut of critical thought processes required across the academic disciplines, complex reasoning tasks such as summarizing, analyzing, comparing and contrasting, evaluating, synthesizing, arguing, and hypothesizing about a multitude of academic topics and issues. In addition, until secondary students uniformly acquire full knowledge of the concepts underlying the modes in which schools require them to write, many will struggle unnecessarily as they try to think, read, and write according to the critical standards upon which secondary and academic achievement now depend. Without this knowledge base, they especially will not understand the changes they need to make to communicate the source-based purposes, specialized knowledge, and critical and abstract reasoning expected of an academic audience. On the other hand, my class's successful dive into transactional writing, in record time, verifies their untapped potential as secondary academic writers and thinkers. Secondary students have the ability and desire to shift from the "self-writing" mode in which many of them remain stuck to the self-expansive "audience-based" mode long before they receive their first academic writing task.

Works Cited

Atwell, Nancie. *In the Middle: Writing, Reading, and Learning with Adolescents*. Portsmouth, NH: Boynton/Cook, 1987.

Berthoff, Ann E. with James Stephens. *Forming, Thinking, Writing*. 2nd ed. Portsmouth, NH: Boynton/Cook, 1988. "Reclaiming the Active Mind." *College English*. 61 July 1999: 671–80.

Britton, James. *Language and Learning*. Coral Gables, FL: University of Miami, 1970. *Prospect and Retrospect: Selected Essays of James Britton*. Ed. Gordon M. Pradl. Montclair, NJ: Boynton/Cook, 1982.

Kennedy, Mary Lynch, and Hadley E. Smith. *Reading and Writing in the Academic Community*. Englewood Cliffs, NJ: Prentice Hall, 1994.

Kennedy, Mary Lynch et al. *Writing in the Disciplines: A Reader for Writers*. Upper Saddle River, NJ: Prentice Hall, 1996.

Knoblauch, C.H., and Lil Brannon. *Rhetorical Traditions and the Teaching of Writing*. Portsmouth, NH: Heinemann, 1984.

Marzano, Robert J. *Cultivating Thinking in English and the Language Arts*. Urbana, IL: NCTE, 1991.

University of the State of New York. Dept. of Education. *Learning Standards for English Language Arts*. Revised ed. March 1996.

Zemelman, Steven, and Harvey Daniels. *A Community of Writers*. Portsmouth, NH: Heinemann, 1988.

Chapter Seven

The Benefits of Grounding Secondary Students in the Literary Mode of Writing

Secondary literature, as a discipline or body of knowledge students are required to learn, has suffered a tremendous setback due to public education's shift from a content- to a process-centered approach to learning. As the most radical consequence of this shift to a process-based literature curriculum, high school students are inconsistently taught to identify, analyze, and evaluate the distinctive elements that make up each literary genre. They can read *Hamlet,* for example, without having to analyze Shakespeare's complex dramatic conventions of characterization and conflict or his intricate language devices for deepening these conventions. In turn, they can no longer evaluate the contribution of *Hamlet* to tragic drama or literary art as a whole, given the thoroughness, novelty, and depth of this play's tragic vision. Without a foundational knowledge of the literary elements shaping this genre during late sixteenth century England, students cannot be expected to evaluate this play by common dramatic standards or grasp its thought-provoking, category-defying perspective on our human condition. With the erosion of the genre-based or inter-textual approach to secondary literature whereby students study a play in the context of a large number of other plays to which they can make constant comparisons and contrasts, and the disappearance of literary standards for interpreting and evaluating literary texts, secondary students are robbed of a coherent body of literary knowledge, as well as an inspirational context of ever-changing perspectives on what it means to be human. The dismantling of secondary courses that present literature from a predominantly literary perspective, whether these be sweeping humanities courses in literary classics, period courses in national literatures, or in-depth studies of a specific genre like short story or contemporary drama, prevents secondary students from viewing and using literature as a much-needed escape valve from the stunted, culture-fed notions of self and identity in which they are enmeshed.

How Non-Literary Approaches to Secondary Literature Affect Learning

As secondary literature trend decrees, the literary classics secondary students once studied within their genre and historical contexts now serve as catalysts for learning processes and objectives extraneous to the subject of literature and applicable to any high school subject. With the new educational focus on how rather than what secondary students must learn, both literary texts and the larger contexts in which they were created—the author's life, the established trends in its genre, the cultural ethos or belief system that informs it, and important social and historical events and conditions—become inferior to the one context to which all students can effortlessly and equally relate: their personal lives. The reader response approach, the popular practice of guiding students to give their personal, subjective interpretations of literature, is now the favored process for learning not so much about literature—its artistic conventions and imaginary perspectives—but about a trendy student-centered way to read, study, and teach literature without necessarily understanding the subject of literature. The common theme running through a barrage of new books zealously and one-sidedly promoting the process approach to the teaching of literature is reflected in Kutz and Roskelly's admonition: "It seems clear that before educators can create an integrated curriculum in English, they must show students how their real lives put them at the center of their classroom lives, how what they do in life contributes to what they do when they read and write" (220). When applied to literature pedagogy, this widely held belief means students must engage in activities that, above all, allow them to impose their full range of experiences—social, emotional, and intellectual—on the created world of a literary text.

Unfortunately, what began as a theory of literary criticism now controls and restricts what students learn about literature. Reader response, just one of many external standpoints from which critics evaluate literature, has become synonymous with the most student-centered and, therefore, indispensable process for learning literature. In this age of the crammed secondary curriculum, this approach to literature reflects the priority that teacher educators and, in turn, teachers themselves now give to helping students cope with their personal worlds.

By now, reader response has become such a mainstay of secondary literature instruction that it has practically replaced the teaching of literary conventions with the imposition of students' views and interests on their texts. As with other more culturally appropriate ways to read and interpret literature, this approach views literature from an external frame of reference, marginalizing the teaching and learning of the literary elements of each genre and the artistic and metaphorical levels of reading and meaning-making afforded by the literary mode. When made the dominant process by which students learn literature, as is now the trend, the reader response approach may help students build greater self-knowledge while valorizing individual views on literature's relevant adolescent topics and issues. However, like other student-centered learning processes, it masks behavioral objectives such as self-discovery, self-esteem, self-determination, cooperation with others, and tolerance of diverse cultures and opinions behind the pretext of literary study. In the long run, the time-consuming nature of reader response prevents students from learning the literary mode of writing and the artistic conventions and techniques common to each genre. This student-centered process of literary study denies students the full intellectual and inspirational benefits of literature just as they are preparing for college and life-long learning.

Until the early 90's, the secondary English program in which I taught required upper-level students to read three or four novels a year including teen classics such as *A Separate Peace, Lord of the Flies, To Kill A Mockingbird, The Catcher in the Rye, In Country, Huckleberry Finn,* and *Great Expectations*, as well as numerous adult classic plays and novels by 12th grade, including *Oedipus Rex, Macbeth, Othello, The Death of a Salesman, A Raisin in the Sun, Wuthering Heights, Pride and Prejudice, The Stranger,* and *Main Street*. During the 20 years that I taught secondary English, however, I never once made the distinction between a teen and an adult literary classic, let alone design a literature course around texts that appeal exclusively to the young-adult, under fourteen category of consumer readers. While lessons on teen classics like *The Outsiders* or *Huckleberry Finn* always invited students to explore and share relevant experiences, the generation of personal responses never became the raison d'etre for studying literature it now threatens to become. Students' personalization of literature evolved out of focused and richly detailed literary contexts, whether it be a character's developing conflict, internal factors contributing to a pivotal decision, or techniques for illuminating a character's inner reality. While students had ample opportunities to relate literature to their adolescent conflicts, friendships, changes, or aspirations, their personal responses and applications grew out of their knowledge of literary genre and techniques and the external factors shaping the author's perspective. When they eventually linked a specific character, event, or symbol with a relevant personal experience, they did so from the greatly expanded view of individual experience which the discipline of literature inspires.

Over the past two decades, the context for learning and understanding literature has shifted away from the evolution, conventions, and aesthetic qualities of literary works and toward the woof and warp of students' personal lives. Now whether literature lessons deal with teen or adult novels and stories, they tend to showcase students sharing wide-ranging personal responses and anecdotes. This practice, moreover, sends students the message that their experiential knowledge is the most valid framework for reading, analyzing, and evaluating literature. While this experiential context from which to make sense out of literature may encourage secondary students to think more analytically and logically about their own lives, it provides weak motivation to rigorously study an author's unique literary craft, or to get beyond self-centered views to the multiple perspectives on human development and potentiality afforded by literature. Secondary students who spend precious classroom time analyzing each other's real-life dilemmas reduce their chance to learn how literary conventions help readers envision new ideas about human experience from literature's imaginary perspectives. Why, they ask, should they work hard for these academic and challenging achievements when they can be rewarded for making subjective responses? Why learn the subject of literature when it is impossible to be wrong about personal feelings and reactions to literary elements? Since secondary education has made the individual needs and interests of secondary students its all-consuming priority, literature's dual function as a rigorous field of study in which students continuously advance in knowledge and skills, and a mode that broadens readers' views by offering hypothetical perspectives of shared experiences has declined when students need it most. According to the secondary gospel of the reader's point of view, the status of a novel or play within its genre, or its literary or artistic merits no longer matter to high school students conditioned to viewing literature as a vehicle of self-discovery and self-validation. Literary study and educational trend could not be more at odds.

Long schooled by untested learning theories and activities that modify behaviors while starving minds, twenty-first-century secondary students are conditioned to value literature, even a play as artistically complex and innovative as *Hamlet*, from the standpoint of whatever happens to be personally relevant. Susie B. is no exception to this pedagogical norm. Following is her journal entry summarizing the "learning experience" she gained from studying *Hamlet* in her 11th grade literature class. Most to the point, it highlights the replacement of close analysis of literary elements with personally relevant and engaging learning processes now becoming commonplace in upper-level secondary literature classes:

*When my teacher first announced that we would be reading **Hamlet** next, I almost died. After hearing so many stories about how long it took to read, how difficult Shakespeare's language is, and how confusing it is to follow Hamlet's character, I expected a terrible time. Boy, was I surprised when the time to read the dreaded play arrived! The first lesson on this play was so cool. Instead of giving us lots of boring notes on the board about the author's background or the different parts of the play we would have to learn, our teacher had us first write a personal journal entry describing a time when we wanted to get even with someone close who had deliberately hurt us. We had to explain the betrayal situation first, and then describe in detail the different feelings that went through our head while thinking about getting even. This way, she said, we would be ready to relate with the terrible emotional conflict Hamlet has when his father's ghost explains he was murdered by his uncle, the man who is both king and husband of Hamlet's mother when the play opens. As if this is not enough to deal with, the ghost also tells Hamlet he must now kill his uncle to get revenge.*

This made me immediately think of a relevant experience of my own involving Abby, the girl I once thought was my best friend. To begin, I explained how one day last summer Abby betrayed me terribly when behind my back she tried to get my boyfriend to go on a date with her. I was fortunate that he liked me enough to tell me what she had done the next day. Now, months later, I still refuse to speak to her in school. As I explained this in my journal, I started pouring out all kinds of pent up anger and feelings of betrayal I never really dealt with at the time; in fact, I wrote about these feelings for the rest of English class, and the next day we each read our entry aloud except for a few too embarrassed to do so. Thanks to those who did, I realized I wasn't the only one who felt extreme rage and resentment after someone tried to steal my boyfriend. Several others described similar betrayals. After sharing our stories, we discussed the different ways we each reacted to our betrayals and drew conclusions about which reactions were positive and negative. I was one of a few that simply dropped the betrayer from my life as my form of revenge; others, unfortunately, described more aggressive methods of getting even. Then as my teacher explained, we were finally ready to identify with the terrible inner conflict with avenging his father's murder that Hamlet goes through in the play. I was glad to know even young people back in Elizabethan times had to deal with shocking betrayals by people they really believed they could trust.

We read the play mostly aloud in class, and each day we had to come up with our personal views on what Hamlet was experiencing as he kept trying to get revenge for his own father's murder. It seemed to me that he was extremely determined and loyal in getting revenge for his father's murder, even though it did not work out exactly as he wanted it to. We also received an activity packet that outlined exciting projects we could do in groups after each of the five long acts so we could better understand and relate to what had happened. One of the projects my group worked on together involved writing a rap song reflecting the basic plot of Act I, so that everyone in class could fully understand the complicated plot in our own informal language. My favorite project was writing my own informal soliloquy, paralleling Hamlet's premeditation speech starting, "To be or not to be," a speech in which I could express my inner anxieties about how to best get even with Abby for her betrayal, the same way Hamlet's soliloquy conveys his inner anxieties and his decision over how to kill Claudius so as to avenge his father's death. Our best learning experience, however, was when my group planned and acted act out the grave digging scene in Act V for our final presentation. Since we spent three class periods rehearsing, our final performance, wearing the costumes and using the props we created ourselves, was a great success.

While Susie B. represents our typical first-year college student, she also embodies our premise that the way a subject is taught and learned has a powerful impact on what students learn in secondary school. The conception and expectations related to literary study that are shaped in high school have an even more cogent impact on how students perceive college literature courses than educators at both levels realize. Specifically, this hypothetical entry is designed to highlight an extreme literary phenomenon that is not that extreme in everyday secondary practice: the literature lesson without content. While Susie's *Hamlet* projects undoubtedly met her need for personal engagement and vali-dation in "learning" this play, her only reference to actual literary instruction and application takes the form of omission. Like a typical high school student, she voices great relief that she and her classmates escaped having to take notes on Shakespeare's literary and historical backgrounds, just as they would if a substitute teacher showed up that day. While she knows a soliloquy can capture a character's "inner anxi-eties" and personal conflicts, she discusses no activities that helped her fully understand the dramatic conventions and ironic language like puns, incongruity, and innuendo by which Shakespeare develops his enigmatic and highly relevant tragicomic hero. She also conveys no indication that a unit that could last four weeks in a school year of less than 40 has helped her understand and appreciate how literature differs from other kinds of writing.

By contrast, what her entry celebrates is the replacement of the liter-ary content of *Hamlet* with lengthy, student-directed non-literary proj-ects. The first, a pre-reading, free-writing activity, lets students generate their collective prior knowledge, in this case a set of relevant examples, definitions, and consequences of adolescent betrayal, that is intended to prepare them, emotionally and cognitively, for studying a complex literary conflict. While this is a typical reader response exercise, it could not be more antithetical to what students need to do to appreciate and learn *Hamlet* as literature. Students spend a great deal of time writing about and discussing their personal, age-relevant examples, but, as Susie B's entry suggests, they acquire a distorted and superficial view of Hamlet's conflict with avenging his father's death; no insights into his complex and ambivalent psychological makeup that is Shakespeare's hallmark; and not an inkling of insight into his character's connection with a belief system that radically opposes the ideology of revenge and power that, ironically, is kept alive and healthy by popular culture.

The second paragraph of her journal entry could easily be confused with a psychology rather than a literature assignment. Given the priority behavioral and process-oriented outcomes they now receive across the secondary curriculum, it is no wonder students spend English class time engaging in activities one would expect to see at a therapy session for teenage victims of abuse and aimed at building coping skills and self-esteem, while eliminating unhealthy defense mechanisms. In lessons like this, literature becomes a springboard for analyzing and resolving real-life emotional conflicts, for preoccupying students with personal traumas when they should be learning literature, and for reinforcing the fallacy that learning is valid only when it is personally meaningful. Ironically, the more students are exposed to such student-centered activities and attitudes, the more resistant they become to the detached, critical thinking they need to study Hamlet's complex character and ironic language in depth. If they worked this way, from the literary elements out, they would achieve a broader, trans-adolescent view of the emotional impact that betrayal, disloyalty, deception, and manipulation have on people of all places and times.

This brings us to the most serious but least noticed learning problem resulting from Susie B's equation of literature with her personal experiences and reactions. This problem, one tied to the current crisis in thinking, involves the greatly reduced amount of time secondary students can dedicate to their literal reading of literature. There are abundant factors that explain this trend: not enough texts to assure all students have their own copy to read at home and in school; no time after school or on weekends for working teens to read their books even if they wanted to; replacement of full-length classics like Dickens's A *Tale of Two Cities* and *Great Expectations* with shorter paperback multicultural novels that are easier to read, more politically correct, and conducive to value-driven projects whether students read them or not; parents who neither model nor instill an enjoyment of reading and discussing complete works; and the cultural shift from print literacy to electronic imagery and stimulation that sends high school students the message that reading the printed word is simply no longer "hip." At worst, the twenty-first century could mark the disappearance of reading for the sheer enjoyment of the story, a habit common when I attended high school, read and analyzed literature, held a part-time job, had an active social life, and still had time to go to the library every month for books I would read for the pleasure of anticipating a new view of life. Whatever factor is blamed, it will not alter the fact that when secondary students are sidetracked by non-literary practices from understanding a work's artistic conventions, they lack the groundwork for analyzing literature and constructing meaningful literary interpretations. This is the most serious long-range impact, implicit in Susie B's journal entry, which needs urgent addressing.

In chapter three, we provided secondary and college level writing samples, reflecting students' inability to grasp a literary work's literal level of meaning from beginning to end. Several secondary essays display the piece-meal, fragmented grasp of literal story line that, in turn, makes it impossible for students to coherently trace a character's internal conflict through its rising and falling phases, or to interpret the character's deeper metaphorical levels of meanings. In these cases, failure to grasp a work's entire literal meaning directly correlates with the students' inability to reason critically, i.e., analyze, synthesize, and think creatively about literary elements. Susie B's journal entry makes only the most obvious reference to the literal conflict Hamlet develops upon learning the circumstances of his father's murder and who committed it at the beginning of the play. That she read the entire play well enough to understand the web of internal and external factors that keep expanding Hamlet's internal conflict with avenging his father's murderer right to the play's catastrophic ending seems unlikely. So does the possibility that she read carefully enough to notice the development of this conflict through several conventional dramatic phases, let alone its unconventional twists and turns. On the contrary, when teachers focus students' attention on processes for learning literature, particularly self-gratifying, non-literary approaches, they deprive students of the time and guidance needed for the thorough literal reading upon which recognition, analysis, and interpretation of literary elements like the main character's internal conflict depend.

According to Northrup Frye, the literal reading is the reader's initial act of reducing literature "to the intentional meaning, attending to what the work explicitly says rather than to what it is" ("The Critical Path" 277). Few would dispute this standard definition. During the literal phase, the reader absorbs a story's or play's simplest meaning, that which it most obviously refers to in the real world. A thorough literal reading of *Hamlet* involves taking into consideration every action or thought relevant to Hamlet's inherited mission of revenge as if it actually happened, from beginning to end. This is not an easy task for today's secondary students. However, Frye goes far beyond this common meaning. To him, this "naive" or "pre-critical" reading is one of direct participation and enjoyment, one that "arises from a habit of reading or theatre-going, and much of this pleasure comes from a greatly enlarged kind of expectation, extending over many works and many years....we are building something up, accumulating a total fund of experience, each individual response being an investment in it" ("The Critical Path" 277-78). Each literal reading, therefore, is not a separate journey through a different fictional reality. Rather, as Frye suggests, this phase involves the reader in the pleasure of recognizing recurring literary conventions; anticipating new versions; and adding to and enriching an existing storehouse of literary devices. He underscores this aesthetic role of the literal reading in his seminal work: "Understanding a poem literally means understanding the whole of it, as a poem, and as it stands. Such understanding begins in a complete surrender of the mind and senses to the impact of the work as a whole, and proceeds through the effort to unite the symbols toward a simultaneous perception of the unity of the structure" (*Anatomy of Criticism* 77). These passages confirm Frye's equation of the literal reading phase with the reader's awakening to a work's artistic makeup and unity. For our purposes, however, this expanded view of the literal reading phase raises serious educational questions about current student-centered habits of reading literature. It especially raises the question of whether popular process-oriented approaches are doing more to stifle than stimulate the secondary reader's literary consciousness.

One can conclude from Susie B's entry that she knows a lot about student-centered methods for learning literature, but has only an inkling of the revenge plot in *Hamlet.* From her watered-down literal reading, she dives into her own experience with betrayal and getting even about which she knows a great deal, abandoning her literary imagination. It is almost as if her learning objective were writing a personal diary entry as opposed to understanding one of the greatest literary works ever written. From Frye's standpoint on literal reading, Susie B's vague grasp of what happens to Hamlet in the play means she lacks the literal groundwork necessary to spark her literary imagination. Had she spent more time reading and reflecting on the literal experience of Hamlet, and had she even a small "fund" or storehouse of tragic protagonists with which to compare and contrast this character's development, she too could have experienced the "pre-critical" excitement of anticipating and contemplating the verbal artistry shaping Shakespeare's protagonist. From this phase, she could then move to the critical phase of analyzing, comparing and contrasting, and interpreting this particular tragic protagonist at the multiple levels of meaning that make this drama a work of literature. Without this "pre-critical" reading, Susie B, like those she represents, remains stuck in a personal frame of mind.

Moving from the hypothetical to the real, evidence of the non-literary nature of secondary literature lessons continues to flow from the contemporary English classroom. Based on my recent supervision of student teachers, current educational theory and methods have had an overpowering impact on the next generation of English educators. Specifically, the replication of full-period literature projects lacking in substantive literary content threatens to come full circle from student, to student teacher, to teacher, and back to student. In my initial visit with each student teacher and his or her cooperating teacher, I carefully review the criteria for planning and implementing effective language arts lessons. My major goal is to build student teachers' awareness of their future students' learning needs. Where literature instruction is concerned, this means emphasizing the importance of planning lessons around specific, grade-appropriate literary elements like setting, conflicts, techniques of characterization, or figurative language, and strategies for helping students increase their literary knowledge from one grade to the next. Despite this strong literary appeal, at least one out of every three or four initial observations confirms the powerful imprint of popular process-oriented lessons on the novice's fledgling pedagogy. These lessons vary in degree to which the teaching and learning of literary elements and their implications are marginalized by behavior-driven activities. Nonetheless, they uniformly reflect a pedagogical shift that is frighteningly anti-literature and anti-language in nature.

In teaching 11th graders a 6-7 week unit on *Macbeth*, one student teacher's overriding goal was to make the literary material relevant to students' lives and interests. Often, this means changing it into a more familiar genre. To teach Act I which they had already read, the student teacher personally engaged students by having them create and read letters to Lady Macbeth from her husband revealing his thoughts and feelings thus far about the witches' predictions, particularly his predicted Kingship. As they read their letters, it was evident that they lacked a basic concept of the tragic hero figure in literature, as well as a grasp of the wide range of mental, emotional, physical, and moral traits that Shakespeare gives his tragic character in Act I. Students, moreover, showed no tendency in reading their letters to quote or paraphrase lines capturing the complex, multi-level changes going on in Macbeth or to integrate the dense background material that enriches this character's introduction.

By contrast, their mock confessional letters tended to display one-dimensional, opinionated views of Macbeth as egotistical, ruthless, and power-hungry and little understanding of his complexity or his powerful relationship with his wife. Obviously, a careful literal reading for the key traits and motives of Macbeth introduced in Act I and an examination of Shakespeare's initial characterization techniques were not part of the students' learning agenda. They began their project by disconnecting themselves from the literary context shaping Macbeth's character, reflecting on this convention from their personal frame of reference, and enjoying playing a role that distorts the literary meaning of Macbeth in Act I. Since the lesson also permitted them to express their views in casual writing and speech genres, it was all the more aligned with their personal needs and learning habits. A text-based activity that guides students to read for a close analysis of the tragic character of Macbeth, particularly his conflicting motivations and traits as revealed in Act I, would prepare secondary students to understand the literary meaning of this convention as it evolves throughout the play. As a bonus, such a close analytical reading would also prepare them for the real-life Macbeths whose potentially deadly ambitions emerge from the similar confluence of inner and outer forces they can and cannot control. While personalized activities like this integrate students' full spate of learning skills—reading, writing, speaking, and listening—do they, we must ask, help students achieve the standards they desperately need to read, write, speak, and think critically about the literary components of literature?

The guided discovery lesson is another popular secondary learning process that, like reader response, is fast becoming a staple of the literature classroom. Both learning approaches are based on the assumption that students learn best when their developmental needs, whether for self-esteem, self-expression, or, in this case, discovering learning concepts on their own, are being met. When this approach is used, as Jacobsen et al explain, "students are provided with information, and through the guidance of their teachers they 'discover' the abstraction the teachers have identified in the objectives" (177). For example, students could be given excerpts from three different novels and asked to work in groups figuring out the specific point of view in each and how it differs or compares with the others. Clearly this approach could be applied to the teaching of any specific genre convention like narrative point of view or dramatic monologue, or any figurative language device.

The chief problem with using this approach to teaching literature, however, is that of time. Many learning experts, including E. D. Hirsch, Jr. and Elaine Wrisley Reed, strongly argue that inductive lessons take too much time to implement while affording no guarantee that students will adequately learn an underlying concept such as point of view in literature. As related to literary study, the kinds of "hands-on" activities students are encouraged to do actually reduce the time they need to spend individually reading, exploring, and interpreting literary conventions and symbols and their multiple levels of meaning or application. In fact, this potentially effective approach can engage the students and teacher so much in the discovery process that they lose sight of the lesson's literary objective. Today's student teachers, themselves products of "hands-on" education and entertainment, can become so excited about designing and implementing their own discovery lessons that they fail to recognize when a learning process supplants genuine literary content.

One student teacher's lesson aimed at preparing students to understand the protagonist's role in Stephen Vincent Benet's "By the Waters of Babylon." To achieve this outcome, he arranged the students in six groups, gave each an unfamiliar, early 20th-century artifact such as a juicer or a bottle cap remover, and guided them through the critical processes of analyzing its parts, comparing and contrasting it with known objects, naming it, hypothesizing its underlying function or concept, and presenting findings to the class. For the entire period, the groups worked collaboratively, displaying the signposts of inductive learning: active, self-directed involvement with an example of an abstract concept, and application of language and critical thinking skills to the process of discovering an object's underlying concept, in this case its twentieth-century function or technology. In addition, the students were "on-task" and self-directed for the entire period.

However, as these motivated students spent the class modeling and grasping the phases of inductive learning, they acquired no new knowledge of their literary objective. Their literary objective remained severed from this learning activity. Since secondary students have so little class time to study literature, this activity should have directly engaged them in analyzing and drawing inferences about literary artifacts, in this case selected passages representing the protagonist-hypothesizer's step-by-step awakening to the frightening implications of modern technology. Because of this activity's misapplication, students were unable to shift their critical lens to the story itself; unable to share and benefit from the protagonist's expanding perspective on the dangers of modern technology. New teachers, raised on the assumption that literature must enhance the reader's self-knowledge, hesitate to immerse students in rigorous, step-by-step analysis of difficult literary elements. Out of habit, many spend valuable time on non-literary activities that prevent students from developing the dense and informed concepts these elements represent. That literature itself is the ideal inductive learning context has not occurred to them.

Throughout my college teaching career, I have read the signs of the deteriorating discipline of secondary literature. The two most corrosive effects of process-driven instructional practices on first-year college students are shallow and fragmented literary background knowledge and a tendency to skim literary works for the bare literal plot as if they were boring information texts. The increasing popularity of the young-adult literature genre in high school is a strong index of students' shift away from literary content and meaning and toward equating literature with other subjects that deal with objective, scientifically observable areas of experience. Students no longer read books for their rich artistic significance and inspiration, but for what they can tell them about their own and others' personal lives. In the long run, the practices that have generated secondary students' misconception of literature have left them doubly deprived: deprived of the opportunity to develop a broad and coherent knowledge of a body of literature—i.e., literary history, literary genres, and a broad grasp of literary devices and conventions that make up each genre; and deprived of the ability to understand and appreciate how to critically read for literary meaning, as opposed to the objective and quantifiable meanings of fact-based disciplines. Students now graduating from high school have grown up with a distorted notion of the literary mode, and how it should be thought, read, and written about in contrast to informative or argumentation texts.

Helping Students Create and Benefit From Literary Meaning

I will always remember a senior's personal narrative about a friend's estrangement from negligent parents. His poignant story never would have been conceived or written had he not first read, closely analyzed, and been inspired by the literary artistry of Salinger's *The Catcher in the Rye*. Prior to writing his personal response, he undertook a disciplined study of the fictional Holden Caufield's account of his parents' self-absorption and hypocrisy. He did not, prior to reading, sit down and describe his friend's personal experiences. Instead he began by critically reading for the full dimensions of Salinger's imaginary parent-child conflict. This also meant tracing the dynamic growth of Holden's first person point of view, from his initial adolescent self-centeredness, to his growing awareness that certain adults have feelings, problems, and needs no less important than the plights of adolescents, and finally to his awakening to the many hidden factors that lock people, teenagers and adults, in stultifying, divisive age stereotypes.

By examining the novel's point of view from beginning to end, my student began to grasp the deeper factors underlying parent-child alienation in the fictional light of Holden's skeptical and expanding consciousness. He soon discovered, by reading from Holden's fictional point of view, an entanglement of personal and social factors—causes, effects, and analogies—against which the fictional and real teenager's perception of adult selfishness and hypocrisy takes on greatly extended meaning. His preliminary reading of the novel involved thorough analysis of Holden's dynamic point of view from beginning to end. As a result, he brought a mature awareness of the multiple factors underlying the key concept of parent-child alienation to his response essay about his friend. This broadened view would not have been possible had he been required to make lengthy explorations, written and spoken, of personal associations and relevant experiences his first connection with the novel. Such a precondition automatically inhibits students' exploration of literature's artistic conventions. It limits their exploration of the full artistic dimensions of a literary point of view like Holden Caufield's; it dampens their desire to explore the metaphorical implications, the range of human possibilities, this convention holds for them. Had the reader's need for making personal responses to literature been the main learning objective, my student would have never grasped Salinger's talent for creating novelistic elements that help all readers, not just teenagers, understand the complex, often uncontrollable aspects of what at first seems to be a blatant case of parental neglect. When students critically analyze a dominant literary element like point of view in *The Catcher in the Rye*, their most important change is the expanding consciousness that comes from viewing a concept they thought they understood through the kaleidoscopic prism of fictional point of view.

Whether or not Holden represents American adolescence, the spirit of alienation and rebellion so captivating to young-adult readers today, held little interest to my student over ten years ago. He could have focused on actions and words linking Holden with the typical self-centered American teenager, particularly his litany of immature reactions to all that others do to "tick him off." He also could have spent this learning experience writing about his personal encounters with such trendy issues as parental abuse, divorce, drug addiction, and unemployment—just as serious causes of twenty-first-century teenage defiance as the materialism and selfishness of Holden's parents. However, he was more engrossed in reading a literary conflict from the inside out, for the detail-packed story of a defiant adolescent; for the highly controlled literary techniques of point of view and symbolism in which Salinger casts this story; finally, for this author's expanded concept of adult hypocrisy in capitalistic America—its many forms, causes, and effects—which only a literary work can quickly generate. Having thoroughly analyzed the narrator's point of view and related symbolism, my student discovered this book was about much more than a realistic portrait of adolescent hipness and rebellion against the world of phony adults. By dissecting and mentally grappling with Holden's ongoing struggle for understanding, he also moved beyond his immediate problems and needs to recognize, via a literary convention, a refreshingly unconventional prototype of adolescent consciousness. By breaking the mold of adolescent self-centeredness and blame,

Holden's narrative can inspire a generation to similarly transcend teenage narcissism and develop the broadened perspective on crucial life-concepts that begins with acknowledging and respecting the views of others, in fiction and in life.

In the long run, rigorous study of specific novel conventions and the author's deeper vision of modern family decay taught my student the same truth Hamlet tries to teach his logic-bound friend, Horatio: "There are more things in heaven and earth, / Horatio, / Than are dreamt of in your philosophy." If only secondary English programs would apply the same wisdom to the multi-faceted movement to personalize and find appropriate psychological strategies in the teaching of literature. Those controlling these programs now have a serious choice to make. They can continue to support the process-oriented approach that reduces literature to a panacea for nurturing the total student and perpetuating self-centered modes of thinking and learning; or they can give today's secondary students the gift of becoming critical and creative thinkers by learning literature from the inside out.

Of all the learning problems, in thinking, language skills, and content knowledge, with which high school graduates now begin college, we believe the most serious but least addressed is their inability to read and interpret the language of literature. Schools that care about ameliorating the crisis in students' thinking and language skills will make the study of the discipline of literature a top priority at the secondary level. When undergraduates thoroughly grasp a work's dominant literary elements such as the tragic protagonist in Sophocles's *Oedipus Rex* or the realistic setting in Lorraine Hansberry's *A Raisin in the Sun*, and are also guided to closely analyze the element's literal and abstract meanings, they do not have to be English majors to achieve the full intellectual and creative benefits of literary analysis. Like successful students in my recent Introduction to Drama course, they merely need to be guided through a "pre-critical" reading of a play in order to recognize a literary element's full literal and artistic dimensions. This literary process, based on the same principles of effective teaching and learning that should pertain to secondary literature, enabled my students to achieve maximum literary knowledge and meaning as their final essays confirmed. Succinctly put, those who participated regularly in the close analysis and discussion of the plays' literary conventions and strategies achieved the same critical and creative outcomes that secondary students should be acquiring much earlier. The specific skills students gained from learning literature from inside out are:

1. An expanded understanding of literary conventions and the common concepts they represent

2. An expanded understanding of the literature's inherent capacity for generating and

3. strengthening analytical reasoning needed across the secondary and college curriculum.

4. The ability to think metaphorically about the multiple frames of reference that a literary element can spontaneously generate and clarify for the reader

5. The ability to synthesize literary conventions in related works and appreciate the broadened view of shared concepts made possible by intertextual study

These intellectual and creative benefits have been confirmed by our combined teaching experiences and insights into how students can best achieve literary knowledge and understanding at the secondary and college level of instruction. The first benefit, conceptual reasoning or concept formation, results from students' disciplined effort to thoroughly explore an abstract idea represented by a literary element. By first analyzing Sophocles's dramatic convention of the tragic hero in *Oedipus Rex,* my entire class made rapid progress in discussing and fluently writing about the classical theme of the individual's struggle to control his or her personal destiny as embodied in the character, Oedipus. Several essay excerpts reflect students' developing, "hands-on" literary understanding of what turned out to be a much less uniform and predictable literary theme than they expected to find. As their textual investigations brought to light, Oedipus's illusions of personal power and magnitude quickly dissolve under Sophocles's careful shaping of his paradoxical protagonist.

The first excerpt captures the student's active concept development as, while she reads and writes, she discovers that Oedipus's opening displays of personal magnitude and power are undercut by Sophocles's intimations of a darker, totally unexpected nature:

In Sophocles's play, Oedipus is a character who is a great leader of Thebes, and possesses the Aristotelian ingredient of magnitude in his role as king. The reader is able to infer that Oedipus's magnitude, or greatness, makes him well respected and admired by his people. One example of this trait occurs early in the play, when the people of Thebes seek Oedipus's help to end the plague that has struck the entire kingdom. The priest, who serves as a messenger for the people, states that Oedipus "is not one of the immortal gods, we know;/ Yet we have come to make a prayer/ as to the man surest in mortal ways/ and wisest in the ways of God" (45, l. 34-7). This passage implies that Oedipus is not only looked upon as a king with magnitude and authority, but his people also equate him with Apollo because of his wisdom. Another instance of Oedipus's magnitude is the way he reminds his people early in the play that he became King of Thebes without, ironically, any connections to King Laios's ancestral line. According to the myth, Oedipus left his homeland, and arrived at the gate of Thebes, as a young man looking for a place to take refuge. However, on his way he solved the riddle of the Sphinx, and the people made him King of Thebes. On one hand, this feat proves that Oedipus is a man who achieves goals like peace for all his people, a goal thought unattainable by most people then, and requiring superior intelligence. It also suggests Oedipus has such magnitude as a leader that he can solve any problem he is confronted with. This development suggests the kind of magnitude as a leader Sophocles believed necessary for the tragic hero. However, it also conveys Sophocles's concept of the tragic hero as a person whose very magnitude ironically results in his fall from greatness. Magnitude becomes a key element in Sophocles's tragic hero formula, since it makes Oedipus's fall from glory all the more catastrophic. While the play begins with Oedipus at the apex of his magnitude and his reign as King, it also begins with his tragic discovery of his true self.

The depth of literary meaning this student has gleaned by closely examining the relationship between the character's development in specific lines and scenes and the underlying concept of controlled destiny cannot be underestimated. It highlights the kind of grappling with the literal level of character and plot that enables students to make the jump to implications beneath the surfaces of fiction and life. From this experience, she learned not only the Sophoclean duality of the individual's fated vs. chosen destiny, but the literary truth that shows of personal power and control always have a conflicting side. Moreover, by the time this student analyzed the greatness, tragic flaws, horrific suffering, and atonement that constitute Oedipus's tragic characterization, she came much closer to sharing Sophocles's detached, ironic view of humankind's ongoing obsession with self-imposed destiny. In fact, she made this initial character study the literary and conceptual touchstone from which to compare and contrast subsequent tragic characters of Hamlet and Willy Loman, Mama Younger and Mme. Ranevskaya. Her eventual synthesis of five tragic views on the idea that humans can control their personal destiny was not only an advanced act of concept formation, but a testament to literature's power to continually defy, in endless variety, the absolutist ideas that stymie human potential.

The second critical benefit of focused literary analysis is the student's growing recognition of his or her power of analytic reasoning. Not only is this thinking skill required across the college disciplines, it is the cornerstone of literary interpretation. Sadly, its erosion is also a main cause of the serious difficulties that secondary and post-secondary students now have understanding information and literary texts. To understand either mode of writing, they must be able to infer the deeper structure or pattern around which a concept is being organized; only then can they move to the next step of this critical thinking and reading process, identifying its various parts or attributes and determining their interrelationship. As Link confirms, this critical thinking process involves "the ability to analyze component parts in order to find how they relate to each other as well as how they contribute to the overall character of the whole they compose" (Link 95). Students' academic success depends greatly on their conscious application of analytic reasoning to a broad range of college textbooks. Unfortunately, those lacking this critical process have serious difficulty noticing and analyzing the pattern around which an author organizes a central concept, whether a historical concept like immigration or racism or a literary concept like characterization or metaphor.

Besides concept expansion, the essay from which the above passage was taken conveys the student's analytic grasp of the Aristotelian tragic formula underlying Oedipus's characterization, the equal and prescriptive parts of magnitude, tragic flaw, suffering, and reversal or ruin that shape the ironic classical view of human nature. Another student's essay provides in-depth analysis of the three roles Jocaste, Oedipus's wife, plays in facilitating her husband's tragic fall from demi-god to pariah. In the following excerpt, she applies analytic reasoning to her scrutiny of Jocaste's role as emotional supporter, thereby stretching and complicating the stereotype.

Jocaste's emotional support involves trying to help Oedipus find out who the killer of Laios is. However, she really plays little part in emotionally supporting her husband out of love. In the beginning of the play when Oedipus wants Jocaste to get the man who knew what the killer of Laios looked like, she attempts to persuade him not to do that. She tries instead to convince him that the shepherd might alter parts of the story, or he might not remember after so many years (58, l. 320-330). When Oedipus persists, Jocaste says, "I would not wish to cross you in anything" (58, l. 334). Jocaste's motives here are strictly to appease Oedipus because she had to. She feels it is part of her wifely duty to listen to what Oedipus says. However, Jocaste's earlier motives for covering up the truth of her infanticide and not sharing her feelings with Oedipus from the time they were married were much deeper. The shepherd was the one she assumed killed her baby. Thus she did not want to bring up anything from the past if she did not have to; her past is riddled with deceptions and self-deceptions. She mainly did not want Oedipus to look down on her for what she did. She also did not want her people to know what she had done. In ancient Greece, a queen should not commit a crime of such horror, especially having a son put to death. Another key instance when Jocaste seems to emotionally support Oedipus occurs when she tries to convince him that the oracle claiming Oedipus would kill his father and marry his mother was insignificant. She says, "since Fate rules us and nothing can be foreseen/ A man should live only for the present day" (60, l. 65). Yet here she is really supporting him for her own agenda. She wants him to remain as clueless as possible; she fears the loss of Oedipus, but more so the truth of her own wrongdoings. If her people or Oedipus find out the truth, she will be ostracized for the rest of her life. Also, if he does not know the truth about her past, then they will remain the royal and revered couple they appear to be. In many aspects, they remind me of Bill and Hillary Clinton. Hillary, although disgusted with her husband, appears to emotionally support him in public. However, if we take a closer look we can see that it is all just a business agreement; there is no love involved. As for Jocaste, not once in the play does this leader's wife make reference to the love she has for Oedipus.

This passage captures the student's dynamic analysis of Jocaste's ambiguous role as her husband's emotional supporter. As she moves from one related example of this role to the next, she continually shifts gears, revising and expanding her interpretation of Jocaste's "support" role in light of new, complicating, and contradictory details as they emerge from the text. Having thought about and connected seemingly unrelated aspects of Jocaste's characterization, she succeeds in extending the classical stereotype of the wife whose main objective in life is to please and obey her husband to include strong hints of subversive and self-serving motives. Analytic reasoning, her interpretation makes clear, becomes a catalyst for expanding students' preconceptions of seemingly fixed cultural ideals. In the process of anatomizing this single character role, the student has made implicit connections between this role and Jocaste's equally paradoxical roles as both the primary enabler of her husband's ambition and a significant contributor to his catastrophic downfall. By the end of her complete analysis of Jocaste's multiple and related character roles, she achieves a more informed and ambivalent concept of the role of the ancient Greek wife. As the student now seems to realize, even in ancient times the wife found subtle but powerful ways to create a meager identity.

The subtext of this telling excerpt is clear: when secondary students are similarly guided to analyze and connect related literary elements, latent concepts rush to the surface, are reassessed, edited, revised, and reconceived through the critical lens of the student's new literary perspective. Their storehouse of ideas, their intellectual groundwork, is continually renewed from literature's mind-expanding context of ideas. Purpose-bound texts, however informative or persuasive, cannot compete with literature's fluid and interactive conceptual framework.

This brings us to the third powerful benefit of students' guided study of literary conventions: their ability to think metaphorically or hypothetically about a range of possible meanings that a literary element, when studied in its entirety, can generate. Here, in the realm of literary hypothesis, there is no right or wrong meaning, only valid vs. invalid applications based on a convention's literal meaning. In contrast to a scientific hypothesis which posits a single connection between two observable and measurable factors, such as large classes and unequal student participation, metaphorical thought generates multiple connections between a literary element and the reader's open-ended imaginative and experiential associations. Rational thought is reductive, purposive, and logical; metaphorical thought is expansive, pluralistic, and associative.

The former follows one line of reasoning, moving convergently from cause to effect; the latter is open to multiple meanings, moving divergently through a range of associations. Metaphorical thought, the dynamic process whereby readers make mind-opening connections between literary conventions and multiple frames of reference, is desperately needed by print-resistant secondary students raised on a diet of spoon-fed, culturally constructed images and views.

The second excerpt culminates with the student's imaginative, free-ranging analogy between an ancient fictional couple and a prominent real-life couple. It captures her thought at the moment a literary character whets her imaginative appetite for seeing something familiar, in this case Hillary Clinton, in a new light that is the essence of literature's generative power. She converts Jocaste to metaphor the moment she associates her with Hillary Clinton. Through her imaginative equation of the duplicitous love of a fictional and real ruler's wife, she unleashes myriad associations that enhance the meaning of both figures and the forms of power to which they must resign themselves. As this excerpt illustrates, a thorough analysis of Jocaste's character generates new perspectives, multiple frames of reference that expand and complicate the concept of female power she represents. Literary meaning begets literary meaning. Unfortunately, many secondary students lack guidance in viewing a literary convention as an ever-expanding source of insight into common concepts and life-experiences.

For their second literary essay, my students compared and contrasted two tragic protagonists who represent different forms of blind devotion to abstract cultural ideals. To culminate their study, they explored their characters' metaphorical values by comparing them with a personal experience or contemporary example. They reconceived again their chosen example from the literary standpoint of characters already analyzed: Sophocles's Oedipus, Shakespeare's Hamlet, Chekhov's Mme. Ranevskaya, Miller's Willy Loman, and Hansberry's Mama Younger. As metaphorical thinkers, they could draw on any of the insights they had gleaned from analyzing and relating these literary figures to clarify, extend, and complicate their personal analogy. They quickly discovered that by juxtaposing a real-life example with a fictional one, many hidden facets and implications of the former spring to mind. Thus they experienced the boundless metaphorical thought process Paul de Man so poignantly describes: "In the manner of a vibration spreading in infinitude from its center, metaphor is endowed with the capacity to situate the experience [being compared] at the heart of a universe that it generates" (235). The following three excerpts present only a few of the creative analogies my students, when inspired by literary characters' metaphorical implications, were liberated to create. The multiple benefits of this creative thought process for today's secondary students, so torn between standardized assessments and personalized learning processes that undermine intellectual and creative growth, should be self-evident.

Many times in life people have found themselves in situations they had no idea how to handle. What would you do if you were in the same situation as Jocaste and Linda [wife of Willy Loman]? Would you have hung on to the very end or jumped out when the sailing became rough? We all have our own ideas of who we are and what we can do. However, many times when we are put in perplexing and complex situations we are unable to make rational decisions. We become tangled up, like Jocaste and Linda; we do not know which way is up. We may not even know if we are the enablers of others' destructive habits of mind or not. My husband, who had five years of sobriety, started drinking again a year ago. If I had not told him to either stop drinking or get out, I would have been his enabler. Now that he has a year of sobriety under his belt, I am thankful he chose a saner state of mind. However, these choices are not always easy. Who should a person remain loyal to—herself or her loved one? I believe Hamlet said it best: "To thine own self be true."

In conclusion, even though there are 2500 years between these plays [Oedipus Rex and Death of a Salesman], some of women's roles are still the same. These fictional wives, Jocaste and Linda, have to starve their internal well-being while being an emotional supporter, enabler, and unfortunately a contributor to their husbands' downfalls. In literature today some of these cultural stereotypes are changing, but clearly not as much as one would expect. Women are still viewed by writers, society, and other women somewhat through shaded glasses, but due to the Women's Rights movement this concept is beginning to change. The shades will have to disappear and the sun shine through on women in literature throughout the world in the next millennium. Any woman can be seen as the protector of her family, but due to increasing psychological knowledge and different support groups, it may be possible for a woman to remain the emotional supporter of those she loves but not the enabler of the illnesses or disorders of her husband. The male and female roles will always be different as they are intended to be that way. Hopefully, in the future the negative connotation of the term "enabler" will disappear, therefore giving women a more positive role in society.

The search for self-knowledge by Oedipus Rex and Willy Loman closely relates to that of the prisoner in Plato's cave because they are both blind to their human potential, and they also made a resolution upon seeing the "upper world" of truth and reason. It is jarring to see how "The Allegory of the Cave" equally relates to Oedipus Rex and Death of a Salesman, the latter written thousands of years ago. Both the symbolism of the cave and the tragic downfalls of these characters relate strongly to our society today. An example of a modern prisoner would be a person who is illiterate. He is chained to the cave of the physical world by things like poverty, ignorance, and dependence on others. Some come out of the cave and enter the light of knowledge, like Oedipus finally does, by going back to school and seeking help. Others continue to delude themselves and, like Willy Loman, live their lives without gaining true knowledge of who they are or can be. Though social conditions change, the story of the cave still holds true because humans continue to choose to blind themselves to their human limits and potential.

These excerpts reflect not so much a fitting conclusion for a focused literary comparison/contrast as they do the third and metaphorical phase in the construction of literary meaning. To reach this level, all three writers have already acquired a literal and literary understanding of two different authors' tragic characters. As pre-critical readers, they have read two selected plays with an eye to gleaning explicit details, specific actions and words, that contribute to the literal meaning of these characters; they have reflected on such a range of attributes for each that they have developed an emotional bond with them, a literary friendship so to speak. This empathy reverberates through these writers' unveiled emotional appeals to their own audience: "What would you do if you were in the same situation as…"; "These fictional wives have to starve their internal well-being while being…"; "they are both blind to their human potential, and they also made a resolution upon seeing…." Upon reading these students' moving conclusions, one can rest assured that the literary characters they selected for their comparison/contrast essay have in some ways become as full, complex, and meaningful as the real characters with whom they live.

Second, these excerpts imply all three writers' shift to the dimension of literary convention; their movement beyond reading for characters' literal meaning to acknowledging and appreciating, in this case, two writers' specific techniques for giving an old and new twist to male and female tragic characterization. Since by this point they have read and analyzed five tragic dramas on multiple levels, they have achieved a broad literary context or what Frye calls a "total fund of [literary] experience" in which to contextualize and more fully grasp two authors' convention of tragic characterization, as well as their innovations. These excerpts further convey what Frye calls the "greatly enlarged kind of expectation" which readers with a "fund" of literary experiences have as they begin to encounter each new version of a traditional element. Appreciation for the author's literary craft resonates from the first writer's grasp of the tragic enabler role played by a modern and ancient literary wife; the second's insight into how Linda and Jocaste tragically contribute to their husbands' downfall; and the third's understanding of the tragic blindness of Willy and Oedipus to their human potential and limits. Had these novice literary thinkers not achieved this more comprehensive knowledge of how multiple authors handle tragic characterization, it is unlikely they could transform this convention into such powerful and expansive metaphors.

As these passages also imply, students' ability to transform literary convention into metaphor is nurtured by careful, preliminary analyses and comparisons of a literary convention shared by authors across time and space. Each excerpt reflects the range of reference points, concrete and abstract, that literary symbol turned metaphor is free to generate. The first writer freely associates Jocaste and Linda with movable frames of reference: her own marital dilemma, the difficulty of all enabling wives to make rational decisions, and the highly abstract message regarding these choices *Hamlet*'s famous line conveys. Just as spontaneously, the second writer views these tragic heroines from two contemporary standpoints—the feminist focus on the "cultural stereotypes" and the "shaded glasses" through which literary wives continue to be viewed and the expanded psychological concept of the modern wife's potential—and also from a future vantage point, one in which women's enabler status has become a positive rather than negative force. The third has already closely analyzed Sophocles's, Miller's, Shakespeare's, and other authors' tragic vision of the human journey from blindness to self-knowledge, including Plato's "Allegory of the Cave." Drawing on this dense literary context, this writer swiftly links the literary journey motif with both a broad philosophical view of life and the gripping real-life condition of illiteracy. The new knowledge that can result from such free-wheeling metaphorical links between and among previously unassociated concepts, conditions, and experiences is impossible to measure. Nevertheless, the creative and knowledge-building benefits of metaphorical thought can be achieved by any secondary student encouraged and guided to learn imaginative literature from the bottom up.

A fourth critical and creative benefit of discipline-based literary study should strongly appeal to secondary and college students today. This is literature's capacity, due to its unique makeup of artistic, literary conventions, to create limitless perspectives on and insights into concepts that continue to shape our human experiences. Students, embedded in the pedagogy of the self, especially the habit of spouting self-centered opinions of no relevance to literature's creative mode, can be released from their thinking trap by guided literary study. Many begin college literature classes predisposed to argue personal positions on a character's decision, a plot's outcome, or an author's choice of dominant symbol, blind to these literary devices' open-ended artistic and metaphorical nature. Clinging to subjective views and personal preferences and used to showcasing these in literature classes, they resist this mode's "critical path" away from self and toward the multiplicity of views it affords on concepts and life-experiences that affect everyone. However, given the chance to study literature from the bottom up—from the literal, to the literary, to the metaphorical levels of meaning—they too can understand the hardest literary truth for students to grasp: as de Man asserts, "The 'meaning' of the metaphor is that it does not 'mean' in any definite manner" (235). In other words, the metaphor of Willy Loman has as many possible meanings to the reader as can be grounded in *Death of a Salesman*'s thematic center and the fluid and open language with which it is created. Yet regardless how plausible a dozen different interpretations may be, the play remains an open-ended source of meaning.

Guided literary study enables students to learn and respect the world of difference between personal reactions to literature and the disciplined, maturing process of creating literary meaning. They also discover and are inspired by literature's inherent capacity to generate and support the reader's divergent interpretations. The full benefits of this pluralistic mode of thought result from navigating two intersecting pathways to literary knowledge. They can study literary concepts intratextually, exploring the multi-layers of meaning within a single text as it spirals outward from literal, to literary, to metaphorical dimensions. By tracing Oedipus's or Jocaste's character through the play's literal, literary, and metaphorical levels of meaning, my students achieved the diverging and thought-provoking insights into human power and deception, as both self-validating and self-destructive that the literary mode inspires. Equally important, the abstract and analytic reasoning skills gained from this literary experience will strengthen their cross-disciplinary and cross-life learning experiences in truly self-expanding ways. Students can also study literary concepts intertextually either by exploring and synthesizing multiple authors' literary elements across time or space, or by examining a single author's literary artistry across his or her body of work. By the time my students had studied four tragic dramas in-depth, they were ready to experience the critical and creative challenges afforded by the intertextual path to literary knowledge.

The following excerpts, from three of my students' literary journals, reflect the dynamic synthesis of views they now could "free-write," having achieved the dense, multiple text pool of literary associations and concepts needed for intertextual study:

*In **A Raisin in the Sun**, Mama's role as a tragic hero can be compared to Oedipus, Hamlet, and Willy Loman. Three of Mama's tragic traits are magnitude, long-lasting suffering, and a tragic flaw or weakness. Oedipus has a great deal of magnitude in Sophocles's play; he is a king and viewed as noble and almighty. Mama also has a great deal of this type of magnitude within her family. She is the matriarch of the family; everyone looks to her for guidance. By contrast, Hamlet and Mama share the trait of long-suffering. They both suffer terribly because they must make certain decisions. Hamlet suffers throughout the play from having to decide whether or not to commit revenge; Mama suffers from having to decide what to do with the family's insurance money, and whether to trust Walter to handle the money. Both of their sufferings develop equally from within their families. Finally, Mama and Willy Loman share an arrogance about their families that is not at all realistic. Willy actually deludes himself into thinking* *he is a great salesman with a great family, while Mama just wants to believe that under her guidance her family will always be fine, that they will overcome any problems. While Willy's tragic flaw is his personal egotism, Mama's is her arrogant belief in her family's goodness and her blindness to Walter's greed and selfishness.*

*Mama's first character trait as a tragic hero is her magnitude. Her magnitude is shown in her age and family tradition. She is the head of the family and holds the family together. Compared to Oedipus, Mama does not have the nobility that Oedipus has; she is not a king or leader of her society. However, she is a leader to her family. She is also a role model for women because she takes the usual role of the male as head of the household. Oedipus is respected by his people because he is a king. Mama, by contrast, earns her respect through her actions and words. Another trait of the tragic hero is the tragic flaw which leads to the suffering of the protagonist. Mama's flaw is her overtrust of Walter; she gives him all the insurance money that is to be used for Beneatha's medical school and the rest to put in the bank. Comparing this tragic flaw to Willy Loman's **in Death of a Salesman**, Mama is in some ways similar. Willy's tragic flaw is his belief that to be liked is more important than who you are. His delusions do not allow him to see his true self. Although Mama does not have delusions to the extreme that Willy has, she does not realize Walter is not capable of handling the money or their home. The last trait of the tragic hero is the suffering he/she must endure. Mama's suffering is the loss of all the money from her husband's life insurance policy. She is so broken-hearted and down. Her suffering stems from having to make the decision whether to give Walter charge of the money or not. This endured suffering is similar to Hamlet's long suffering in his own mind whether to kill Claudius or not. They both undergo internal suffering from these difficult decisions.*

Oedipus, Willy, and Hamlet all share some of Mama's traits. Although each character is unique in the way the author portrays them, they each share ancestral commitments, pride or hamatria, destruction of oneself in one way or another, and each suffers. They all meet with catastrophe.

Oedipus learns who he is and makes thing right. Willy cannot accept who he is and commits suicide, and Mama gives up her place in the family to her son. This causes a family catastrophe as Walter risks and loses their money. In all three of these plays, the families go through suffering along with the tragic hero. Oedipus reflects the ancient belief system of many gods, and the oracles or fate, Willy reflects a modern belief system of the American Dream, Hamlet the belief system of revenge and his responsibility to avenge his murdered father's killer, and Mama the belief in God who she prays to so that things will be taken care of. All these characters are forced into some sort of belief system that controls their lives and their suffering. All these systems were not a positive ideal for these characters to follow. These pieces of literature also have an undercurrent of death. Oedipus murdered his father and caused his wife's suicide, Hamlet eventually kills Claudius, Willy Loman commits suicide, and Mama gets the insurance money only because of her husband's death. With each death, the author implies something which each reader can interpret differently. My feeling is that death has a way of either making good things happen for these families or something horrible. Two of these deaths can be taken positively. Willy's suicide freed his family from him. Mama's husband died, but the insurance money helped get them out of their small apartment. Hamlet and Oedipus seem to portray death as negative, it is associated with murder. Oedipus kills his own father, and Hamlet's father is murdered, therefore causing the deaths of the uncle who murdered him, the wife who married the uncle, and the eventual death of the father's son, Hamlet himself. While death is portrayed very differently in all these pieces, there are still some amazing similarities.

What happens when students view the recurring tragic ingredients of magnitude, hubris or self-love, self-deception, and long suffering, concepts that shape the tragic vision of human experience, from the standpoints of multiple characters, each representing different individual drives and cultural trappings? These three journal entries capture the intellectual and creative benefits of this intertextual approach to tragic drama. The first is simply understanding the interdependence of literary works. Students learned this by drawing on their knowledge of multiple tragedies to synthesize or create common links among these works' literary conventions. From this widened literary perspective, they experienced "hands-on" the interconnected nature of tragic dramas, as they began to infer how all four characters closely relate in their tragic makeup. These entries also reflect the further extension of an underlying concept's meaning, made possible by synthesizing literary conventions in multiple dramas. By studying the protagonists of different works and times, they greatly expanded their grasp of the entire tragic hero convention, especially the concepts of magnitude and power, self-deception and blindness, and various internal conflicts underlying the pattern of tragic downfall and suffering. Also, as they synthesized these common qualities, they realized that each protagonist is both a recreation and an extension of preexisting forms.

As these entries confirm, students immediately recognized some of the different twists and adaptations each author gives to the hero's tragic destiny. Oedipus, believing he is an omnipotent monarch, is cursed by a distant ancestor as well as by his own fatal flaws; Hamlet inherits the tradition of revenge, but not the mindset to carry it out; Willy inherits a fantasy of material success that almost completely severs him from his humanity; and Mama Younger inherits from her husband and from God the power to guide and emotionally support her biological family through life's hardships. However, by the time students synthesized the primary traits of magnitude, fatal flaw, suffering, and reversal of character, they grasped a deeper commonality at the center of the western tragic hero convention, the obsession with carving out a personal destiny that all but Hamlet, the quintessential literary anomaly, seem to share. This intertextual framework also allowed students to focus on, contrast, and compare a broad array of self-deceptions causing the protagonists' suffering: Mama's inability to accept her son's weaknesses; Hamlet's inability to cope with both his uncle's betrayal of numerous ancient taboos and family bonds and his inherited duty of revenge; Willy's refusal to accept his father's abandonment, his adultery, and his personal limitations; and Oedipus' refusal to accept his place in the predetermined scheme of ancestral fate and communal atonement. This focused, cross-textual synthesis eventually brought another tragic constant to light. Mama, Hamlet, Oedipus, and Willy suffer equally from believing they can fix or conceal a horrific act of family betrayal which they caused and/or are permanently affected by. As cross-textual synthesizers, these students could not have been more absorbed in discovering, hands-on, the changing faces of the unchanging dilemmas at the heart of great literature.

For my students, the second and creative benefit of this cross-textual enterprise was their growing appreciation for the limitless human possibilities represented by literature's imaginative conventions. The third journal entry in the previous set reflects the student's anticipation of the metaphorical dimension toward which her synthesis of multiple tragedies invariably leads. Having internalized the full cycle of literary analysis, she moves fluently between synthesizing literary conventions and investing four tragic figures with metaphorical significance. Imagining broader possibilities, she immediately associates the pride and blindness of three of these "heroes" with the suffering family: "In all three of these tragedies, the families undergo suffering along with the tragic hero." One association triggering others, she then connects the downfalls of all four tragic heroes with the larger belief systems in which they are embedded and which ultimately control "their lives and their suffering." She makes yet a broader association with death itself, the ever-present and ambivalent reality that most informs tragedy and that, as she implacably states, "has a way of either making good things happen for these families or something horrible." Suffering families, absolute systems of thought, and death itself—these metaphorical associations perfectly capture the process that Cullers describes as the "questioning of the self and of received modes of ordering the world which has always been the result of the greatest literature" (289). By adding my student's metaphorical insights to Cullers's, it would seem that great literature has the capacity to raise serious questions about how concepts like selfhood and identity align with the needs of the family and with the ever-present reality of human mortality. Needless to say, genuine literary study can stimulate this type of concept expansion in secondary students when they need it most.

Works Cited

Cullers, Jonathan. "Structuralism and Literature." *Contexts for Criticism.* 2nd ed. Donald Keesey. Mountain View, CA: Mayfield, 1994. 280-89.

de Man, Paul.: *Blindness and Insight: Essays in the Rhetoric of Contemporary Criticism.* 2nd ed. revised. Minneapolis, MN: U. of Minnesota, 1983.

Frye, Northrup. *Anatomy of Criticism.* Atheneum, NY: Atheneum, 1966. "The Critical Path." *Contexts for Criticism,* 2nd. ed. Donald Keesey. Mountain View, CA: Mayfield, 1994. 271-79.

Hirsch, Jr., E. D. *Cultural Literacy: What Every American Needs to Know.* New York: Vintage Books, 1988.

Jacobsen, David, et al. *Methods for Teaching: A Skills Approach,* 4th ed. Upper Saddle River, NJ: Prentice Hall, 1993.

Kutz, Eleanor, and Hephzibah Roskelly. *An Unquiet Pedagogy: Transforming Practice in the English Classroom.* Portsmouth, NH: Boynton/Cook, 1991.

Link, Frances R. "Instrumental Enrichment: A Strategy for Cognitive and Academic Improvement." *Essays on the Intellect.* Ed. Frances R. Link. Alexandria, VA: ASCD, 1985. 89-106.

Reed, Elaine Wrisley. "Projects and Activities: A Means, Not an End." *American Educator.* 21.4 Winter 1997-98: 26+.

Salinger, J. D. *The Catcher in the Rye.* New York: Bantam Books, 1951.

Chapter Eight

What's to Be Done on the College Level? The Way We Were, Are, Can Be

Should you think that we are merely being nostalgic for a time that never existed, in which students wrote well and thought clearly, here are a few examples of college in-class papers, final exams that were selected randomly twenty years ago. The wps ratio was no higher than today, but just compare the following two passages:

1998:	1978:
Willy spent all his life making friends in the business world. From his job in the city to his trips to Boston there were always people waiting to see Willie Loman. When Willie kills himself he believes that all these people will come to see his funeral. When Willie dies there are not many people at his funeral, just his family and his friend. That is what is ironic, all the friends he made throughout his life, and none of them were actually his friends in the end.	The world that was predicted that seemed the least attractive to me was the world or planet of Topaz in *Foundation*. The reason it is so unattractive to me is the idea of a whole race of people who prefer to live underground and are afraid when they see the sun. I don't like the idea of breathing piped in air and living in artificial sunlight. By living in an underground world you become too dependent on your machines.

The difference between these two excerpts isn't just a matter of sentence length but the complexity of the thoughts and the conciseness of expression.

The first clear contrast between the two passages is the relative poverty of word-choice in the later compared to the earlier example. The word "friend(s)" is used four times, "people" three times and "Willie" four times. In contrast, the only word repeated in the 1978 essay other than common forms of verbs and pronouns is "world," three times, and in one case it is accompanied by a synonym, "planet." But what is more striking is the contrast in the development of an idea. In the 1998 essay, the first two sentences can be combined into one; sentences 3-5 repeat the same idea, the third and fourth almost literally starting with the same construction: "When Willie kills himself…," "When Willie dies…." The writer from twenty years ago moves logically from one sentence to the next, intoducing his thesis in the first; giving his reason for his choice in the second; applying this reason in the third to his personal tastes—but *connected* to a text, not divorced from it—; and advancing a conclusion to support his point in the fourth. The writing has more vitality, more awareness of an AUDIENCE. Incidentally, both essays received the same grade, C+.

Another contrast between the two essays is in the vigor of the earlier work compared to the tentative, almost fearful expression in the first. The writer of the 1978 essay seemed eager to introduce his opinion into his writing but not divorcing it from what he was writing about: "I don't like the idea of breathing piped in air and living in artificial sunlight." The next sentence extrapolates from the particular statement and opens it up to a generalization: "By living in an underground world you become too dependent on your machines."

The 1998 writer seems to cling to the one idea of proving the irony of Willy Loman's funeral being only attended by his immediate family and best friend. It is almost as if the two middle sentences were written by a non-native speaker trying to write English "safely." "When Willie kills himself he believes that all these people will come to see his funeral. When Willie dies there are not many people at his funeral...."

Further examination of in-class papers written twenty years ago reveal much of the same tendencies when contrasted with contemporary student writing. Following is a sample of randomly selected lines from these 1978 essays—the first complete sentence after the fourteenth line: the papers received anywhere from an A to a C+:

1. *I would much rather see the future world in a sense that everything reverts back to more of a pioneer type situation where people actual have to rough it again in order to survive.* *(C+)*

2. *In a world of chemical manipulation people have no control over what they see, or think. All visions are illusions and chemicals in the water and air control emotions.* *(B)*

3. *The machine has already survived nuclear holocaust and seems to be self-sustaining. It will run forever and is capable of keeping you around that long.* *(B)*

4. *Everything these people did was actually decided by someone else since the very way they viewed the world was controlled. Another thing disturbing about this world is the total lack of human interactions.* *(B+)*

5. *What Lem is saying here, about religion today is that it is no longer as strong as it was many years ago. This can be seen in the widespread use of birth control, even though the Church is against it.* *(B)*

6. *The only people who really know what is behind everything are the small elite group that refuse to allow anyone else to know the truth. The rest of the people have become less than human through this. They resemble monsters out of children's nightmares.* *(B)*

Two other papers are short stories, an option I provided students twenty years ago which I know would no longer be considered a viable essay choice today. (I know this since the option was discarded because students no longer chose it at all.) Here are some excerpts from these students' work:

7. The violinist stopped his music, and there was sputtered applause from the restaurants patrons. We had a cozy little table in the corner, and by the candelight, Lola's eyes twinkled incessitatly. Her gold hair, in the long braid, made her appear so lovely, almost too good to be true. We were talking small talk over Chianti, and I felt the time was right (B).

8. Fearfully, I went up to one of the strange, ghost-like people and asked, "Excuse me, but could you tell me where I might get something to eat?"

A harsh, scratchy voice answered, "Use your nose, can't you smell your way around?" His face was blank, and I noticed for the first time he had no eyeballs, simply black sockets. (A-)

Although the first may be unoriginal, there is a delight, almost PAS-SION in the way the student creates a scene and chooses image-bearing words. In both imagination and an enjoyment in language is clearly revealed. These papers may be coming from self-selected students since the course I was teaching was an elective—Science Fiction—but this could be said as well about students in my Jewish-American literature course 20 years later. Here is, again, a sample of their writing beginning on the fourteenth line from their essays:

1. He finds the Rabbi Lipschitz who makes the crown and asked about them. The rabbi informs him that the crown only works if the people have faith in it. Albert, after much debate in his head, gets the crown but feels very uneasy about it (B-)

2. His brother, the boy's father, was not even there with his son when he was dying and Leventhal felt that was very wrong and that he should have been there with his son. All of those problems that he was having only contributed to the fact that Albee was herassing Leventhal (C).

3. He was very excited about buying the crown, and was willing to hand over a lot of money to make it possible. However, he became quite skeptical when he thought he had been hypnotized, and when he was told that he could not see the crown (B+).

4. Sarah had her name switched several times. She really never had a say in what she was being called. All the men in her life had a powerful effect on her. When she got married, she was told she had to change her name (C+)

5. That's where he went wrong from the beginning. He didn't want to do something for his dad because he loved him, he wanted to do it so that his conscience would be cleared if he did (B-).

There might not be as striking a contrast in form between the two sets of papers. Sentence length, grammar, punctuation are not markedly different in quality. It is in the complexity of the thoughts, the ease with which the group of students twenty years ago applies its knowledge to the text, something that students in the Jewish-American lit. class could have done as well.

Among references extrinsic to the text is the "pioneer type situation" to which we can "revert back" (1), the reference to the Church's opposition to birth control in a discussion of religion (5) and an awareness of an "elite group" that can control the rest of society (6). There is also a marked contrast in the conciseness and vigor of expression:

"All visions are illusions and chemical in the water and air control emotions" (2); "The machine has already survived nuclear holocaust and seems to be self-sustaining" (3); "They resemble monsters out of children's nightmares" (6). Compare this to: "Albert, after much debate in his head…" (1); "…the boy's father …was not even there with his son when he was dying and Leventhal felt that was very wrong and that he should have been there with his son" (2); "Sarah had her name switched several times. She really never had a say in what she was being called. All the men in her life had a powerful effect on her" (4). Even from this small sample, it is clear that the contrast in the twenty years shows a falling off in language, a lack of energy in the prose, and, in some instances, even a lack of logic: a definite decline in student writing. But perhaps the most significant difference between the two sets of excerpts is that too many students today seem only comfortable when they are *summarizing* material; twenty years ago they were *interpreting* it.

Certainly, there are students I could select from the papers I now receive that write good, serviceable prose; some even excellent prose. But their numbers are few, and their writing is no better than that of what might be closer to the average student of 1978. More noticeable, however, is the fact that the "average" student today in our writing classes is very much below the average of twenty years ago. There is really no middle anymore: very good, bad, and awful. As Yeats said in another context:

"The center cannot hold

Mere anarchy is loosed upon the world."

If this were the anarchy of mediocrity, it would be manageable, but the anarchy we see is one in which so few students seem to be able to express themselves clearly and competently, at least as reflected in their writings, that their ignorance could prove perilous to the future of democracy in this country.

One possibility to explain this decline is that the students we are presently admitting are not up to the standards of the ones twenty years ago. If that were true, this would be reflected in the SAT and class rank of students now compared to them. From the data we have through our Admissions Office annual reports, this is simply not the case. In 1979, the mean verbal SAT score was 435; in 1995 before the "new" SAT scores were calculated, the mean was 429, statistically insignificant. If anything, SAT verbal mean scores were generally lower in the early 1980's than when they peaked at 452 in 1993. We don't have data for class average until 1984 but in that year some 70% of the freshman class had had high school averages below a B while only 51% had below a B average in 1997. Unless we acknowledge that the standards as a whole, nationally, are going down in terms of what is expected of high school students, there is no other way to explain how our students today have higher class averages, similar verbal scores, and considerably lower achievement.

Both of us over the years have, through trial and error, managed to develop ways of teaching that have proven successful in giving students a chance to develop their writing and thinking skills. Unfortunately, too often, these methods are not followed up in subsequent courses and are generally unpopular because they involve intensive work with students, especially one-on-one conferences.

Last summer, I was involved in a six-week "Summer Institute" which is run by the Educational Opportunity Program here at Cortland. In that six-week period, a number of these students, who have generally been under-prepared for college-level work, showed remarkable progress in their writing and thinking skills. The students met with me for one hour every day. They always had a writing assignment of some kind, they had to keep a journal, and they had to write three drafts each of four papers and two in-class essays. In many instances, after two or three weeks, their writing was comparable or better than that of students who have been taking my sophomore-level drama course, many of whom are juniors and seniors. There were also only ten students in one section of this course, nine in the other. As little as I believe in standardized tests, they still measure something. By the end of the six-week period, many of these students showed a two-grade advance in their reading speed and comprehension scores on the Nelson-Denny reading tests, some as many as four grades.

From our experience, we have culled the following principles that should be followed in teaching good writing and critical thinking in the classroom, and these could apply to high school students as well as college freshman:

1. Class size must be capped at fifteen students.

2. Each student must keep a journal with relevant exercises supplementary to the tasks in the classroom.

3. A significant amount of writing must go on in the classroom, with close teacher supervision.

4. The texts should come from the classic and modern literary works that have been the traditional literature of the "old school." However, multi-cultural texts should be introduced, but ONLY after students establish a knowledge base from the classics.

5. In high school the extent of the reading should be accelerated to include at least one new text every week or two weeks, depending on the length. Students don't find reading interesting not because they are incapable of being engaged, but that the snail's pace rate of the reading is BORING.

6. Students should have their papers returned within one week of submitting them and have a mandatory conference with their teacher prior to submitting a final draft and after each paper.

7. Peer evaluation, collaborative learning, and other "innovative" methods of teaching can be used but only when there are clear, demonstrable goals for each of these activities that show a measured objective in improving students' work.

ANY OTHER GOALS, OBJECTIVES, DESIRED OUTCOMES MUST BE SUBORDINATED TO THE PRIMARY TASK OF GETTING STUDENTS TO READ THOROUGHLY AND CAREFULLY CLASSIC TEXTS, WRITE DEVELOPMEN-TALLY, AND HAVE THE OPPORTUNITY TO THINK CRIT-ICALLY ABOUT THE ISSUES THAT ARE DERIVED FROM THE LANGUAGE AND MEANING OF THE TEXT.

Of course, the most difficult of these suggestions to implement may well be the first; few if any school boards took seriously President Clinton's call for a reduction in class size as one of the challenges for the improvement of education. But if it is not done, all but the best and the brightest will have the skills to be able to function competently in what will still be the print-centered culture of the future. Regardless of the medium, the message still requires a comprehension of a vocabulary which includes a wealth of cultural allusions and a variety of words that goes beyond the average sixth grade vocabulary in which most newspapers and directions are written. If the intellectual and educational elite are the only ones to master these cultural tools, they will be that more easily able to manipulate the rest whose interests are best served through their own knowledge.

Significantly reducing class size nationally would require a massive investment in building new schools as well as making the $300 billion-worth of repairs on schools that are presently in need of them. It would also require an enormous effort to recruit new and effective teachers, something that at present has been so unsuccessful that recently states have recruited science teachers from Austria! Imagine their surprise—and the students'—when these teachers walk into a classroom with their level of expectations of what the students should already have learned and what they are supposed to teach.

But in order to have new and good teachers, the teacher's colleges themselves must be reformed as well as able to recruit top students into their programs. This would require, as happened in the 60's, a marked increase in teachers' salaries and an improvement in the anti-teacher atmosphere that too often taints the political and cultural scene when education is discussed. In other words, to improve student thinking and writing, you must start with Utopia! Yet if we were to argue that any-thing less than a radical change in attitudes and conditions of teaching and teaching teachers were necessary in order to make real improve-ments possible, the little nudge in the direction of "personalized" learn-ing would not even be conceivable.

By "personalized" learning, we do not mean learning that deals with the "whole child" or any other social agenda. We mean that each student should have a definite set of goals and objectives in mastering texts and writing about them that is reflected in the teacher's understanding of the *intellectual* strengths and weaknesses of the child. Too often intellectual and affective behavior are commingled or confused and the result is a child who is being told how to "feel good" about herself rather than "think" about what she is learning. The direction in which schools must take students who can then become successful in college work is toward more focused, task-oriented learning that emphasizes writing and thinking about reading difficult, demanding texts in a developmental schema.

As it is, the trends are very much in the other direction: multi-culturalism is the "in" thing from the left; traditional values, which is often a vacuous excuse for an elitist agenda is the watchword from the right; and "distance-learning" and the "net" are being pushed as panaceas by the educational tech managers from almost every direction. Certainly, as we have said, say and will say and still be misunderstood despite our saying it: *there is room for multi-culturalism, and even teaching religion in the schools—as a subject, not indoctrination—so long as these agendas are subordinated to the students' need to read widely and deeply, write extensively, and think through the texts they are learning about.* And that requires small classes, well-informed teachers who themselves know how to write well, and an educational and political establishment that values good teaching and solid learning as the backbone of a democratic society. It is, unfortunately, unlikely that any of these things will happen, but at least we feel that it is more of a possibility if a few of us yell loudly enough that we are merrily careening down a cliff when we think we're ascending to Parnassus.

To us it is clear that although there are some benefits to the new educational technology that has developed over the past several decades, in the hands of those who will purchase these technologies, the superintendents and school boards there is one priority: SAVE MONEY. So long as schools are dependent on property taxes for their funding, they are subjected to the whims of their constituents. And in many parts of the country today's public schools are being abandoned by the middle class who will have even less of a stake than ever in supporting public education. How this problem of funding can be solved is not the provence of this book: that the ed tech advocates are trying to solve it by pitching the money-saving aspects of educational technology as a selling point—covert as it sometimes can be—is abundantly clear to us. Evidence of this comes from reports of computer labs and other technological wonders going unused, underused or misused for lack of competent staff to teach students how to use them.

Besides, the most important thing a student can "feel" is that someone she respects is aware of her existence and willing to help her—in intellectual as well as emotional issues. Smaller classes can make that possible; larger ones highly unlikely. In almost every autobiography written by "disadvantaged" writers—whether through race, poverty, or both—there is always some "guiding light" that took the youngster in hand and showed him or her a way of making the most of talents and opportunities. Machines can supplement but simply cannot substitute for people. This is a truism that seems to be lost on the technological geniuses whose "philosophy" often interfers with educational goals. The many studies showing that students improve in their work in almost every area when in smaller classes are still ignored or contradicted by the politicians who want to pretend that the solution to these problems lies in family values when many today have no real families and few positive values.

Recently, the Mayor of New York City, Rudolph Giuliani, in response to criticism of the unconscionably large classes of forty, fifty and more students in the inner city schools argued that when he was going to school as the son of immigrants from Italy, he, too, was in large classes. Since I am a contemporary of Mr. Giuliani and attended public schools in New York City at about the same time as he did, I can honestly say that I do not remember any class with more than thirty students and, if my elementary school was typical, probably less. And the students who attended school when I and the Mayor were there had not had their early years cluttered by television, certainly not television that was available twenty-four hours a day on fifty channels. The teachers who taught us were generally highly intelligent, devoted single women who had themselves been raised at a time when even the radio was not that readily available and where print was the primary, if not sole, source of information.

The students of today to which Mr. Giuliani refers are literally raised on television; they don't have to know how to read, they believe, because everything they are interested in isn't conveyed through print but images. And the teachers they have are often poorly trained, not very often in the top of their class, and have little of the core knowledge that teachers of generations ago could convey to their students. One of mine, Mrs. Decker in fifth grade, had an anaconda skin hung across the front wall of the classroom, a snake that had been personally killed by Theodore Roosevelt, a family friend of her childhood. She wasn't kidding: she had pictures of herself sitting on Roosevelt's lap when she was a girl. Naturally, among other things, we got a little first-hand knowledge about Theodore Roosevelt. Not that Mrs. Decker, who was the science teacher for the school, was at all typical of my teachers, but certainly, the cohort from which she came were first and foremost readers.

The students of today that the Mayor is so confident can learn the basics in hall closets, bathrooms and classrooms with falling plaster and crumbling walls are being taught by teachers who themselves were raised on television, the first generation to do so. That is perhaps, from a demographic point of view, the major difference between the generation of students who wrote so much better twenty years ago and today's. This earlier cohort was born from 1958-60 which means that NONE of their teachers could have had a television in her home before they had learned to read since the youngest of such teachers could not have been born before 1936. Students today are being taught by teachers who, for the most part, were born after 1945, most after 1950. The overwhelming majority were "taught" by television **before** they learned to read.

This is one of the many reasons that class size must be small: the students must have an optimal chance of being reached by teachers who are far less well-equipped to teach than those of two generations ago. But there are other good arguments for small class size:

1. Teachers can more readily remember students' names, an important "affective" factor in getting them to feel that the teacher cares who they are.

2. Teachers can evaluate papers more quickly and frequently to give students necessary feedback in order to improve their writing.

3. Teachers can have time for making greater contact with students who need the one-on-one hands-on learning in order to be able to achieve their best.

4. Teachers will be happier, last longer, have less "burn-out" (at present the burn-out rate nationally is about seven years for grade-school teachers; three or less for those who teach in inner-city schools), and feel they have actually made a measurable difference in the intellectual lives of their students.

5. Students will feel more welcomed in a classroom where they are "known" both in the emotional and intellectual sense by their teachers and fellow classmates.

6. Students will have a far more favorable learning environment than one in which mere survival is the main objective of their teacher each day.

7. Therefore, students will LEARN how to read more deeply, write more competently, and think.

We are certain that there are a host of objections to this proposal to limit class size to fifteen, the foremost being economic. But if that is the most important consideration, we can only argue that in the long run, it will be cheaper to invest in a future that can promise a decent way of life for the overwhelming majority of our young people than invest later in what will, we believe, inevitably become a police state, the word "democracy" a cruel mockery of what it once was, or could be. You pays your money and you takes your choice; you don't pay your money, no choice.

In addition to studies about the efficacy of class size, some anecdotal examples from our experiences will illustrate the urgency of our point. For five years I (Shatzky) ran the honors program at Cortland. One of the mandatory courses was a weekly seminar limited to ten students in which academic issues that were brought up during the previous week could be discussed. A second required class was the weekly "great ideas" course which we called "The Artist in Modern Society" which was team taught by faculty from the arts and English. Classes were limited to fifteen. This was also true of the number of students in the freshman comp. course we taught which was basically a "great books" course. The works read were by Goethe, Standahl, Dostoyevsky, Kafka, Camus and Fowles, as I already indicated.

These classes, particularly the freshman comp course, were quite lively; most of the students kept up with the readings although admittedly not all; and the quality of both class work and written work was generally quite high. Samples of their papers are comparable in quality to the work of the better students today at the college, as well they should be, and thus comparable to the random sample of the papers written twenty years earlier. They chose and wrote on such topics as a critical analysis of Standahl's *The Red and the Black*, a comparison of the novel and film version of Fowles *The French Lieutenant's Woman*, teenaged drinking, and a study of Salvador Dali. The class, as I mentioned, was limited to fifteen.

BUT when a number of the students in this class-about half- took my regular intro to drama course with an enrollment of thirty, their participation noticeably diminished, and even the quality of their writing was not nearly as sharp and lively as it had been in the other course. There may be many other factors besides class size to account for this phenomenon: the subject, the influence of the other students in the class, the time at which it was taught. But I was able to determine from talking to a number of them candidly that the size of the class was an inhibitory factor in their participation in discussion.

I have also noticed that among the students in the Summer Institute who were also quite active in the small class atmosphere reticence in participating in the larger classes which I taught. I believe that fifteen in a class is an optimal number, however, because it provides enough students to have some chance of a variety of views in an atmosphere in which most feel free to participate. Very small classes of under ten can be inhibitory as well as those over twenty. But studies have borne out my own experience and impressions well enough.

Perhaps the essays submitted in class can evolve out of journal writing; perhaps new ideas can be engendered through careful reading of a text and using the journal to "brainstorm" interpretations. But even the concept of "brainstorming" can be self-defeating unless the brain has some clear content and context to "storm" about. This means that journal assignments must be task-oriented with expected outcomes from the effort; and they must always be connected to class readings in a way in which the student must look carefully at the text in order to respond in the journal.

In-class writing is a necessity. Too often, students write when they are up against a deadline or are distracted by people and situations around them, or, more than likely, they just can't concentrate. In a writing class, that is, any class in which some form of writing is being stressed, regardless of the subject, often half of the class period should be taken up with writing. Once again, the task, the objectives, the source of the text to which the writing responds must be clearly laid out. And the instructor must not only go around the room to supervise the writing to make sure it is being done, she must also know what to look for in the writing to be certain it is done correctly, that is, with a clear objective in mind. One of the most successful classes I ever had was one in teaching students how to teach drama. In order to be sure that they were given a syllabus that would most motivate them, I checked with our department teacher supervisor to find out the list of the most frequently taught plays in the New York State high schools and based most of my play selections on that list. I then taught the class with a minimum of lecturing and maximum of collaborative learning for specific literary objectives. Although the number of students was above the optimum, 24, they were highly enough motivated to provide the necessary atmosphere of relaxed yet concentrated effort to make this number of students effective. They also all knew each other from three years of previous classes so a number of the advantages of small class size was accomplished. This situation, of course, is not typical but almost ideal.

I divided the class into groups of four, giving each one a text-based question from a scene or act of the play being studied. They then had to work together to answer the question, but each was responsible for some aspect of the answer. In this way, there were few, if any "free-loaders," especially since all had the incentive to participate as they were going to be applying the methodology I was giving them the next semester in student-teaching. I found that properly set up, I could leave the room and return half an hour later to find all of the students still on task, almost oblivious of my presence but ready to respond to the questions, the answers of which they had carefully written out.

The following is an example of the methodology I provided as a model:

METHOD OF TEACHING A PLAY

l. Introduce the concept of a play by distinguishing its component parts from those of a novel or short story.

    a. Plot of a play versus story.

    b. Dramatization of an event versus description of an event.

    c. Dialogue as a whole versus dialogue as a part.

    d. The role of the actor: Gesture: vocal expression, facial expression, movement

    e. Role of director and technical assistants: Costumes, props, sets, lighting, sound, stage

ll. Use the class as the basic resource for the drama.

    a. Choose those students who would be willing—or least reluctant—to read aloud in class.

    b. Try slowly to introduce other students to the practice of reading aloud.

    c. Choose non-threatening (unambiguous) roles at first to give the students confidence.

d. Get them to read in front of the class so that there is attention and focus.

e. NEVER have students read from the page while others are reading the dialogue aloud.

f. AWAYS involve the "spectators" by asking their advice on how the "actors" should interpret their lives and movements.

g. Choose relatively brief excerpts, no longer than one or two minutes, that are both dramatically and thematically essential to the play.

h. Use the device of "blocking" by making copies of these excerpts and giving each member of the class a chance to do some directing.

lll. Analysis of a scene: Opening segment of Ibsen's *Ghosts.*

  A. The action: Engstrand's entrance.

    1. How does he look?

    2. How would he move? Ask for volunteers to demonstrate.

    3. How would Regine look and talk in contrast?

  B. The plot and characterization: The conversation.

    1. What does Engstrand reveal about himself?

    2. What does Regine reveal about herself?

    3. How do you think she would deliver the line: "Sailors have no savoir-faire"?

  C. The setting

    1. What kind of place serves as the setting for this play?

    2. What is the weather like?

    3. If you were to draw a sketch of the set, what would be the most important thing to include in it?

  D. The structure

    1. Why is this first scene between Regine and Engstrand necessary?

    2. What information is conveyed by the characters?

    3. What motive causes Engstrand to leave the room?

    4. How would you direct these two characters to make their lines interesting?

    5. On what specific lines would you have them move?

  6. Demonstrate what you would do by "directing" two "actors"
   through this first scene.
 E. The theme
  1. How does the conversation, setting, characterization and
   plot in this scene create an idea that could be considered part
   of a theme?
  2. How could the actors be directed to emphasize this theme?

Choose only about four or five highlights throughout the play in order to use this approach effectively. DO NOT READ THE WHOLE PLAY THIS WAY. These highlights can be used for you to reinforce the discussion of the rest of the play.

In order to teach the play effectively, it is helpful to divide each act into "scenes" which are generally determined by the entrance or exit of a character. Each "scene" can then be used as a point of focus to show how it contributes to the whole, not only *thematically* but *dramatically.*

Note that although there are many directions, few, if any ask the student to "react personally" to the play but rather use the text as a basis for any development of ideas. Reader response is only valid after the student has mastered the text. Even then, it must be used very carefully; the instructor must always return the student to the text in order to defend an interpretation. The greatest problem, as well as the greatest temptation, in an instructor's method of teaching the interpretation of literature is to allow the student to wander from the text into flights of her own fancy under the instructor's mistaken notion that she is letting the student be "creative." Creativity is based on a mastery of content; Keats had read Chapman's Homer before he could write "creatively" about it.

Although to some instructors classroom writing may seem to be time-consuming, what I do to move the process along is to give a very limited amount of time to each task, three-five minutes each. This way, students know they have a short amount of time and must concentrate if they want to be able to show some results from their efforts. And giving them a short and limited amount of time makes them aware that in an in-class essay exam, they have to learn to think quickly and efficiently. The overall objective of such a method is to give them practice under the best of conditions in which they would be writing—in the classroom— so that they can make their mistakes when they are not penalized for them and feel that they can free up their writing by not fearing making those mistakes. The analogy to sports is clear enough to them: you don't get the basketball for the big game and expect to do well if you've never practiced. But if one considers the enormous amount of writing any successful author has done prior to actually making a break-through, it would be absurd to expect students with their limited interest and talent in writing to do as well without at least as much practice.

The primary idea is not to try to make the students better writers through limited and concentrated efforts, but by one giving them writing assignments to do in class every day, they become used to writing, and by systematically working with each at intervals on things that they must practice, they eventually overcome their fears and become so used to the act of writing that they can eventually improve very much on their own.

Learning a foreign language can be child's play if you begin as a child and practice each day in a foreign country in which you must speak the language. Learning a foreign language as a teen-ager, as we often absurdly insist is the time to learn, is very much a hopeless task for most students since they never practice speaking the language, often not even in the classroom. If children started writing regularly, every day, when they are small, and are properly supervised by trained writing teachers who could spot weaknesses and disabilities when the children were at an early age, after twelve years of writing, the likelihood of success in the college classroom would be considerably increased. But that means WRITING EVERY DAY.

The reason most students who write poorly react the way they do to criticism of their work—defensively and at times resentfully—is due to their fear of the unknown. Since it has been so rarely practiced by them, and is too often either unhelpfully criticized or mindlessly praised, the act of writing is plunging into alien territory, as foreign to many of them as the Cyrillic alphabet or Chaucer's English: unknown, unexplored, fraught with peril.

We believe that teachers on the secondary level can do much to make their students improve their writing and thinking. But they must be given the resources and instruction to do so. We feel that the present trend of "student centered" teaching is promoting the "thinking crisis" that exists among today's students. We believe that the only way to deal with this problem is through a more holistic approach we have advocated throughout this book.